The Wisdom of the Four Wise Men

Finding Personal Truth
in the
too-much-information age

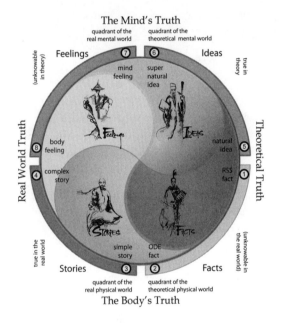

Book II: Unraveling
Human Nature

Steven Paglierani

published by

The Emergence Alliance™

Nanuet, New York

Published by
The Emergence Alliance Inc
55 Old Nyack Tpke., Ste 608
Nanuet, NY 10954

SAN 859-5380

http://FifthWiseMan.com (this site explores the wise men's map. You can buy
the book here, as well as on Amazon and Barnes and Noble.)
http://theEmergenceSite.com (This site contains the discoveries which
preceded this book. And while I've since refined many of my terms and ideas,
some may find it of interest. You can also buy the book here.)

Paglierani, Steven. T., 1946-
        Finding Personal Truth (in the too-much-information age)
        Book II: Unraveling Human Nature by Steven Paglierani

Includes bibliographical references.

ISBN 978-0-9844895-1-0 (hard cover, jacket)
ISBN 978-0-9844895-7-6 (ebook edition)

1. Personality 1. Human Nature 2. Personal Truth 2. Personal Growth
3. Personality Tests 1. title

303 pages. 110,000 words.

PSY023000   PSYCHOLOGY / Personality
PSY042000   PSYCHOLOGY / Assessment, Testing & Measurement
SCI075000   SCIENCE / Philosophy & Social Aspects

Library of Congress Control Number: 2010943495

Printed in The United States of America

Printing Number
        16 15 14 13 12 11   10 9 8 7 6 5 4 3 2 1

Dedication

To my grandfather, Stefan, for awakening in me the desire to hear people's stories. And to my grandfather, William, and my uncle, Louie, for instilling in me the importance of education. Even from a distance, each of you has changed my life.

Thank You

To my friend and comrade in arms, Brit Paterson, for his years of insisting that I be myself. I couldn't want for a better brother.

To my dear friend and fellow therapist, Lauren Saletan, and to my equally dear friend and fellow musician, David Snider, for their ever-present faith in my ability to find answers.

To my students and friends for patiently enduring my frequently odd sense of humor and lengthy diatribes.

To my friend and editor, Avital Spivak, for her continued support, encouragement, guidance, and willingness to argue with me for her truth.

A Note to the Reader

Were you to feed this book into a readability program—the Coleman Liau index, for instance, or the Flesh Kincaid Grade Level, ARI (Automated Readability Index), or SMOG—you'd find the reading level of this text is fifth grade. Likewise, Book I. Thus as far as the words, these books are easier to read than most.

Unfortunately, I'm told the content is so dense—and the ideas so counterintuitive—that despite being written at a fifth grade level, these books challenge even good readers. Indeed, people tell me Book I has numerous similarities to the mind-numbing power of Umberto Eco's writings and that trying to read it can hurt people's heads.

At first, I admit, these reports were unsettling, to say the least. The last thing I want is for my books to make the too-much-information age worse. Then I began to work with people on their ability to read Book I and to my utter astonishment, doing this even one time caused life changing emergences in some people. It seems learning to read in a personally meaningful way not only improves people's ability to read the written word. It also alters their ability to find personal meaning in all words—whether spoken, written, thought, or implied.

The upshot of this is that I've begun to create a program intended to teach people to read, speak, and hear words in a personally meaningful manner. Here there are only two goals—to either have personally meaningful pictures for each and every word *or to at least feel curious as to what it would be like to have such a meaning,* given you can't find this meaning.

What's in it for you? One woman earning her second masters told me in tears that she had just written the first paper in her life wherein she was on the page. Another found the words to have conversations she'd been wanting for years to have with her long-time boyfriend. Another told me her self confidence had dramatically improved. And another said that for the first time in her life, she felt her opinion mattered.

What I'm saying is, this book is largely a technical book in that it contains many, many ideas. Know that helping you to find your personal truth means far more to me than your retaining these ideas. With this in mind, I've been developing a way to teach people this style of reading. Hopefully by year end, my third site, http://FindingPersonalTruth.com, will be up. There I'll have videos showing what it's like to read this way.

My hope is that these videos will enable you to reclaim some of your love of learning. To this end I pray that, like me, this happens to you and to all those you love. And that you too find your personal truth.

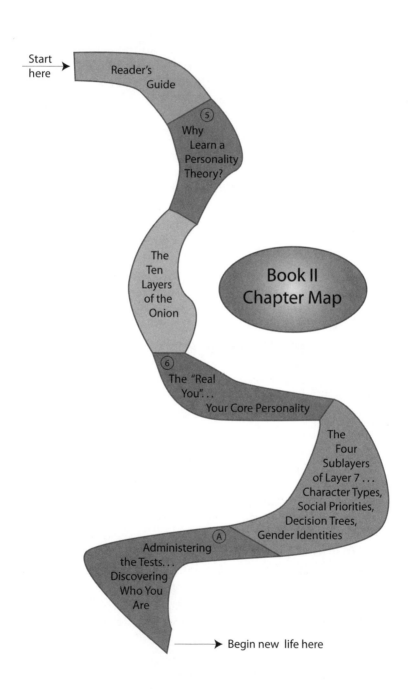

Start here

Reader's Guide

⑤ Why Learn a Personality Theory?

The Ten Layers of the Onion

Book II Chapter Map

⑥ The "Real You"... Your Core Personality

The Four Sublayers of Layer 7 ... Character Types, Social Priorities, Decision Trees, Gender Identities

Ⓐ Administering the Tests... Discovering Who You Are

Begin new life here

Table of Contents

Chapter 6

Discovering the Real You (Your Core Personality) 353

Appendix

Administering the Personality Tests 479

Introduction

Reader's Guide to Unraveling Human Nature

My Awakening

Life changing events rarely announce themselves. The one that happened to me when I was twelve was no exception. My grandfather, who was close to ninety, had come for Sunday dinner. He had done this only twice before.

In large part, this was due to my mother's condition. She could tolerate only the most perfunctory talking and no loud noises at all. Because of this, we lived in monastic stillness rarely speaking, including at meals which were almost always eaten in silence.

When dinner was over, my grandfather got up and went outside. Minutes later, my mother directed me to go sit with him. I remember feeling nervous as I opened the door. What do you say to a man to whom you've never spoken other than to utter hello? Moreover, having been raised in near silence, I had no idea how to have a conversation.

Worse yet, there were only two chairs behind my house. This left me with one option—to sit right next to him. Nervously, I sat, and as I did he spoke my name. Even now, I can hear his gentle voice. And although I had no way to know it at the time, this conversation was about to change my life.

What happened next never fails to make me well up with tears, not so much from what he said but rather, because of how it made me feel. For the first time in my life, someone spoke to me as if what I thought mattered. As if I was not invisible. As if I existed as a person of some importance. Indeed, I have no words for what I felt other than to say I felt alive.

Can you picture me, a pathologically-shy twelve year old hanging on every word? My grandfather was eager to tell me about his life. And I was hungry to hear what he had to say. But just as I began to settle into what I felt sure was to be the most important conversation of my life, the back door slammed open and my mother shouted, "shut up, pop." At which point, we resumed our silent poses. Fade to black.

Today, I know my grandfather was a disciple of the empirical wise man. My grandfather was a storyteller. Sadly, I met no other until I entered AA more than twenty years later. I mention this as it seems to have been the event which kindled my obsession with unraveling human nature. Indeed, from that day on, my hunger for people's stories has never lessened. And along with it, my need to uncover the mysterious patterns hidden within these stories.

This book is a compendium of the patterns I've discovered so far. What you'll learn is that it takes only five of these patterns to completely describe the core personality of any person on the planet, including you. Indeed, of the roughly six billion people on the planet, only one hundred twenty are just like you. More important, tests based on these five patterns can determine your core personality *with one hundred percent certainty*.

In this book, you'll learn what's behind these claims, as well as how to administer these tests. Can you imagine the possibilities? Students and teachers precisely matched. People who love their careers. Marketers who speak to your inner self. And people seeking romantic partners, well, you get the picture.

Who Are the Four Wise Men and What is Their Map?

In this book, I introduce a new personality theory, which is to say, a new way to know yourself. Moreover, unlike prior theories which largely resemble ad hoc collections of loosely-related ideas, in this theory, everything connects to and looks like everything else. Sort of like the layers of an onion, or the dolls in a Russian nesting doll set, or the folds of an almond croissant.

Why would you want to invest time learning a personality theory?

Before I get into this—and in case you have not yet read Book I—a few introductions are in order. For instance, this book's cover refers to four wise men and to their "map of the mind." So who are these four wise men and what's so great about their map? Let's start with the map.

The Four Great Truths

(© 2007 Steven Paglierani   The Center for Emergence)

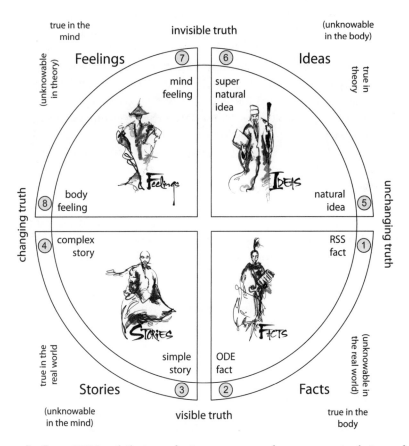

In June 2008, while introducing a new student to my work in and around personality and human consciousness, I accidently discovered a way to map the mind. This is possible because all minds are based on the same underlying design. In this way, our minds are similar to our bodies. Only where our bodies have things like lungs and hearts and toenails, our minds have things like a character type and social priorities.

The problem is, minds are invisible. So you can't see this design. Indeed, as you'll soon learn, this invisibility is the main difference between your body and your mind. And this is where the map comes in.

Like squirting water on an invisible man reveals the man, the map outlines the design of the mind. This allows you to see the inner workings of your mind in new and exciting ways.

For one thing, it reveals the four ways all human beings seek truth—through facts, stories, ideas, and feelings. For another, you see proof that to find truth, you need all four.

What does this map actually look like? I've placed a version of it on the previous page. In it, all expressions of the mind have been divided into the four categories of truth I just mentioned. What makes this map special then is how it defines these four truths—and the relationships between them. But before I can tell you about this, you'll first need to know a bit about the map's design.

To begin with, two crossed-lines divide the map into four quadrants. Moreover, each line has a question assigned to it. The question assigned to the vertical axis? *Is the truth you're seeking visible?* And the question assigned to the horizontal axis? *Does this truth change over time?*

Why these two questions—and where do the answers go?

The vertical axis question determines whether a truth arises from the body or from the mind—whether it's a *physical* truth or a *mental* truth. Physical truths are visible and tip towards the lower part of the line. Thus they go into one of the two lower quadrants. Whereas mental truths are invisible and tip towards the upper end of the line. Thus they go into one of the two upper quadrants.

The horizontal axis question then determines whether this truth changes or not—whether it's a *real world* truth or a *theoretical* truth. Real world truths do. So they tip towards the left end of this line and into one of the two left quadrants. Theoretical truths don't. So they tip towards the right end of this line and into one of the two right quadrants.

Overall then, there are two things to see here. First, both these questions have only two possible answers. Either a truth is visible or it's not—and either it changes or it doesn't. Second, between the four possible answers, every potential outcome is accounted for. Thus together, these two questions account for everything in the mind.

This then is what makes this map so special. The answers to these questions are complementary opposites. In other words, each answer contains none of the other. Yet together, they account for every possibility.

What's the big deal?

If you now combine answers from adjacent arms on this cross, you define all four truths with incredible precision. To wit, *facts*—the materialist wise man's truth—become *visible unchange*. *Stories*—the empirical wise man's truth—become *visible change*. *Ideas*—the rationalist wise man's truth—become *invisible unchange*. And *feelings*—the spiritual wise man's truth—become *invisible change*.

According to the map then, if the truth you seek is visible, then you're seeking a physical truth. This means you're seeking truth with your body. But if the truth you seek is invisible, then you're seeking a mental truth. This means you're seeking truth with your mind. And if the truth you seek never changes, then the truth you're seeking exists only in theory. A theory, once posited, never ceases to exist in that exact form. But if the truth you seek constantly changes, then this truth exists only in the real world. Nothing in the real world stands still.

Does this sound like verbal diarrhea? Then try defining these words yourself. What do they mean to you? Now go ask several people you trust and respect to do the same thing. Then compare notes. Finally compare the relationships between your definitions—or between anyone's four definitions—and the ones in the wise men's map. Do any of them contain the kind of elegant relationships which exist between the four wise men's truths?

In part, this elegance is what makes the wise men's map so powerful. Logically, the map accounts for all expressions of the mind. At the same time, it manages to define them perfectly. Not bad for a bit of logical geometry.

Finally, a good way to understand what's making this possible is to picture a square. Now imagine that your truth is on a table in the middle of this square. Now picture four seats, each located on a corner of this square and facing inward. Now imagine you are sitting in one of these seats.

The thing to realize here is that regardless of where you sit, you get exactly the same amount of view—90 degrees. Moreover, to see the whole 360 degrees of your truth, you must sit in all four seats. The four truths in the wise men's map function in exactly the same way. Each covers 90 degrees of the mind. Thus together, they account for all possible truths.

Keep in mind that none of this would mean much were this map not based on tipping points. Which means what exactly? Let's see.

What is Tipping-Point-Based Math?

Admittedly, most people will balk at these claims. For instance, how can anyone claim they can define the full scope of the mind? Here the answer lies in the type of math which underlies the map's questions.

What's so great about questions based on tipping-point based math? Just one thing. These questions function like coin tosses. And to see what this means, ask yourself this. Once a coin lands, how certain are you of the outcome? It's obvious. One hundred percent. Either it's heads or tails. At the same time, when a flipped coin lands, it can't be both heads and tails. Nor can it be anything other than heads or tails. Thus the outcomes of coin tosses are always a pair of complementary opposites which define all the possible outcomes.

The wise men's map does the same thing for the content of the mind. It completely describes the possible outcomes with one hundred percent certainty. This is possible only because the map derives entirely from a pair of tipping-point-based questions. Moreover, because the possible outcomes of these questions are complementary opposites, these two questions not only define all possible *theoretical* outcomes with one hundred percent certainty. They also define every possible *real world* outcome this way as well. Try doing that with statistics.

This then is what makes what's in this book so different. Everything in it is rooted in pairs of tipping-point based, complementary opposites. Moreover, each of these pairs of opposites is also part of a quadrant of tipping-point based, complementary opposites. And yes, grasping the implications of quadrants of tipping-point based, complementary opposites can at first be overwhelming. Even saying this phrase is hard. But the only thing you need to see at this point is that nothing this elegant could possibly be accidental or ad hoc.

For something to be in this book then, it must be tipping-point based. Moreover, these tipping points must all be like the layers of an onion—they must fit together in self-similar patterns. I challenge anyone to find a scientific theory which can live up to this standard. Indeed, were you to put current theories to this test, you'd find, few survive.

How the Map Explains Human Nature

Obviously, none of this would mean much if it didn't offer real world benefits. And to see what I mean, consider how this book uses a variation of the wise men's map to define the relationships between the four social learning disabilities—Autism, OCD, Asperger's, and ADHD.

The map? Question one—the horizontal axis question—is, where do your distractions come from, from inside you or from outside you? And question two—the vertical axis question—is, do these distractions occur mainly in your body or in your mind?

Now watch what happens when we answer these two questions.

Autism gets defined as a social impairment wherein internal physical sensations distract the person. In effect, these folks get distracted by an inability to manage sensation itself. Whereas OCD gets defined as a social impairment wherein external physical sensations distract the person. These folks suffer from an intermittent inability to manage the things they sense.

The Four Social Distractions

(© 2007 Steven Paglierani   The Center for Emergence)

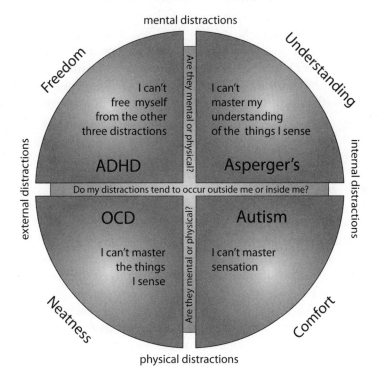

mental distractions

Freedom

Understanding

Are they mental or physical?

I can't
free myself
from the other
three distractions

I can't
master my
understanding
of the things I sense

external distractions

internal distractions

ADHD

Asperger's

Do my distractions tend to occur outside me or inside me?

OCD

Autism

Are they mental or physical?

I can't master
the things
I sense

I can't master
sensation

Neatness

Comfort

physical distractions

Vertical Axis Question:
Are they mental distractions or physical distractions?

Horizontal Axis Question:
Do my distractions tend to occur inside me or outside me?

Asperger's then gets defined as a social impairment wherein internal mental sensations distract the person. These folks struggle with an intermittent inability to manage how they think about the things they sense. Finally, ADHD gets defined as a social impairment wherein external mental sensations distract the person. These folks suffer from an intermittent inability to extricate themselves from the need to manage the other three experiences.

Now ask yourself this. When you get distracted, does this distraction feel like it's coming from inside you? If so, then you have things in common with folks who have Autism and Asperger's. But if your distractions tend to feel like they originate outside you, then you have things in common with folks with OCD and ADHD. Moreover, if these distractions occur mainly in your mind, then you have things in common with folks with Asperger's and ADHD. Whereas if they tend to occur mainly in your body, then you have things in common with folks with Autism and OCD.

Do these definitions sound arbitrary and unscientific? If so, then consider how this quadrant of complementary opposites describes the succession of life skills children must master during their first four years.

To wit, the first life skill babies must master is their bodily sensations. They do this during their first six months of life. Failing this, their bodily sensations randomly overwhelm them. Worst case, they end up with the condition therapists call Autism.

The next life skill babies must master is organizing the things they sense. Sans this, the things they sense become external physical distractions. Generally, by the end of the second six months, babies have this well in hand. But if they don't, they become like little Felix Ungers. Which is to say, they develop the condition therapists call OCD.

Next up on a baby's developmental to-do list is learning to assign meanings to the things they sense. They work on this in the second year of life. Deficits here result in internal mental distractions. And in extreme cases, babies end up with the condition therapists call Asperger's Syndrome.

Lastly, in the third and fourth years of life, children must master the ability to coexist with other beings. To do this, they must learn to free themselves from their own sensations. Failing this, external mental distractions constantly cause them to lose focus, resulting in the condition therapists call ADHD.

Now consider the elegant way in which this map reveals connections between these four conditions. For instance, because Autism and Asperger's are both internal oversensitivities, we could say that having Autism is like having Asperger's of the body—and that having Asperger's is like having Autism of the mind. Whereas since OCD and ADHD are both external oversensitivities, we could say that having OCD is like having ADHD of the body, and that having ADHD is like having OCD of the mind.

In addition, because people with Autism and OCD both suffer from oversensitivities to physical things, we could also say that having Autism is like having an internal version of OCD—and that having OCD is like having an external version of Autism. Similarly, because folks with Asperger's and ADHD both suffer from oversensitivities to mental distractions, we could say that having Asperger's is like having an internal version of ADHD, and that having ADHD is like having an external version of Asperger's.

Know that every aspect of the personality theory presented in this book functions similarly. Everything lives within a quadrant of complementary opposites which is tipping-point based. This is to say, everything in this book is based on a variation of the wise men's map. And because it is, this book is filled with these kinds of previously unseen, elegant truths.

Not bad for plugging a few words into the wise men's map.

Why We Must See All Four Wise Men

Of course, you'll need completed maps in order to uncover these kinds of connections. And to have completed maps, you'll need input from all four wise men. The problem is, we each favor one wise man and tend to ignore the rest. And while most times this isn't a biggie, at other times this can even lead to life threatening situations.

Take me. For years I dreaded going for my annual physical. I'd been seeing an arrogant, patronizing doctor who pooh-poohed my questions and concerns. Worse yet, he often manipulated me with worst case scenarios, claiming this was how he motivated people. And on several occasions, he'd submitted false claims to my insurance, this despite my telling him to stop doing this.

Why didn't I just switch doctors? Two wise men had given him a thumbs up. I'd had friends tell me good things about him—the empirical wise man's truth; stories. He'd been open to alternative treatments and seemed intelligent—the rationalist wise man's truth; ideas. But he didn't send me for any medical tests. So I'd ignored the materialist wise man's truth; facts. And I'd dreaded going, but kept going anyway. So I'd ignored the spiritual wise man's truth; feelings. End result. I knew I should have changed doctors, but I kept going anyway.

In the end, this doctor insulted and ignored me one too many times. So I began to seek a new doctor. Two months later, I found someone so open to my questions that at first I felt uncomfortable. He also treated me like a person of importance in that he welcomed my involvement. For instance, when I asked if I could bring in my home blood pressure machine to see if it matched his readings, he excitedly agreed. At the same time, his thoroughness scared me. For instance, besides the usual blood and urine tests, he sent me for ultrasounds and an MRI. He said he needed to get a baseline for my health. These tests revealed a lot of problems, including two possible cancers—both eventually ruled out—and that I'd lost 100% function in one of my kidneys. Can you imagine not knowing that.

Should I have blamed my previous doctor? At first, I did. For years, he'd explained away kidney-related anomalies in my blood tests as mere dietary problems. Translation. He never sent me for tests. Had he, in all likelihood, I'd still have two working kidneys. Not a pleasant thought. In truth though, the problem lay more in the way I'd surrendered my personal truth. I'd had doubts and concerns, and I knew he should have sent me for tests. But I was scared and couldn't talk about this. So my fears overrode my truth.

Has this kind of thing ever happened to you? Have you ever questioned what your doctor told you only to have him or her dismiss you or worse—tell you you're being difficult? If so, did you then keep your questions to yourself rather than risk provoking more criticisms? Or maybe like me you fear medical procedures and so, welcome alternative treatments. They're less painful, right? Talk about a lack of truth.

Why This Book is the Second in the Series

Before we begin, I need to remind you that this is the second book in a series of three books, all titled, **Finding Personal Truth in the too-much-information age.** This book is **Book II: Unraveling Human Nature.** The previous book is **Book I: Solving the Mind-Body Mystery.** And the final book will be **Book III: Solving the Mysteries of the Universe.**

Know I'd originally hoped to publish all three books under one cover. However, as facing an 800 page tome can discourage even the most adventurous reader, I decided against it.

At the same time, since these three books are still one long book, I've opted to retain the original, single-book, chapter and page numbering scheme. And while you're welcome to read these books in any order you like, reading them in numerical order would be best, as the order in which you read them will greatly affect how much you retain.

As for what we discussed in the previous book, in Book I we looked at a number of things. For one thing, we looked at the four ideas that ground this entire series of books—that we all seek truth, that there are only four ways in which human beings seek truth, that in order to find your "personal" truth you must have access to all four, and that a map of your mind and a method for using this map can give you access to your own wisdom.

Why did I focus on a map and a method, rather than on telling you "the" truth? For one thing, because no matter what people tell you, there is no "one-size-fits-all" truth. For another, because even if there was, one book couldn't possibly hold it all. Mainly I did this though because even the smartest people fall prey to self doubt at times. And because there are only one kind of stupid people—those who blindly accept other people's truths rather than seeking their own. Thus we all need this map and method in order to find our personal truth.

Overall, you should have come away from Book I having discovered two things about yourself. One. You should know which wise men you favor and which you ignore—your biases when it comes to where you look for truth. Two. You should know your mind body orientation—your biases as far as how quickly or slowly you take in this information.

A Few Words About This Book's Content

All books have a theme. This one does too. Finding personal truth in the too-much-information age is this book's theme. Along with this though are a number of auxiliary themes, the main one being that to find this truth, you'll need a method. This book's method centers on making wise men's maps.

In addition, there are assertions I make without which this book could not exist. That personality, like all living things, is fractal, not linear. That synchronicities do not prove all things happen for reasons. That our perception of time is what creates the mind body duality. That startles program blank spots into our minds that only epiphanies can heal.

In addition to these assertions, I make a number of assumptions as well. That all babies are born with an innate capacity, and desire, to find their own truth. That all people suffer injuries to this innate capability. That it takes more than logic and compassion to heal these injuries. That we all deserve this healing. And that only by doing this, can we get the lives we want.

Then there is the thing about how I write. I have Asperger's. This means I use words differently than most people. For instance, there are places in this book where you may feel annoyed by what appear to be redundancies and repetitions. In truth, I'm not repeating myself. I'm merely restating things in different words in order to add shades of meaning.

I also tend to redefine words a lot, starting with the four wise men's truths—facts, feelings, stories, and ideas. However there are literally hundreds of other words which I have felt the need to clarify or redefine. The Asperger's thing again. Know that like Nobel prize winning physicist, Neils Bohr, I agonize over every word. So if something doesn't make sense, know it's probably because of the fussy way I define words.

Why tell you this? Because despite the fact that I've tried to write this book in clear, everyday language, there will be times wherein you'll find yourself getting lost. Indeed, while software tells me this book is written at a fifth grade level, to be honest, you may get lost a lot. When you do, be sure to remember it's not your fault. Or mine, really. Rather, it's likely you've been thrown off by a familiar word or phrase which I have felt the need to refine. Here a little patience and remembering how I've agonized over these words may help.

Then there are the strange diagrams you'll find throughout the book. In these drawings, I marry classical geometry with aspects of fractals and chaos theory. By doing this, complex truths become recognizable geometric shapes and shades of grey. So if you have an art background—or a math education—this will definitely be a plus. And even if you don't, if you relax and just let them seep into your mind, you'll grasp far more.

Know too that I'll do my best to treat you like my grandfather would have—as a person of importance. In all likelihood, the world's been too hard on you, especially when it comes to finding truth. Know the wise men's map can be the remedy for this. So please do give it a try.

Finally, there are three things I'd like to suggest you keep in mind as you read this book. Read slowly and in small gulps. Copy the diagrams and key points into a notebook. And personally imagine yourself in every example.

Why slowly? Because there's far too much information in this book to read it quickly. An unfortunate irony considering this book's title.

Why use a notebook? Nothing paces the flow of information in the mind as well as having the body simultaneously write and draw it. Indeed, even if this is the only thing you learn from this book, by book's end, you'll have significantly improved your ability to grasp all things.

And why personally imagine being in the examples? Because if you don't, you'll likely come away with nothing but frustration. It's personal truth you're seeking here, remember? So please take your reading personally.

Last Thoughts Before You Begin Your Adventure

In a moment, we'll begin our journey together—exploring what it means to be human. Hopefully, by the time you've finished this book, you'll feel the same amazement I feel. At the same time, because we haven't met—and while this may make you uncomfortable—I have something to say to you before you begin.

I believe in you.

I also believe you have it in you to find your own truth, and to use this truth to leave this world a better place for your having lived. This said, it's unlikely you'll read another book like this for the rest of your life. Books normally don't contain this many original ideas. I've literally attempted to explain the essence of everything we experience as human beings, a "theory of everything personal," so to speak. And while I knew I would never succeed, I've tried anyway.

Try anyway.

Steven Paglierani

Chapter 5

A New Way to Look at Who We Are

Fractals, Personality, and Personal Truth

In Book I, I introduced you to the four wise men, explored the four realms of the Axis Mundi map, and used this knowledge to solve a major mystery. In this book, I'm going to take things to a whole new level. I'm going to use what I've shown you so far to composite all of human personality into a single diagram. One diagram. An entire theory of personality. Does this sound impossible? It would be, were we not using the wise men's map and fractals.

What does this theory of personality have to do with finding your personal truth? To begin with, the word *personality* is just a fancy way to refer to who you are. It's everything you think, feel, say, and do. So when you look for personal truth, your personality shapes the whole process, affecting everything from what you'll look for and where you'll look to how you'll interpret your results.

Conversely, since a lot of what we look to find is the truth about ourselves, there is no way to separate personality from personal truth. On the one hand, your personality determines where and how you'll look for truth. On the other, what you find determines a lot about your personality—who you are. Which brings us to the focus of this chapter.

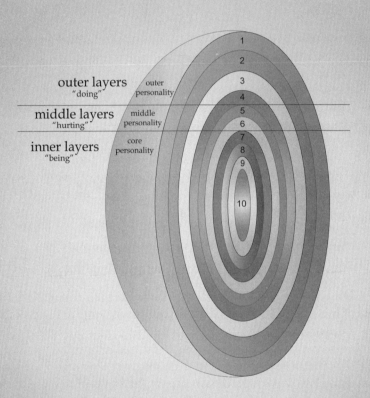

Personality as a Ten Layered Onion
(according to Emergence Personality Theory)
(© 2007 Steven Paglierani The Center for Emergence)

outer layers
"doing"

outer personality

middle layers
"hurting"

middle personality

inner layers
"being"

core personality

1
2
3
4
5
6
7
8
9
10

The Ten Layers of Personality
1 - connections to nothing (personal non existence)
2 - punishing questions, excuses, and explanations for not punishing
      (impersonal non existence)
3 - time limited punishments (temporal duality)
4 - eternal punishments (temporal non existence)
5 - symptoms (hypervisual duality)
6 - blocked needs (visual non existence)
7 - pure needs (disconnected duality)
8 - disconnections / aloneness (universal non existence)
9 - personal connections (connected duality)
10- connections to the "all" (universal existence)

Since finding your personal truth requires you to know a personality theory, I'm going to introduce you to one. Moreover since everything in this theory is based on the wise men's map, it manages to honor all prior theories while resolving their shortcomings and blaming no one. Sound intriguing? Hard to believe? You have no idea.

We All Want to Know Ourselves

From the cave paintings at Lascaux, France, to the female figurines of Catalhoyuk—for as long as we humans have walked the earth—we've been searching for ways to describe our world. In truth, a good portion of everything we've accomplished or created has either been tied to this goal or been a side effect of failing to reach it. Perhaps this is why, were you to study our ancestors, you'd find their searches have much in common with ours today. Including the one thread which flows through all these searches—that the more satisfying ones involve fractals.

What exactly have we been trying to describe? Arguably, the main thing has been who we are. Human personality. For me, this search began at an early age, as most of my childhood memories involve attempts to describe people and how they work. No surprise here. My mother was a schizophrenic who died of anorexia at 48. Her mother spent most of her life in the locked ward of a mental institution—I still have no idea why. I, myself, like half my family, have alcoholism, but am one of the few to actually stop drinking. And as if this is not already enough, I also have Asperger's and a freakishly high IQ.

Why the personal stuff? Because as I've said, there is no way to separate who we are from our personal truth. Since this theory is my personal truth, it may help to know a bit about me and my life. No surprise then that this theory derives entirely from two ideas—[1], that the primary drive in human nature is to avoid suffering, and [2], that personality manifests itself as a series of nested fractals, each of which describe the degree to which we experience this drive.

In a moment, we'll begin to look at how these two ideas play out in your life. Before we do, we'll first need to explore a few of the assumptions which make this theory different. One, we'll need to look at why a personality theory must be fractal. Two, we'll need to talk about how this theory is divided into two parts—the *container* and the *content*. Three, we'll need to look at the idea that to be a proper personality theory, it must benefit us in the real world. And four, we'll need to look at the questions this theory must resolve in order to benefit us. What qualifies something as a theory of personality anyway? What does it need to do?

Sound like a tall order? It is. But what else is new. Good thing the wise men love talking about this stuff. So while I don't think they'll be singing Kumbaya with us any time soon, I doubt there will be any bloodbaths in this chapter either. One can only hope.

Okay. Ready to be amazed by how easy it is to learn new things about personality? Alrighty then. Wise men, will you please dim the lights?

Personality is Fractal

Like all things which describe natural repetitions in the real world, personality is fractal. By this, I mean that everything about us—who we are and what we do—is based on recognizable patterns which always repeat differently. Breaking this phrase down, there are three things to see. One, by *recognizable patterns*, I mean naturally occurring visual patterns like gender and romantic attraction which, once recognized, can easily be identified. Two, by *always repeat*, I mean these patterns are always present. All personalities include the qualities of gender and romantic attraction, even if this means having the tendency to avoid expressing these things. And three, by *always differently*, I mean these patterns resemble snow flakes and oak leaves in that no two will ever be alike. No two people will ever express their gender, or be romantically attracted, in exactly the same way. Nor will any individual ever express their gender, or be romantically attracted, in the same way twice.

Applying these three ideas to people in general, we now get a way to define personality. Personality is *the sum of all the recognizable patterns of human experience and behavior which always repeat differently*. This also gives us a way to define what is not part of personality. At least in theory. What is not part of personality is the sum of all human experience and behavior in which the patterns are either unrecognizable or linear. Finally, I've qualified this second statement as true *only in theory* because, in the real world, there is always the possibility that we will, at some point, become able to recognize a previously unrecognized pattern.

Personality Has Two Parts: the Container and the Content

Having defined the scope of our endeavor, we now come to the first quality which defines personality, the continuum on which all of personality exists. Here the basic idea is that everything about personality can be divided into two piles—the things which explain how we are alike, and those which explain how we are different. I call the first category—the things which are the same in all of us—the *container* for personality. And I call the second category—what is different in all of us—the *content* of this container.

What do I mean by *container* and *content*? To see, consider store-bought bedroom dressers. Have you ever thought about how many people buy the same style bedroom dresser? Obviously, quite a few. At the same time, despite the obvious similarities, none of these dressers will ever contain the same arrangement of clothes or other things. Nor will the contents of any single dresser ever be the same twice, although strong similarities may exist at times. Personality is similar in that, like having the same kind of bedroom dresser, we all store our life experiences in a container of the same design. And similar to the way that no two dressers will ever contain the same content, no two personalities will ever contain the same content either. Nor will the overall content of any single personality ever be the same twice, although, like the content of dressers, strong similarities may exist at times.

Here then is where the drawing I previously mentioned comes in. In the theory of personality I'm about to share with you, the composite drawing will represent the container, and the examples will represent the content. Together, these two things will represent an entire theory of personality. Moreover, before anyone balks at my claim that this one drawing represents a whole theory of personality, know that like all things which represent naturally occurring fractal patterns, this theory has infinite levels of stochastically (non-deterministic) self-similar detail, much of which becomes visible only when we zoom in. Thus similar to the kinds of drawings engineers make, we'll begin with a single, zoomed out drawing, then use "detail" drawings to zoom in.

Adding these two qualities—container and content—to the two definitions we've used to define the scope of personality, we now have the rudiments with which to construct a theory of personality. Moreover, any theory of personality which does not include these rudiments will have more in common with a messy-teenager's bedroom floor than a scientific theory.

In other words, the purpose of a theory of personality is to help us to have good lives. All theories of personality include this in their goals. However, to be useful, this theory must give even lay people clear and distinct *in situ* methods with which to uncover specifics and organize the results, as well as ways in which to make sense of both our triumphs and our failures. The theory I'm about to show you accomplishes all this and more, and does this in ways in which the basics become immediately accessible and useful, even to children. And lest this last comment trigger a round of hoohas from the four incorrigibles, know that at some point in the next chapter, I'm going to tell you a story about a seven year old boy who, after briefly being exposed to parts of this theory, once taught these things to his teacher and classmates, impressing even his teacher. Can you imagine a personality theory so accessible that even a seven year old could share it with others? Or would even want to?

Personality Theories Must Reflect Real World Practice

Speaking of things which are accessible and useful, perhaps this would be a good time to be a bit more specific as to what we're about to explore. We'll do this by asking two things about personality theories in general—what kinds of questions must a personality theory address, and how finite must the answers be?

To begin with, to have any hope of arriving at real world answers, a personality theory must limit the scope of the questions it asks. To do this, it needs to eliminate from it's questioning whole areas of human nature. For example, personality theories should not, in any way, try to posit truths about philosophy, religion, politics, or psychology. At the same time, these theories must describe personality in a way in which we can clearly understand how these four areas of human nature come into being. What makes us so passionate about philosophies, religions, political systems, and psychological theories, and why are these things so ubiquitous? And why isn't personality a subset of these four things?

Next, personality theories should not claim to be therapies. Professional remedies for human suffering, by definition, need be focused on the pragmatic and the technical. At the same time, no therapy can hope to help people with their suffering without deriving theoretical reassurances and professional guidance from a personality theory. Thus personality theories should lead to pragmatic therapies. And these pragmatic therapies must continuously validate and enliven these theories.

Stated in the wise men's language, to be considered a genuine personality theory, this theory must emerge from and integrate ongoing input from all four wise men in the form of facts, feelings, stories, and ideas. To do this, the theory must form a theoretical to real world feedback loop with a therapy. No coincidence, all of the great personality theories do this in spades, while all of the still aspiring to be great personality theories either avoid this entirely or substitute contrived research situations for actual case studies, claiming the lack of control in real life situations invalidates the research results.

In truth, the only thing these contrived research situations accomplish is they guarantee the researchers will still have jobs. Moreover, these attempts to force fit the messy roundness of human nature into the square dry holes of statistics and logic prove once again that given the chance, the wise men can get even the smartest people to fall for the dumbest ideas. Nothing in the real world is linear. Thus any test situation which leads to linear results guarantees these results will never translate to the real world, let alone become the basis for a functional therapy. To be considered a theory which describes real people then, a personality theory must lead to pragmatic, real world results. These results must then be used to test and enhance the theory.

Personality Theories Must Answer the Five Big Questions

This brings us to the next requirement—connecting the metaphysical to the pragmatic. Here we're talking about being able to answer the five big questions in human personality—What are wounds? What is healing? What is learning? What is consciousness? And what is love? In other words, to be considered a personality theory, this theory must define, in a logically clear and factually pragmatic way, these five qualities in human nature. And lest you hear this as mere quixotic rhetoric, try describing human nature without defining even one of these concepts, the idea of wounds, for instance.

What is a wound anyway? Is it having symptoms like depression and anxiety or rage? Many people think so. But if this is true, then does getting rid of symptoms heal wounds and if so, how can you tell the difference between a wound that has been healed and one which is asymptomatic? Obviously, if you define wounds as symptoms, you can't.

But if wounds are not symptoms, then what are they?

Some people define wounds as the outcome of painful experiences— what happens to you when you get raped, for example. And certainly, getting raped wounds people. But if we define wounds as painful events, then why doesn't every rape victim suffer the same symptoms? In truth, they don't. Not even close. In fact, despite this sounding counterintuitive, in my experience, assuming a rape victim will suffer sexually is a serious mistake. Do they suffer? Of course. But not necessarily sexually. We'll look at why in Book III: chapter ten.

The point is, we base our diagnostic manuals—psychological, medical, and so on—on symptoms and painful events. Yet neither of these things could possibly define our wounds. Can you see why not? If personality comprises both a *container* (what is the same in all of us) and *content* (what is different in all of us), then symptoms and painful events cannot be wounds. They are both content. Whereas the wounds themselves must be something which happens to the container.

Defining Wounds as "Damaged Containers"

Are you having trouble seeing this? Then consider our bedroom dresser metaphor again. What would have to happen to a bedroom dresser for us to consider it "wounded?" Would filling it with soiled underwear and undarned socks qualify? Or would the actual dresser itself have to be damaged? The answer is obvious. For us to consider a dresser wounded, it would have to have sustained some sort of permanent damage. Human beings are no different. To be considered wounded, we must have sustained some sort of permanent damage to our container. This in fact is why we experience symptoms. They derive from our attempts to put normal content into a damaged container. We'll address this idea later in the chapter.

The point is, to be considered a true theory of personality, the theory must define *wounds*. It must also do this in a way in which you can use this knowledge to heal these wounds. And lest you see this as me being too hard on theorists, consider how the lack of this one definition would affect the rest of the five big questions.

Answering the Rest of the Five Big Questions

Without a clear and distinct way to define wounds, how do you define healing? Or being unwounded. Or know the difference between these two states? And if you yourself need to heal something, how do you choose a doctor? Or a therapist? Or a spiritual healer? Shouldn't these folks be able to do more than identify and treat your symptoms? Shouldn't they know what your actual wounds are?

If you don't know what your wounds are, then how can you tell if your doctor knows? Because you feel better? Because she's knowledgeable? Because the symptoms go away? What makes a good doctor anyway, or a good therapist, or a good social worker, or a good spiritual healer? Does it really come down to having a superior intuition or a big heart?

Then there's personality theory's really big "H" word—health. What is health? With no real way to define wounds or healing, then how do you know when you're healthy, let alone decide what will make or keep you healthy? For instance, what exactly is it about processed foods which makes them bad for us and unprocessed foods better? Does learning to be more articulate really make our relationships healthier? Do medicines lead to health or do they just hide our wounds, and if they do lead to health, then what explains the placebo effect? Can placebos lead to health? And how do you know that all health is not just the result of the placebo effect?

Then there's learning. What is learning? And what are learning disabilities? For instance, when someone has trouble learning, how do you know whether she's being resistant to the process or if she has wounds which prevent her from enjoying the process? Without knowing what wounds are, you cannot know, let alone hope to help her learn.

What proves you've learned something anyway? Is it passing tests? Is it being able to generalize knowledge? Is it having fancy degrees? If so, then why do even people with advanced degrees forget most of what schools claim they've been taught in less time than it takes for a breeze to diffuse a fart?

Then there's personality theory's really big "C" word—consciousness. What defines human consciousness anyway? Is it having learned life lessons? Is it being able to live what we've learned? Is it having the answers to all of life's questions. Is it some elevated state of mind? And yes, I'm well aware that some pretty smart people have been coming up short for thousands of years now in their efforts to define consciousness.

So am I claiming I can define consciousness? From the viewpoint of personality, yes, I am, albeit, this in no way means I have an absolute definition for consciousness. At the same time, this definition gives us ways to understand everything from why our feelings for people change when they die to where the meaning in life comes from. We'll explore this in depth in Book III: chapter nine, when we look at how all it takes to define human consciousness is four simple algebraic formulas, this and a little psychophysical topography in the form of another composite drawing.

Finally, we have personality theory's really big "L" word, and no, it's not "lesbian," although lesbians feel this too. Here we're talking about what some folks see as the one thing which heals all wounds—love. What is love anyway? Is it longing? Admiration? Altruism? Something more? And if we can't define love, then how can we hope to find it? Or know for sure if it's our wounds which prevent us from getting it? Do we leave it to fate? Do we hope for a meaningful accident? Do we spend our lives seeking less dysfunctional partners? Do we resign ourselves to settling?

All this from not being able to define one word—wounds. Are you beginning to see what makes personality theories important and why I'm claiming that, to be considered a genuine personality theory, this theory must define these five qualities in ways in which these definitions better our lives? Moreover, while no personality theory should promise you'll master these kinds of things—or even claim it can define them absolutely—it should at least offer you some kind of a picture for them, as without this picture, you'll have a hard time getting the life you want.

Summarizing What We've Said About Personality Theories

So let's summarize what we've said so far. What makes something a theory of personality?

We started by defining the scope of personality. Personality is *the sum of all the recognizable patterns of human experience and behavior which always repeat differently.* This makes a personality theory a system of recognizable patterns of human behavior, experience, and consciousness which generalizes, in fractals, who and what we are as persons. Human behavior is what we do. Experience is what it feels like to do it. Consciousness is what allows us to do things and feel what it's like to be doing them.

Next we defined the overall structure of personality. Here we divided personality into two categories, *container* and *content*, with the container being the things which are the same in all of us, and the content, what is different. This means personality theories must divide their hypotheses into these same two categories, and do this in ways in which even lay people can see the difference.

We then discussed the need for personality theories to generate real world results, including that they must form a theoretical to real world feedback loop with a therapy. This is true because, while people-oriented scientific research certainly has its place in things like psychology and politics, in personality theory, it cannot substitute for real world case studies. After all, we're talking about person-ality theories—theories which explain us as living breathing individuals, and not people-ality theories—theories which merely generalize all of us and what we do while never actually describing us as living, breathing persons. This, by the way, is the main difference between personality theories and the four big classes of people-ality theories—philosophy, religion, politics, and psychology.

Finally, we spoke about the need for personality theories to connect the metaphysical to the pragmatic. Know this is just a fancy way to say they must connect the mind to the body. Here we spoke about the five big questions a personality theory must answer—what are wounds, what is healing, what is learning, what is consciousness, and what is love? We also looked at how the lack of a way to define any one of these things would affect our overall ability to find personal truth, in particular, how the inability to define wounds would affect the remaining four questions.

Now let's begin to look at what the wise men have to say about personality. What kind of a personality theory could fit in a single drawing anyway? The answer? A mighty powerful one. Or so say the four know-it-alls—the rationalist, materialist, empirical, and spiritual wise men.

Section One

The Inner Layers
of
Personality:

"Being"

Metaphors as Clothing for Ideas

In Book I: chapter four, I mentioned that personal truths must result in composite drawings. There the example I used was the composited drawing of the four philosopher's views on the mind body mystery. How the heck could anyone be expected to put all of human nature into a single composite drawing though? Isn't this asking too much?

Like everything else the wise men have to teach us, when you finally understand how this drawing works, you'll be amazed by how easily fractals can simplify complex subjects like personality. But because the four blockheads like to make us work for things, and because they want to remain mysterious, they prefer to use metaphors rather than telling us their teachings directly. Unfortunately, because we so rarely take metaphors seriously, these lessons more times than not remain hidden in plain sight.

For instance, consider my two favorite ways to express the composite drawing for personality—the Onion metaphor and the Russian nesting dolls metaphor. We've been using these metaphors to represent personality for a long time now. Rarely do we take them seriously though. Surprisingly, either metaphor is capable of compositing the entirety of human personality in a single drawing. The thing is, in this chapter, we'll be using both metaphors. So in case this makes it sound like we'll be using more than one drawing, allow me to point out a few things about metaphors.

Metaphors function like clothing for ideas. What I mean is, with clothing, you can change your image by changing what you wear. Wearing different outfits shows different sides of you. Changing metaphors does the same thing for ideas. By using more than one metaphor for the same idea, in effect, you dress up this idea in different clothes. This increases the chances people will understand this idea, by offering them different ways to look at it.

Why must we use metaphors? Because ideas, in and of themselves, are invisible. At the same time, as I told you in Book I, all ideas are based on stories and stories are visible. In addition, all metaphors are stories, which in part explains how they can reach us in ways which far exceed words. This means, when I call these drawings, "composite drawings," I'm referring to that they use metaphors to composite whole systems of ideas into a single drawing.

As for the idea that I'll be using more than one drawing, it's simple. This theory does indeed fit into a single drawing. However, because composite drawings more refer to the underlying concepts than to the clothing they're dressed up in, I've dressed this theory up in more than one metaphor so as to improve your chances to understand it.

Composite Drawings as Containers for Theories

Now consider how this explains why the four wise men's composite drawings are such an integral part of their teaching theories. Theories are extensive collections of interrelated ideas. Thus like having a bedroom dresser with an unlimited capacity, a composite drawing can, in a compact and well organized way, contain a theory. Know this capacity, in and of itself, does not guarantee a theory will be correct. However, since all metaphors are fractal, basing a composite drawing on a metaphor forces this theory to either fall apart or take the form of an interrelated group of fractals.

As for the idea that composite drawings can contain infinite amounts of detail, as I've already mentioned, to see this detail, we'll need to do something similar to what architects and draftsmen do when they use breakout drawings to clarify construction details and technical functions. Only in our case, because what we're zooming in on is fractal, these zooms will more resemble opening a nesting doll, or peeling layers of an onion, in that what we'll be looking to see will be the stochastically self-similar aspects of human nature. Said in simpler terms, we'll be using these detail drawings to expose the kind of non linear repetitions which exist within all living things—smaller versions of the same design.

Now let's begin to look at the actual theory. What does a fractal personality theory look like anyway? We'll start by talking briefly about the overall nature of the container. Its structure. We'll then look at how this container comes into being. How do we get a personality? Finally, we'll touch on a few of the implications of this theory. If personality is fractal, then what does this mean about theories that are not fractal? Are they wrong? Here I'm sure you can guess the answer—they're all true in their own way. How can this be? We're about to find out.

The Container for Personality: the Basic Design

On the next page, you'll find the Russian nesting dolls version of the composite drawing. In it, you'll see a cross section of a ten doll matryoshka set. Here each doll is numbered, 1 through 10, with doll number 1 being the outermost doll, and doll number 10 the innermost doll.

Know these numbers have a meaning. They represent the logarithmic intensity of what we see on the screen of our mind. Thus doll ten is the most visually and personally intense, and doll one is the least. In addition, the order of these numbers also has a meaning. Doll ten represents the first part of personality to appear and doll one, the last.

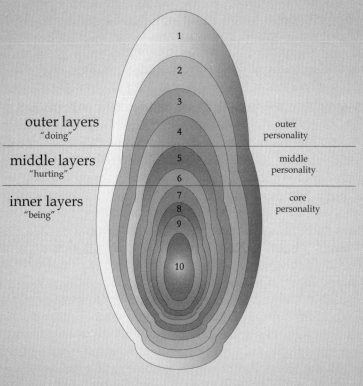

Personality as the Ten Russian Nesting Dolls
(according to Emergence Personality Theory)
(© 2007 Steven Paglierani   The Center for Emergence)

outer layers
"doing"

middle layers
"hurting"

inner layers
"being"

outer
personality

middle
personality

core
personality

1
2
3
4
5
6
7
8
9
10

The Ten Layers of Personality
1 - connections to nothing (personal non existence)
2 - punishing questions, excuses, and explanations for not
punishing (impersonal non existence)
3 - time limited punishments (temporal duality)
4 - eternal punishments (temporal non existence)
5 - symptoms (hypervisual duality)
6 - blocked needs (visual non existence)
7 - pure needs (disconnected duality)
8 - disconnections (universal non existence)
9 - connections to persons (connected duality)
10 - connections to the "all" (universal existence)

Now notice how these dolls are referred to as "layers," not dolls. This has been done so as to maintain a consistent method by which to refer to the parts of this system. Thus beneath the nesting dolls metaphor lies an even more fundamental system, the essence of which are the two ideas I mentioned at the beginning of this chapter—[1], that the primary drive in human nature is to avoid suffering, and [2], that personality manifests itself as a series of nested fractals, each of which describe the degree to which we experience this drive. Here the dolls represent the ten major fractals, and these fractals are called *layers*.

Why layers? Because this personality theory was originally dressed up in the onion metaphor and onions have layers. However, because the onion metaphor can only represent personality in the real world—and because all truths, even theoretical truths, exist somewhere on a horizontal axis from real world to theory—I also needed a theoretical metaphor. The nesting dolls metaphor represents the theoretical version of this system.

Now notice how these ten layers have been divided into three groups. Here the outer group describes what it's like to be "doing" things, the middle group what it's like to be "hurting," and the inner group what it's like to just "be." Know that even this grouping has a specific meaning, much of which we'll discuss later in the chapter. We'll also discuss the number of layers in each of the three groups—four in the outer layers, two in the middle layers, and four in the inner layers. Here again, these numbers have a meaning.

Finally, notice how each of the ten layers have been assigned both a theoretical name and a real world name. You'll find these names listed below the nested dolls. For instance, the theoretical name for layer 10 is *universal existence*, while its real world name is "connections to the all." And the theoretical name for layer 1 is *personal non existence*, while its real world name is "connections to nothing."

In a moment, we'll begin to discuss what all these names and numbers mean. Before we do, did you notice how these two layers, 10 and 1, form yet another pair of complementary opposites—*universal existence* to *personal non existence*, and *connections to the all* to *connections to nothing*? In part, this kind of symmetry is what makes this personality theory unique. Every part of the theory is theoretically symmetrical to every other part (like the nesting dolls), while at the same time, being stochastically self similar in every real world aspect (like the onion).

By the way, like the layers, this personality theory has both a formal name and an informal name. The formal (theoretical) name is Emergence

Personality Theory, while the informal (real world) name is the Four Wise Men's Personality Theory. Use either name. The wise men won't mind.

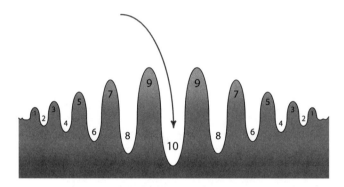

Personality as Pond Ripples
(the ten layers of personality)
(© 2007 Steven Paglierani The Center for Emergence)

The Ten Layers of Personality
1 - connections to nothing (personal non existence)
2 - punishing question, excuses, and explanations for not punishing
(impersonal non existence)
3 - time limited punishments (temporal duality)
4 - eternal punishments (temporal non existence)
5 - symptoms (hypervisual duality)
6 - blocked needs (visual non existence)
7 - pure needs (disconnected duality)
8 - disconnections (universal non existence)
9 - connections to persons (connected duality)
10 - connections to the "all" (universal existence)

Personality as Pond Ripples

If you picture a rock being thrown into a pond, you'll have a pretty good idea of how personality comes into being. Except with personality, there are only ten outwardly-directed ripples. If you now add to this that there are always things floating on the surface of this pond, you have a pretty good picture for how life events shape our personality.

We'll have a lot more to say about this metaphor later in the book, especially about how the peaks and troughs represent the yin and yang qualities of the various layers. Even a casual look though reveals good-to-know things like that layer 10—universal existence—is the only yin unity, while layer 9—connected duality—is the only yang duality with no yang space in it.

Does this already sound like gibberish? Most of the stuff in this chapter will at first. Don't worry. By the end of the chapter, you'll probably be asking yourself things like why you haven't paid more attention to Taoist philosophy and the physics of transverse waves. Or not. Either way, all that matters is that you emerge from this chapter with a good working sense of how to explore your own personality. And the personalities of those around you. And if you're patient and take your time, you will.

Early Personality: the First Three Access Sequences

Now turn to the drawing on the next page, *How Personality Comes Into Being*. This is one of the detail drawings I mentioned earlier. In it, you'll find a sequence of three groupings of nesting dolls—[1] the pre-personality stage, [2] the birth separation moment, and [3] the personality begins stage. Here each grouping represents a stage in the early development of personality.

What exactly happens to us in these early stages, and why make such a fuss about them? In short, the *pre-personality* stage creates the pattern for being in love, the *birth separation moment* creates the pattern for how we get wounded, and the *personality begins stage* creates the pattern for our core personality, the layers in which we are just "being ourselves."

Keep in mind, we're talking containers not content here. Thus these nesting dolls do not represent life experiences. Nor do they cause them to happen. They only *contain* life experiences. At the same time, whenever we access the content of these containers, or put new content into them, the order in which we make these accesses does cause life experiences. Big time. Including the most significant life experience of all—the birth separation moment sequence.

Know I'm not saying that being born is the most significant life experience. I'm saying that the access sequence we experience during the birth separation moment is. This brings us to the first big thing to know about how the ten layers of personality affect us.

To wit, while it obviously matters which layer we're in as each layer holds a different kind of stuff, the order in which we access this stuff matters too. Moreover, of all the possible access sequences we can or will ever make, the most powerful—and painful—involves going from layer 10 to 9 to 8 to 7. This access sequence literally underlies all of human personality, driving who we are, what we do, and how we think and feel.

How Personality Comes Into Being
How Our Core Personality Forms (The Inner Four Layers)
(© 2007 Steven Paglierani   The Center for Emergence)

[1] the pre-personality stage
(before birth, we have a two layer personality
and so, have never felt separation)

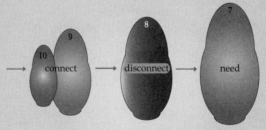

[2] the birth-separation moment
(this access sequence and the pain it causes defines what it means to be human)
connect — disconnect — need

[3] the personality-begins stage
(we now have a four layer personality)

At the same time, it also hurts like hell to access these layers in this order. So I doubt you'll be surprised to hear that it's also what's behind the "stick" half of the famous carrot and stick style of motivation.

What's behind the carrot half then? The pre-personality sequence wherein we cycle between layers 9 and 10. Here we're talking about the times wherein we feel we love someone or something, regardless of the object of these feelings. Obviously love is a strong motivation, to be sure. But next to the hellish 10-9-8-7 stick half of this dynamic duo, as a motive, love pales by comparison. Thus we tend to place a higher value on avoiding the pain of 10-9-8-7 accesses than on feeling the joy of 9-10 accesses. Hence our problems with intimacy and ambivalence, including our two biggest fears—the fear of commitment, and the fear of abandonment.

Did what I just said make sense to you? When we make pre-personality accesses (9-10), we feel love. And when we make birth separation moment accesses (10-9-8-7), we get or relive getting a wound. This makes the birth separation moment access sequence the most painful experience we can have, and the pre-personality access sequence, the sweetest. Moreover, since we must risk experiencing the dreaded birth separation access sequence in order to feel love, we tend to admire love from a distance, preferring the safe distances of the outer layers (4, 3, 2, and 1). We'll talk about why these four layers make us feel safe later on in the chapter.

The "Five Big Questions" Access Sequence

Finally, like everything in our world, the key to understanding these two access-sequence patterns is to look at their opposite. Here I'm referring to the access sequence of 7-8-9-10. What is this access sequence like? For one thing, it is the only access sequence which can momentarily trump the birth separation moment access sequence. However, because all 7-8-9-10 accesses are followed by birth separation moment access sequences, we tend to avoid 7-8-9-10 accesses too.

Can you guess what kind of life experiences this sequence refers to? Its name should give it away. Its called the "five-big-questions" access sequence, as it defines all experiences wherein we [1] discover the true nature of a wound, [2] heal this wound, [3] learn, in the permanent sense of learning, [4] become more conscious, and [5] fall in love. You might also be interested to know that this access sequence is what's behind all spiritual epiphanies, personal aha's, self realizations, scientific discoveries, and emergences in general. Thus this access sequence gives us a clear and distinct way to define these things. Can you imagine?

The Five-Big-Questions Access Sequence
(the metafractal sequence for all positive permanent change)

(© 2007 Steven Paglierani The Center for Emergence)

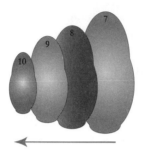

the five-big-questions access sequence

Layer 7 - pure needs (disconnected duality)
Layer 8 - disconnections (universal non existence)
Layer 9 - connections to persons (connected duality)
Layer 10 - connections to the "all" (universal existence)

A First Look at the Inner Layers

Now let's look at how these initial four layers come into being. We'll begin with the first stage in the development of personality, the pre-personality stage. We'll then look at the two layers which make up this stage—layer 10 which holds all the life experiences wherein we feel "connected to the all," and layer 9 which holds all the life experiences in which we feel "connected to persons." Or voiced as theoretical descriptions of what it's like to access these layers, the state known as *universal existence* (layer 10), and the state known as *connected duality* (layer 9). Finally we'll look at the birth separation moment. What is it about this access sequence that makes it so powerful anyway? And why do I keep referring to it as what underlies all of personality?

To see, we'll look at the two layers which emerge in us during this moment, layer 8 (universal non existence) which holds all the life experiences wherein we disconnect from something or someone, and layer 7 (disconnected duality) which holds all the life experiences wherein we feel the results of these disconnections—pure need.

Universal existence. Connected duality. Universal non existence. Disconnected duality. It all sounds a bit grandiose, doesn't it? To be honest, this is part of why the wise men so love talking about this stuff. They just love feeling that what they know is important. Then again, don't we all?

Okay then. I think we're ready to rock and roll. Wise men, would you please dim the lights?

Conception to Birth: Our Pre-Personality

"Happily-ever-aftering."

Finding "the one."

"Soul mates" and "twin flames."

"Someday, my prince will come."

Have you ever wondered why so much of what we long for involves an ideal connection to another human being? The answer to this question lies in the idea of *pre-personality*—the state we lived in between conception and birth. What was this state like? If you can access a memory in which you felt totally and completely in love, you're well on your way to knowing. Now add to this mix the most important ingredient of all—that you've never felt any other way. You now have a good idea of what pre-personality was like. Dreamy, safe, warm, protected—not a care in the world.

Does it sound like I am idealizing pre-babyhood? In reality, I'm not. But to see this, you'll need to imagine never having felt separate, abandoned, or alone. Not ever. Not once. Now consider how the idealistic longing implicit in the things I opened with all derive from the relief we would feel to never be alone *again*—happily-ever-aftering (after what?), finding "the one" (you've been looking?), soul mates and twin flames (ditto), and "someday, my prince will come" (someday?).

Can you now see what's so special about never having felt alone? No? Then think about this. Imagine never having eaten a meal alone in your whole life—more, having shared every meal with the one you love. Add to this that you have always worn matching outfits, and always held hands, and always felt this person snuggling next to you.

Does this description sound over the top? If so, then remember, we're talking about sharing the same physical space here—the same air, the same blood, the same food, the same everything.

Can you imagine being that close to anyone? This much in love?

The point is, we all did feel this way once, in the days between our conception and birth. And yes, we also probably faced our share of distress during this time—intermittent discomfort is a human norm. But imagine never having to face discomfort alone?

This is what I mean by the state of pre-personality—the state of total love. Truly, we all once had a soul mate and had found "the one." And together, we happily-ever-aftered in paradise.

Layer 10: Universal Existence (connections to the all)

Now let's look briefly at the innermost container in this stage of our development, layer 10. What do I mean when I say this container holds all the life experiences wherein we feel "connected to the all?"

To begin with, when I say *connected*, I do not mean this to sound like once separate things have now been reconnected. Rather, in this, the state of *universal existence*, we feel that we and all else in the universe were, are, and always will be one and the same. In a way then, this state much resembles Spinoza's theoretical pantheistic view. Or to put it in real world terms, it's like being a part of what Fritjof Capra calls, the "web of life."

Whatever we call it, the thing to see is how it feels to be in layer 10. Here, rather than sensing an external connection, i.e. that we and all other people, places, and things are separate entities now reunited—instead, we more feel an internal connection, in effect, that we and all other people, places, and things are different aspects of one and the same thing. If you then choose, like Spinoza, to personify this state by calling it *God*, you've defined spiritual/empirical means and methods as the source of your personal truth. And if you choose, as Spinoza also did, to simultaneously not personify this state by calling it *nature*, then you've also grounded your searches for personal truth in materialist facts and rationalist logic as well.

Either way, layer 10 is literally what underlies our metaphoric references to heart, soul, God, and nature. It is the alpha and the omega—the beginning and the end—the first and the last. As such, it is the universal truth underlying all things, including us. Hence, like Spinoza's description of the one substance with infinite attributes, the content of layer 10 is experiences of the infinite variety.

At the same time, like Spinoza's description of our limited access to this ineffable all, we experience the contents of layer 10 only through the attributes of extension and thought. Said in the wise men's language, we experience it in only two ways—through the experiences we call *impressions* (our experiences of physical things), and through the experiences we call *thoughts* (our experiences of the lack thereof). And whenever these thoughts and impressions feel universal, we're accessing layer 10.

Layer 9: Connected Duality (connections to persons)

Now let's take a brief look at layer 9. To begin with, I'm using one of those philosophically difficult words—duality—in the formal title. Moreover, this word is being used in a somewhat non obvious way. To wit, in most cases, the word duality refers to an inherent separateness. And this is true here as well. However, because layer 9 holds only experiences wherein we feel both an internal duality and an external duality, the duality of layer 9 is a special kind of duality—a "connected" duality. Here the internal duality originates from our having once felt connected to the all, but now, knowing this only as an observer. And the external duality comes from knowing that we and our mothers were once both separate beings and at the same time, one being.

Does this sound like a lot to take in? You have no idea. Or maybe you do and like me, you realize it's nearly impossible to put this sacred experience into words. Suffice to say layer 9 is the origin of all two-sides-by-one-coin things, the state in which unity and duality combine into what the wise men call, a "two-that-are-one" state.

How is layer 9's "two-that-are-one" state different from that of layer 10?

In both cases, we feel the total absence of aloneness, hence, the absence of suffering. However in layer 9, we feel intimately connected to only one other being. This is sort of like having an identical twin and watching sunsets together. Hence my saying that pre-personality is the origin of our belief in soul mates and happily-ever-aftering.

At the same time, unlike layer 10 wherein we're connected to all things, in layer 9 we feel disconnected from all things *except* for this one other being. This experience much resembles what it's like to be newly in love and wanting to spend all your time away from the world with this one other being. Thus unlike what you feel when you're in layer 10, wherein being separated from any part of the world feels like an intrusion, in layer 9, experiences of the "outside world" are the intrusion. Hence the informal designation, "connections to persons," rather than connections to people, places, and things.

Overall the thing to see is that, in layer 9, we feel both the total lack of aloneness and the total lack of connection to all else. Thus layer 9 is the source of all falling-in-love feelings, while layer 10 is the source of all being-in-love feelings.

The State of Pre-Personality

If we now nest these two layers, we get a sense of what the state of pre-personality is like. Moreover, in case you have yet to read Book I, layer 10 derives from our psychophysical experience of the brain in the gut (a single unity), while layer 9 derives from our psychophysical experience of the brain in the head (a connected duality). Even knowing this though, it's difficult to imagine being in this state.

The Pre-Personality State of Being
(layers 9 and 10)
(© 2007 Steven Paglierani   The Center for Emergence)

pre-personality (before birth)

The Two Layers of Pre-Personality
Layer 9 - connections to persons (connected duality)
Layer 10 - connections to the "all" (universal existence)

For example, try to imagine what it must have been like to have been in layer 10 before birth. Most people, when they do this, inadvertently retain their identity, the result of having a layer 9. Unfortunately, this is a gross, but understandable, misconception. Since separateness does not exist in layer 10, retaining an identity in layer 10 is impossible.

Know that this very conundrum underlies many of our struggles to find peace, especially when we seek the kinds of connected states spiritual practitioners aspire to such as the Buddhist's dissolving ego or the mystical Christians' merging with God. In this way, pre-personality defines the joy of surrendering ourselves to God, nature, and another being. At the same time, it's also the source of much of our post-birth fear—especially the fear that we'll lose ourselves. Here needing to choose between having an identity (layer 9) and being connected to the "all" (layer 10) causes a conflict to arise. And because we're programmed to desire both, we forever dream of returning to the state wherein we once did have both—the state of pre-personality.

Finally, please note that while my choice of words might make it sound like I'm biased toward the spiritual wise man, I, in no way mean to give you this impression. The spiritual wise man's truths derive entirely from a post-birth view. Whereas the pre-personality viewpoint I've just offered is more my bravely ventured—but admittedly flawed—theoretical attempt to describe what we feel like between conception and birth.

Realize, this same difficulty is what we encounter when we try to describe experiences like aha's, epiphanies, and self-realizations. Here again, our view is filtered though the imperfect lens of personality. At the heart of this imperfection lies this same layer 10/layer 9 ambivalence—the desire to retain an identity while at the same time, dissolving into the all. And because we once had both—but without this conflict—we are forever trying to return to the pre-personality state.

When Does Personality Begin?

Now we come to the pivotal moment in all of personality—the moment in which we're forcibly and without warning ejected from paradise. To address this, we'll need to face a question most theorists avoid—whether personality begins with conception, or whether it begins in the birth separation moment. This question—when does personality begin—is truly one of the more controversial and thought provoking. But to be a proper theory of personality, a theory must address this question.

So what do most theorists say?

Modern theorists, and most people in general, believe personality begins with conception. In Plato's time though, many believed it began with the birth separation moment. Unfortunately, since none of us can—at least not with anything like scientific or spiritual certainty—remember what happened in the birth separation moment, we tend to avoid this question and defer to current assumptions. And since all these assumptions ignore the obvious—that the answer rests entirely on how you define personality—they leave us with no way to know for sure what they think makes you a person. Definitely a strange omission for theories purporting to be person-ality theories.

Strangely, novelists have done better. For instance, take Issac Asimov. In his 1976 novella, *The Bicentennial Man*, he poses this very question when he asks what would make a robot, a person. His point? That this quality is inordinately difficult to define. No kidding.

So when do we become persons? The wise men claim this occurs in the birth separation moment. Admittedly, it may take me most of this book to explain why they feel this way. At the same time, please know, this in no way implies we might have been nothing before this moment. Indeed, even a casual glance at the previous subsection shows their respect for this time in our lives. However, to call someone a "person" is different than to say he or she is alive, albeit, to see why, we'll need to look at how being alive in the state of pre-personality (or before that, if your beliefs are so inclined) differs from being alive after the birth separation moment.

Whatever the truth here, to be a personality theory, this question—what makes us persons—must be addressed. So when does personality begin? Do you have a strong opinion? If so, do you have an equally strong supporting argument—a personal truth about this? Let's see.

The Birth-Separation-Moment Access Sequence
(how layers 7 and 8 come into being)
(© 2007 Steven Paglierani The Center for Emergence)

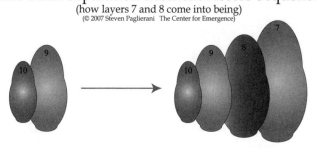

This change is caused by the birth-separation-moment.
(the metafractal sequence for all of personality)
[1] connection, [2] disconnection, [3] pure need

In this moment, the Pre-Personality Layers divide and multipy.
(the first two layers expand into four layers)

Layer 9 - connections to persons (connected duality)
Layer 10 - connections to the "all" (universal existence)

Layer 7 - pure needs (disconnected duality)
Layer 8 - disconnections (universal non existence)
Layer 9 - connections to persons (connected duality)
Layer 10 - connections to the "all" (universal existence)

The Birth Separation Moment: Our First Broken Heart

Imagine going from a state of total love to a state of total need with no warning whatsoever? One minute you're happily sunning yourself in the Garden of Eden. The next, you're free-falling into a smothering pit of darkness. A moment later, you wake up—blind, naked, and confused—and all on your own for the first time in your life. And yes, you're still alive and you suspect this might be a good thing. But you've never been away from home before. So you have no idea what you're supposed to do.

To top it all off, you have no coping skills whatsoever, not even the ones most grown-ups use to deal with free-falls into darkness—philosophy, religion, politics, and psychology. In truth, those things won't begin to exist in you for at least another half decade. And obviously, you can't wait.

So where does this leave you?

With the same humiliating options you'll be faced with later in life when someone breaks your heart. You can either beg, whine, and whimper until someone new comes along. Or you can seek more accessible solutions like folding into a good old fetal position, or desperately sucking down food. Or escaping into sleep. Glorious sleep.

Was this painful eviction really necessary, you wonder (in symbolic language, of course)? Did you treat her all that badly? What did you do that was so wrong anyway?

The truth? Yes, you did treat her that badly. In fact, you were beginning to be a real back & ball breaker, regularly hogging the whole bed, stealing the blankets, and tossing and turning all night. Sometimes you even kicked her. Hard. Oh, boy. The things mothers put up with for love.

Humor aside, the thing to realize here is something we normally don't consider—that the birth separation moment was our first breakup; our first broken heart. Think I'm kidding? I'm not. You literally once had a soul mate and the two of you lived in paradise. Then with no signs or warning, she broke up with you. Good grief! She even threw your stuff out in the street. No wonder you're afraid to take chances. This was your welcome to the world!

The main thing to come away with here is that this painful breakup—and the 10-9-8-7 access sequence which underlies it—are the first things we experience as physically-separate human beings. Hence my saying, this access sequence is the fractal from which all of personality forms. Moreover, given that this event is so painful, is it any wonder we're afraid to love? After getting hurt like that, who wants to risk it again?

Now let's turn our focus to the two new layers which emerge during this event—layers 8 and 7. How do these two layers change paradise into hell on earth? And how does avoiding the painful aloneness of our first broken heart emerge as the main drive in personality?

Layer 8: Universal Non Existence (disconnections)

Is it beginning to dawn on you why so many people feel they once lost something important, but can't say what—or that life is a struggle and inherently unfair—or that the world is by nature a dangerous place—or that they'll never find a place they can call "home?" We all had a perfect love once. And a perfect home. Then it all got taken away and replaced with what philosopher Jean-Paul Sartre called a God shaped hole, a huge emptiness wherein our most painful experiences reside—our experiences of *universal non existence*. "Universal" as in everything we know. "Non existence" as in, none of it exists.

What is it like to feel that nothing exists? As I've said, we feel like we are free-falling into a smothering darkness, albeit, my use of the word *feeling* here is somewhat misleading. Thus similar to the way even light cannot exist in a black hole, even feelings cannot exist in layer 8.

What kind of experience could possibly cause such a hideously painful state? In a word, *annihilation*—the total destruction of all we know, including ourselves. And this last part is the problem. You see, in order to be able to see what being in layer 8 is like, we must somehow cease to exist and still be able to experience being in this layer.

Are you beginning to see what makes layer 8 so terrifying? And so hard to put into words? We simultaneously experience the loss of all we know, the loss of all we might know, and the loss of ourselves. And lest you think this is logically impossible, consider this.

Entering layer 8 is the underlying goal of all Zen meditations. It is what lies immediately beyond the demons of Buddha's final temptation, but before nirvana. It is also what lies just beyond Christ's temptations, inbetween heaven and earth. It is also the psychological hell we suddenly enter whenever we lose access to someone or something we love. As well as what we physiologically experience in the instants in which our breathing changes direction from in-breath to out and back.

Of course, the part that's hard to describe is how we could feel no sensations whatsoever and still know we're accessing layer 8. Who is doing this knowing, and how could we possibly "feel" the total absence of sensation? In reality, we can't even feel needy in layer 8. These kinds of feelings—and actually all painful feelings—do not begin to exist until we enter layer 7.

So how could we possibly know layer 8 exists? Again, it's kind of similar to how we know there are black holes. Because no light can escape black holes, we can't actually see or measure them directly. We can, however, see and measure what is happening around them. The same thing holds true for layer 8. We can't actually see or measure it directly. But we can see and measure what happens to us as we enter and exit this layer.

What this leaves us with then is that if there is a hell, truly, it must be layer 8. And being that layer 8 forms a moat around layers 9 and 10, we now have an explanation for why we're so afraid to seek love. Who, in their right mind, would consciously choose to cross or even approach this moat? Even demons can't exist there. Which is why, even with years of sincere personal effort, at best, we can manage to enter layer 8 only for the briefest of instants. And even then, more times than not, we fail to realize it. Moreover, since time as we know it ceases to exist in layer 8, we can't even tell how long we were there. For an instant? A lifetime? For eternity? More?

This leads us to one of the most important things to know about personality. When I told you that the primary drive in human nature is to avoid suffering, I wasn't just talking about pain in general. Rather, the pain I was referring to is the experience of layer 8. Thus avoiding layer 8 is the drive beneath all human motives.

Why call this motive, *avoiding suffering*? Because layer 8 is a theoretical construct and I wanted to voice this drive using real world terms. Unfortunately, in doing this, I had to face yet another limitation—that there are no words to describe the horrific experience of being in layer 8, as even the word *suffering* is too vague. In the end, I decided to call this prototypical suffering *aloneness*. Why aloneness? Because of all the words in the dictionary, none comes closer to what I perceive this agony to be—so totally alone that you don't even have yourself to talk to.

Admittedly, even this word fails to describe layer 8, as implicit in the word *aloneness* is the idea that we somehow exist. Since being in layer 8 is *the total lack of experience*, however, this cannot be. Thus the main thing to take away about layer 8 is how it affects our motives. To wit, moving outward and away from layer 8 is the most powerful motive in human nature—while our secondary motive—reclaiming pre-birth love—lies only across the moat of aloneness, in the opposite direction.

Layer 7: Disconnected Duality (pure needs)

You're one second old. Can you imagine? You've just survived personality's big bang and a terrifying trip through layer 8, only to end up in some place almost as bad—helpless, scared, and needy. So what is being in layer 7 like? In essence, it's like the worst heartache you can ever imagine and then some. In many ways, you feel like you just got the wind knocked out of you and you're desperately sucking for air. Literally, you feel compelled to cry out but can't find your words. You're also still naked, blind, and confused, and urgently longing for your soul mate. But something is different. Very different. You now have a self. Your own little personality, complete with all the thoughts and impressions you hope will guide you back to paradise. Little do you know that the closest you'll ever come will be to fall in love. Even here though, this relief will never last for more than the blink of a proverbial eye. Moreover, since falling in love always results in repeatedly reliving the birth separation moment, even though love is wonderful, you'll soon learn to avoid it like the plague. Or at least learn to be very freakin' cautious when you see it coming your way.

How does layer 7's desperate neediness compare to the terrifying void of layer 8?

In layer 8, we experience the total loss of all we can know. Sensation, connection, even thoughts and impressions—all cease to exist. Thus compared to layer 8, layer 7 feels like warm summer breezes and lemonade while being gently rocked on a hammock.

Compared to the sated fullness of paradise, though, being in layer 7 is like the worst ache you can ever imagine. All sensations, thoughts, and impressions focus on only one thing—finding something to ease the pain. This is why layer 7 is called the state of "pure need." It's the state in which nothing exists except need. Thus the difference between layers 8 and 7 is, in layer 8, nothing exists. But in layer 7, nothing but need exists. Indeed, if you're at all familiar with the tenets of Buddhism or Hinduism, you've likely heard of this layer, albeit, by another name. Both systems personify layer 7 and call it "the hungry ghosts" or "the ghosts of wanting."

Whatever you call it, the thing to come away with is that layer 8 is the opposite of layer 10, while layer 7 is the opposite of layer 9. Thus, in the birth separation moment, the two layers of paradise get mirrored in the two layers of hell—including that we see no way out of this hell. At the same time, because we have a mother, we do have a way out. She can guide us back to paradise. And whenever we connect to her, we're there.

Unfortunately, because it's inevitable for these connections to be followed by disconnects, each time we reconnect, we're doomed to cycle once more through these four layers, in essence, reliving the birth separation moment—10-9-8-7. Thus in no time at all, we become immersed in the grail journey we'll stay on for the rest of our lives—how to somehow get back to paradise—and stay there—without going through layer 8.

In the next chapter, I'll have a lot more to say about what this journey is like, including that you'll learn how personality tests based on layer 7 are the closest we can come to being able to describe our core personality. Indeed, by the end of that chapter, you should be able to—in only five words—describe your core personality, so accurately in fact that you should be able to predict the basics of every relationship you'll ever have and the essence of every interest you'll ever feel. And yes, I'm fully aware of what I've just promised. In five words? Impossible, right? Then again, why should I start worrying about appearing humble now. (Oh, great wise men, please don't fail me now.)

Personality Begins: Layers 10, 9, 8, and 7

Now let's take a few minutes to explore a bit of the technical side of our first personality. What is it like to have a four layer personality, two layers in heaven, and two in hell? To begin with, you still have your original two access sequences, 10 to 9 and 9 to 10. However, because you've added two layers, you now have more than a hundred possible access sequences, including the dreaded 10-9-8-7. Moreover, because your entire core personality gets formed from these hundred plus initial access sequences, a baby's personality can seem quite complicated. That is, until you compare this to the over 40 million possible access sequences you'll have acquired by puberty. Compared to that, one hundred is nothing.

Our First Personality: the Experience of Being
(layers 10, 9, 8, and 7)
(© 2007 Steven Paglierani The Center for Emergence)

personality begins (post birth)
(the first four layers of personality have formed)

The Four Inner Layers of Personality
7 - pure needs (disconnected duality)
8 - disconnections (universal non existence)
9 - connections to persons (connected duality)
10 - connections to the "all" (universal existence)

If you then remember that access sequences are not, in and of themselves, life experiences, but rather, only patterns which underlie life experiences, you begin to get an idea of how complex personality really is. At least until you recall that personality is fractal. Thus all you really need to come away with is a good working knowledge of how 9-10 and 10-9 accesses (pre-personality accesses) differ from 10-9-8-7's (birth separation moment accesses) and 7-8-9-10's (five big questions accesses).

Finally, if you then add to this that some access sequences are rare, you make it even easier still. Here I'm referring to the near impossibility of remaining in layer 8 for any length of time. This means all access sequences which end in layer 8 are rare indeed. As is the one which originally caused layers 8 and 7 to be formed—making *abrupt* 10-9-8-7 accesses.

Section Two

The Middle Layers
of
Personality:

"Hurting"

Shit Happens: the Medical Layers—6 and 5

As I just told you, whenever we make *abrupt* 10-9-8-7 accesses, we get—or relive getting—a wound. In effect, reliving the birth separation moment *is* what wounds us. Over time, this also causes the layers where we store our wounds and symptoms to appear. Hence my calling these two layers—the *medical layers*—they contain everything medical people deal with. To wit, in layer 6, we store all the experiences wherein getting startled permanently impairs our ability to see certain aspects of our needs—resulting in what most folks call *wounds* (blocked needs). And in layer 5, we store all the experiences wherein having these wounds causes us to consistently fail to meet these needs—resulting in the visible evidence most folks call *symptoms*.

Obviously, what I've just said is a lot to take in. Especially in one paragraph. In effect, I've just described the nature of getting wounded and how wounds cause symptoms. Then again, if you were a newborn baby, none of this would matter to you. All you'd really want to know is, after all the shit you've just gone through, what else could possibly go wrong?

Why use such a disgusting word, let alone suggest a baby might say it? My answer may surprise you. To be honest, I love swearing. I truly do. Including the word *shit*. Indeed, I find this word perfect for those special occasions wherein I slam my freakin' thumb with a hammer, or slide a finger across the edge of a freshly cut piece of paper. I also love it when referring to bigots, racists, sexists, and those who abuse or molest children, albeit, I have to admit, I've had a few nightmares regarding my saying it at the wrong time. Usually, I'm on Oprah when this word escapes my lips. Not that I expect to ever be on Oprah, mind you. Still, I surely would not want to lose control and do this in front of the whole world.

Why mention my swearing-in-public phobia? Because, as you'll learn in Book III: chapter ten, my positive feelings about swearing prove I've healed a wound in and around swearing. This points to yet another important thing the medical layers explain—how to know when you've healed a wound.

Here then are the questions we'll begin to explore in this section. What is a wound, and why call wounds "blocked needs?" What are symptoms, and how do wounds cause them? What is healing, and how do we know for sure that it's happened? And how do *abrupt* 10-9-8-7 accesses lead to the formation of the two medical layers—6 and 5?

Finally, know we'll spend all of Book III: chapter ten exploring wounds and healing in depth. So for now, all you need be concerned with is getting an overview of how layers 6 and 5 begin.

How Being Startled Wounds Us
(we store these experiences in layer 6)

(© 2007 Steven Paglierani   The Center for Emergence)

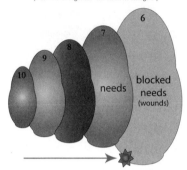

abrupt 10-9-8-7 accesses lead to startling experiences
(this access sequence is the fractal for all wounds)

- abrupt connection (hyperawareness)
- abrupt disconnection (startle)
- abrupt onset of pure need (shock)

These startling experiences eventually accumulate and become layer 6

- Layer 10 - connections to the "all" (universal existence)
- Layer 9 - connections to persons (connected duality)
- Layer 8 - disconnections (universal non existence)
- Layer 7 - pure needs (disconnected duality)
- Layer 6 - blocked needs (visual non existence)

Layer 6: Visual non Existence (blocked needs)

Can you recall ever having been startled? Does this same thing still startle you now? This one-two punch—being startled, and your reactions to being startled—is what underlies layers 6 and 5. Here the script of everything about the startle gets stored in layer 6, including [1]—the last things you witnessed right before the startle, [2]—the actual frozen moment of the startle, and [3]—the involuntary shock and blankness you felt right after the startle. This script is the wound. And all reactions which result from experiencing this script—both those immediately following the first time you go through it, and those which develop in the years which follow—then get stored in layer 5. These reactions are the symptoms.

How does being startled wound us? To see, let's look at a common example—hating to eat certain foods. Know this hatred always stems from having been startled. For instance, did you ever suddenly react to the taste of something, say curdled milk or old eggs, or suddenly realize that what you were eating was disgusting, perhaps a rotten apple or a tomato with a still wriggling green worm in it? If so, how often did you eat this food again? Ever? At the very least, you reacted badly to even thinking about eating it for a long time afterwards. At worst, even knowing it was part of a meal you were about to eat impaired your ability to enjoy that meal.

The parts of this experience which got stored in layer 6 are the few frames of life you've been reacting to (being startled by a bad taste, or by the disgusting appearance of a food). The parts of this experience which got stored in layer 5 are your immediate reactions to these few frames of life (revulsion, gagging, vomiting), plus the cumulative effects of any ongoing reactions (e.g. any interpersonal difficulties arising from your refusals to eat this food, any health problems resulting from your never eating it).

Another example. Have you ever been in a car accident during a snow storm or on black ice? If so, did you then find yourself being overly cautious and looking for excuses to not drive or stay home because the weatherman said it *might* snow or that there *might be* black ice?

If we plug these experiences into the three part wounding sequence, the parts of them which would get stored in layer 6 would be [1]—a hyper-vivid memory of the last things you saw right before the car accident impact (e.g. snow, black ice, other cars, the time of day), [2]—the startle and resultant frozen moment, and [3]—the blankness which followed this startle. And the parts of it which would get stored in layer 5 would be all your reactions to this startling experience, both back then and since (e.g. tensing up at the thought of driving in snow, any back or neck pain resulting from this tension, feeling scared or terrified when driving on icy roads).

Here then are the two ways being startled affects us. First, it permanently programs us to, under certain life circumstances, suddenly and involuntarily [1]—become hyperaware, braced, and tense, [2]—get startled and freeze, and [3]—go blank. This programming gets stored in layer 6. Second, this tendency to suddenly and involuntarily react under these certain circumstances then generalizes to any and all similar circumstances, impairing our ability to make healthy choices whenever we're in these certain life circumstances.

In effect then, startles program us to react to any and all similar life circumstances as if they will invariably turn out as badly as the original event. We believe there's nothing we can do to change the outcome. And this belief then leads to having chronically unmet needs and ultimately, to the visible evidence of these chronically unmet needs—symptoms—all of which get stored in layer 5.

The thing to pay special attention to here is how symptoms and wounds get stored separately. This is why alleviating symptoms doesn't heal wounds. Symptoms are merely the visible evidence that a wound exists. Thus getting rid of symptoms only eliminates the evidence. The wound itself still exists.

Most Wounds Occur During Ordinary Events

Another thing to know about the experiences we store in layer 6 is that the majority of them do not occur during what most of us would consider traumatic life events. Understandably, this may seem counterintuitive. We expect wounds to occur during painful—or even violent—events. But in truth, only a small percentage of wounds occur during traumatic events.

The majority occur under ordinary life circumstances—such as when we're tasting food, or having conversations, or having our picture taken. Ironically, most folks would not consider things like flash photography to be violent acts. Yet few if any people exposed to it emerge unscathed.

To wit, imagine a wedding photographer has you posed for a group photo and has just told the group to "say cheese." How would you react? Most people involuntarily wince as they imagine being blinded by the flash. Moreover there are two things to notice here, and both indicate a wound. One—it's the photographer's suggestion, not the flash, which sets off the wince. Two—this wince occurs *whether the flash goes off or not.*

Know the expectation of pain in ordinary life circumstances is never normal—and always indicates a wound. Indeed, there is always a time before every wound wherein people do not expect to suffer. For instance, think of babies being thrown into the air, or swung, with no fear whatsoever. Think of eating eggs or apples or tomatoes with no concern about getting a bad one. Now try to imagine a photographer telling you to "say cheese" and feeling no urges to wince. Or hearing your spouse say, "we have to talk" and expecting a good conversation.

In a way then, the expectation of pain in ordinary life circumstances is a good way to identify your wounds, as once wounded, most people so expect bad outcomes that they find it hard to imagine ever feeling any other way. Babies, once wounded, expect to fall. We expect the once bad tasting food to always taste bad. People expect to be blinded by the flash. And spouses expect the words, "we have to talk" to preface an argument.

What about you? Can you remember a time when a photographer asked you to "say cheese" and you did not feel urges to wince? If so, can you remember wondering to yourself why everyone around you was wincing? I can. Once blinded by that first flash, however, I knew for the rest of my life. In fact, even as we speak, I am wincing just from picturing a photographer asking me to "say cheese." I also can't imagine the flash not going off, let alone not being blinded by it.

Wounds as "State-Dependent Learning"

What is it about being startled that programs us to expect pain? A lot of it has to do with that wounds are a kind of learning. With learning in general, we come to expect that certain associations are true, for example, that ripe apples are red and that e=mc². And with wounds, we come to expect that being in certain environments will inevitably lead to pain, for example, that hearing someone say "we have to talk" means we'll fight—or that not knowing what to say means we'll be laughed at or ridiculed.

No coincidence, psychologists have a name for these associations. They call them the "state dependent" property of learning. Here the classic example involves learning math while intoxicated, then trying to recall what you've learned when sober. People often can't. But give them a few drinks and retest them, and they have much better recall.

The idea, of course, is that the closer you come to being in the state in which you originally learned something, the easier it is for you to recall what you learned. Conversely, the further you are from being in that state, the more effort it takes to bring what you've learned there to mind.

With wounds then, since wounding teaches us to expect pain in a certain environment, state dependence is one of the more important things to know. Moreover, the closer you come to being back in the original state, the more you'll expect to feel pain. Conversely, the more you can avoid being in that state, the less you'll expect to feel pain.

State dependence is also what underlies our desire to train those around us to avoid doing—or saying—certain things in our presence. For example, when we say things like, "you know I hate it when you do that," what we're really doing is trying to get someone close to us to help us to avoid a state and by doing so avoid reliving a wound.

Wounds as "Associations to Everyday States"

What's especially important to realize here is what I mean by the words "state" and "environment." In effect, I'm pointing to everything we see, hear, smell, taste, touch, think, and feel *in the second or so immediately preceding a startle*. And while at first glance, this may appear to be an overwhelming amount of data, it's not as bad as it sounds, as after a startle we go blank and this blankness functions like a fuse.

In effect, going blank limits the damage by preventing further input. Thus none of that post-startle data gets associated to the wound.

For example, say you recently got blinded by a flash camera for the first time. In all likelihood, the next time you faced a flash camera, you'd wince when asked to say cheese. But add to this that at the time of this injury, you were posed for a group photo shoot at an outdoor wedding, on a beautiful day in the late fall. Say, too, that in the seconds just before you got blinded by that flash, you looked down to see if your still stiff black pumps were scuffed, then quickly looked up. Then, as you looked up, you noticed that the woman standing to your right had on a beautiful lavender and white dress. Moreover, say you were hungry and in this moment, thought to yourself you hoped you would eat soon. And to top it all off, say that in the minutes right before you posed for this picture, you got into a fight with your two year old. And in the blinding instant, you heard her screaming for you.

Have you ever considered this idea then—that at any given moment, you have a heck of a lot of semi-consciously sensed balls in the air? The sum of all these balls is the state you are in. Moreover, since the energy of startles is not selective, the experience of a blinding flash adds a painful charge to each and every thing you are sensing in that moment.

At the same time, not all these things would get the same level of painful charge. In general, those things closest in time to the startle would get the highest amount, in all likelihood, that dreaded, bluish flash camera bulb. Then again, if something distracted you in that blinding instant, like your two year old running toward you, much of the charge would get associated to seeing her running toward you. Not such a great thing for a mother to be programmed to go blank in and around.

The point is, every detail in a wounding state gets charged with the pain of the startle, and those things closest in time to the onset of the startle get the worst of it. Indeed, were you now at another wedding, and were you to re-experience all these of things at once, your expectation of pain might be so high that you might try to beg out of the photo shoot. No surprise, this happens a lot.

Wounds as "the Source of Common Dislikes"

Equally important—though much less obvious—is what would happen to you if, years later, you were in a situation wherein you experienced several of these cues but without the main one—no flash camera. For instance, say your two year old is now a grown woman and that this is her wedding day. Say, too, that the wedding is being held outside, that it is a beautiful fall day, that you are hungry, have on tight new shoes, and can hear the cries of a needy two year old somewhere in the background. Now add to this that your daughter's bridesmaid has on a lavender and white gown and is standing right in front of you, trying to get your attention. It's not hard to imagine that you might get so distracted that you wouldn't notice her, let alone have any idea why.

No big deal, right? After all, it wouldn't be like you intentionally hurt her feelings. But say, instead, you're attending a business dinner at the city's most expensive restaurant, and that this dinner is being hosted by your husband's new boss. Say, too, that it's a beautiful fall day and you're all seated outside, on a veranda—that you have on gorgeous new shoes, a bit tight, but as yet perfectly polished—that after looking down to check your shoes, you look up and notice the boss's wife has on a stunning lavender and white jacket—that the restaurant has been slow to bring your appetizers and you're famished—and that you hear the sound, way in the distance, of a crying baby. How might this wedding photo wound sans flash camera cue affect you this time?

Here the list of possibilities is impossibly complex. On the one hand, you might have a hard time finding your words, perhaps, missing conversational cues or even appearing aloof. On the other hand, you might hate the restaurant or being seated outside. Or you might inadvertently insult your husband's boss while he was standing right behind you by complaining about the service. You didn't see him, right? So much for the wifely good impression.

At the very least, you'd have a hard time being yourself at dinner. Worst case, you'd look absent, or feel irritable, or perhaps be downright rude. Moreover, no one, including you, would have a clue as to why you were acting like this. And lest you think this story is totally absurd, before we end this chapter, I'm going to tell you a true story involving this very kind of thing, something which no amount of talk therapy sleuthing could have ever hoped to uncover, and something which could have easily ended an important new business relationship. And yes, one story does not a theory prove. However, I've literally encountered thousands of these stories during the past decade and a half. Which is why we'll spend almost the whole of Book III: chapter ten exploring these kinds of stories.

The point is, wounds can teach us to avoid, resist, hate, ignore, fear, and otherwise react badly to what, in truth, are benign things. Experiences like the feeling of wearing stiff new shoes, or being in a formal setting, outside, on a fall day, or seeing your two year old run toward you when you're hungry, or seeing someone wearing lavender and white.

Finally, consider this. Had I asked you at the beginning of this section to speculate about how a flash camera might affect someone, chances are you would not have said any of these things. According to the four wise asses though, being startled can make us dislike even things we're only vaguely aware of, including the most ordinary, seemingly insignificant details in life—like the time of year, the kind of day, certain colors, sounds, smells, and so on.

Wounds as "the Source of Anticipatory Tension"

Tensed muscles. Furrowed brows. Wincing. Holding your breath. One of the worst things wounds do to us is they cause us to brace for pain. Indeed, because wounds associate what are otherwise ordinary people, places, and things to the pain of being startled, whenever we encounter one of these ordinary things, we unconsciously expect pain. So we brace ourselves.

I call what we do here, *anticipatory tension.* Can you see how it might affect us over time? No? Then try tensing one of your forearms for a full minute then suddenly relax it. Now notice what this arm feels like. Tired? Stiff? Weak and limp? Now consider how, over time, this kind of tension could lead to stress-related, compensatory injuries.

We'll talk more about anticipatory tension in future chapters. But for now the thing to see is that, in some ways, this tension makes reliving an injury worse than getting an injury, as before you're wounded, these situations don't cause you to wince, tense, brace yourself, or stiffen.

This also makes anticipatory tension a good way to find wounds. If we brace only when we expect pain—and if being wounded is what teaches us to brace—then anticipatory tension is a sure sign you're reliving a wound. No wound. No sure and certain expectation of pain. Thus, no anticipatory tension.

Wounds as a Type of "Learned Helplessness"

Another thing wounds do to us is that they teach us resistance is futile. Since we're certain the outcome is predetermined, we brace for the inevitable pain. Like "state dependence," psychologists have a name for this condition as well. They call it, "learned helplessness." In other words, because we've learned to expect pain in these certain situations, any and all choices to avoid this pain seem futile to us. Here an example would be those times wherein you're certain you know how someone will respond to you. Your boss, for instance, were you to ask her for a raise. Or your spouse, were you to ask him for help.

Ironically, this other person may at times even come right out and reassure you, saying things like that you shouldn't worry, that he or she would welcome the request. Friends and family may also reassure you or offer further reassurances that all will turn out well. They may even offer to intervene on your behalf or make what in reality are legitimately helpful suggestions, only to have you respond with something like, "Thanks. I know you mean well. But I'm sure it won't make any difference."

What makes us certain these experiences will turn out badly?

In large part, it's because we go blank when we try to imagine any other outcome. That we then react even when nothing bad actually happens—e.g. wince when the camera doesn't flash, or tense when the boss does give you a raise, or feel rejected even when your spouse does help you then says he's glad you asked—only further reinforces this belief. This makes learned helplessness one of the worst things wounds do to us. Thus state dependence is not the only "wounded learning" wounds teach us. They also teach us to expect that any and all attempts to change are doomed to fail—in effect, that we are helpless to change these situations.

How Being Wounded "Magnetizes" Us

Something else to know about getting wounded is how this experience resembles iron being magnetized. Here if you place an unmagnetized piece of iron in close proximity to a strong electromagnetic field then suddenly turn off the power, the pattern of the field coursing through the iron permanently records in the iron. In truth this is what "magnetizing" iron means. By abruptly interrupting a state wherein a field is affecting iron, you "teach" the iron to remember the pattern of the field.

This same thing happens to us whenever we get startled. The abrupt onset of the startle causes the psychological and physical state we're experiencing at the time—the "field" of our experience—to permanently record in our mind and body. It also permanently associates the energy of the startle to the details of this recording, and this programs us to be startled in any and all similar situations.

Now consider how what I've just told you explains one of the greatest mysteries about wounds. You would think that once we were wounded, we'd avoid these situations like the plague. And most times, we do. But sometimes, we end up feeling almost magnetically drawn to these kinds of people, places, things, and events, such as when people marry their alcoholic fathers or verbally abusive mothers. Moreover, contrary to what most self help books say, we should not consider this behavior dysfunction. Dysfunction is a condition wherein things do not lead to health. And this can happen. However, once you understand the nature of wounds and healing, these situations can—and often do—lead to health.

How Iron Gets "Startled"
(magnetizing iron as a psychophysical parallel to getting wounded)
(© 2007 Steven Paglierani The Center for Emergence)

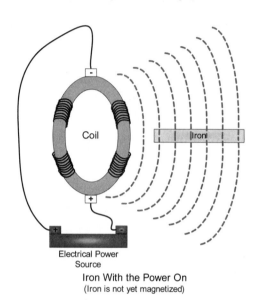

Iron With the Power On
(Iron is not yet magnetized)

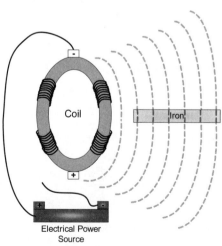

Iron After the Power Is Suddenly Turned Off
(Iron has been startled into being magnetized)

So am I telling you that to heal a broken heart you should deliberately throw yourself under the romance bus? To some degree, yes, I am. You see, in order to heal, you must re-experience the psychological and physical state you were in *but without getting startled*. This, in fact, is what healing means. No coincidence, this exactly parallels how you *demagnetize* iron. Putting the magnet back in a strong electromagnetic field then gradually reducing the strength of the field erases the pattern. And back in the day, this is part of how reel-to-reels, cassettes, and 8-tracks worked. They used iron-based tapes which got demagnetized each time you wrote new information onto the tape.

This then is how you heal a wound. You return to the state you were in when it occurred, then relive the wound while trying not to get startled. No coincidence, nineteenth century therapists, some of them quite famous, often tried to use hypnotism to heal wounds this way. Moreover, when you realize how closely hypnosis parallels magnetism—and how hypnotist's cues resemble wounding cues—you begin to see why. As well as why those early hypnotherapists were often called, "magnetizers."

Now let's take a closer look at how these three processes resemble each other, especially how stage hypnosis resembles getting wounded.

How Wounding Events are Like Stage Hypnotism

How does being implanted with a hypnotist's cue parallel what happens to us when we get wounded?

Start with that being given a suggestion while we're in a hypnotic state very much resembles what I've told you about putting unmagnetized iron into an electromagnetic field. Here the way a suddenly collapsing electromagnetic field magnetizes iron parallels the way a hypnotic "field" suddenly collapses when hypnotist's snaps us awake. In the case of the hypnotist, this leaves us programmed with a hypnotic suggestion.

Know this same process parallels what happens to us when we're suddenly thrust into an intense life circumstance then get startled. The intensity of the life event acts like the hypnotist, putting us into an hypnotic state. The startle then functions like the hypnotist's snap, causing us to record the state we're in. And this sequence then turns the things we experienced at the time into painful, hypnotic cues.

Afterwards, whenever we encounter these particular circumstances, we react to them as if they are hypnotic cues. Moreover, much like the cues in stage hypnotism—wherein we can feel as if we've somehow been transported to another place and time—when we relive wounds, we respond to them as if we are experiencing entirely different circumstances than the ones we're currently in. Only with hypnotism we're reliving an innocuous event, whereas with wounds we're reliving a painful event. Including that we feel the same hyperawareness, the same startling experience, and the same sudden blankness—even when it's not there.

Blocked Needs Cause Symptoms
(we store these experiences in layer 5)

(© 2007 Steven Paglierani   The Center for Emergence)

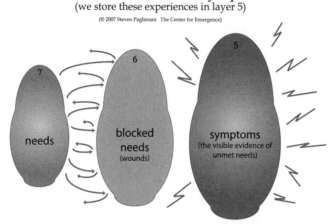

unmade layer 7 accesses lead to layer 5 experiences
the metafractal access sequence for all symptoms

Why Abrupt 10-9-8-7 Access Sequences Hypnotize Us

Now let's look at this from the perspective of layer accesses. How do abrupt 10-9-8-7 accesses do the same thing to us that a rapidly collapsing magnetic field does to iron and a hypnotist's snapping fingers does to his or her subject?

To begin with, I need to tell you a bit about what hypnotists call, "inductions." Hypnotists use this word refer to the things they do to put people under. Moreover, while there are many ways for a hypnotist to induce a hypnotic state in a person, we can divide all these techniques into just two piles—those which occur slowly, and those which occur rapidly.

How fast are rapid inductions? Almost instantaneous. For instance, when I was studying hypnosis, I was amazed to learn that you can hypnotize some people just by having them sit and dropping their limp arm onto their leg. Contrary to what you've seen on TV then wherein being hypnotized is a slow process, sometimes people go under instantly.

Being startled functions much like these rapid inductions. Layer wise, at the onset of the startle, you abruptly enter layers 10 and 9. Here you make universal and personal connections. This explains why people trust hypnotists. In the case of getting wounded however, a suddenly-induced hypnotic state connects you to whatever you're currently aware of—the time of day, your surroundings, your state of being, and so on.

When the Whip Comes Down: How Wounds Occur

To explain this part, I need to change the subject to cowboys and whips. Why? It turns out that the timing of how startles unfold, in many ways, resembles the dynamics of a cowboy's whip. Here I'm referring to how the cowboy's arm draws the whip back then rapidly changes direction, causing a curl of force to travel down the length of the whip. Then when this curl reaches the end of the whip, it suddenly flattens and the whip snaps.

Startles affect you similarly. First the rapid induction causes you draw back, then pause to connect. Then your focus changes direction from inward to outward, causing this connection to deepen. Finally, when the snap of the startle breaks this connection, the hypnotic field which surrounds the event abruptly collapses. This then propels you and your experience of this event first into the black abyss of layer 8 (disconnections), then into the abject neediness of layer 7 (pure need).

Where does the memory of this wound get recorded? It gets stored as a hypnotic script in layer 6. Moreover, since layers 10 through 7 nest within layer 6—wounds do not damage these inner layers. Nor the content of these layers. And this is good news. Your core self never gets damaged.

The bad news is, whenever you get wounded or relive a wound, you go blank inside and lose access to these inner layers. This prevents you from seeing any needs you have at the time. You also become unable to make healthy choices or feel love. Moreover, since the wounding scripts you store in layer 6 are fractal, these blind spots—and the inabilities they cause—then generalize to all similar life events. And since these scripts cause you to go blank *even when nothing bad happens*, eventually, you come to see the pain you feel as inevitable.

This idea—that wounds generalize to all similar situations—has been known in psychological circles for well over a century. In essence, being wounded convinces you that all similar life events are fated to end the same way. Ergo the anticipatory tension and learned helplessness we spoke about. What has not been known however is the first part of what I've just told you—that wounds do not injure your core self—that they injure only your access to this part of yourself. Indeed, the only way for you to see this is to know that personality forms in nested layers.

As for why I call what you store in layer 6 *blocked needs* rather than wounds, it's simple. As I've said, whenever you get startled, you go blank inside. This blankness temporarily renders you unable to meet your needs—you can't meet a need you can't see. It also charges the small details which immediately precede this startle with the mind-emptying power of the startle, turning each of these small details into a hypnotic cue.

Later, whenever you encounter one of these cues, you involuntarily relive this wounding event including the startle. Moreover, because the blankness which follows being startled prevents you from recognizing the nature of these cues, you have no way to know they're the real source of your suffering. And as you'll find out later on in this chapter, your inability to see these cues then leads you to posit some pretty strange explanations as to why you don't meet your needs. This then results in all manner of urges to resent, blame, punish, and avoid these situations.

In effect then, whenever you make abrupt 10-9-8-7 accesses, you get wounded in a number of ways, the worst of which is that you become unable to see and thus, meet certain of your needs. You also become unable to accept love in these times. You simply see no need. Moreover because being startled always empties the mind, you have no way to see what is causing these problems. Nor a way to explain your inability to see and make better choices in these particular circumstances.

As for why you don't always jump inside when these startles occur, it's that the blankness can numb both your mind and body.

By the way, can you now see why *abrupt* 10-9-8-7 accesses wound you, whereas slow 10-9-8-7 accesses do not? As unpleasant as these slow trips through hell may feel, because they're slow they don't startle you. And if the whip doesn't snap, you don't get wounded.

Layer 5: Hypervisual Duality (symptoms)

Now let's talk about how layer 6 causes layer 5 to fill with symptoms.

To begin with, recall where you store your experiences of need—in layer 7. And where you store your experiences of being startled—in layer 6. Now realize that everything you store in layer 6 aligns itself to a corresponding class of needs in layer 7. This explains why startles cause symptoms. Since startles blind you—and since what you store in layers 6 and 7 always align—whenever you get startled, you become unable to see these needs. Over time then, since you can't meet needs you can't see, these unmet needs result in symptoms. Hence my saying, Layer 6 causes layer 5.

Now consider how the placement of layer 6 affects the inner layers. Because we store the damage-producing part of wounds—startles—in layer 6, and because the four inner layers nest within layer 6, startles never damage the inner layers. This means wounds more resemble scorch marks on the window to your inner self than actual damage. In the places where the glass walls of layer 6 are clear, you can see and meet your needs. And in the places where the glass is scorched, you not only lose your ability to see and meet your needs. You also lose your ability to make healthy choices and to feel love.

This then is where your symptoms come from. They come from the needs you repeatedly overlook—because they're not visible. This includes everything from not eating well and not resting enough to not hurting people's feelings, not speaking up, and not believing in yourself.

How Blocked Needs Cause Symptoms

(© 2007 Steven Paglierani, The Center for Emergence)

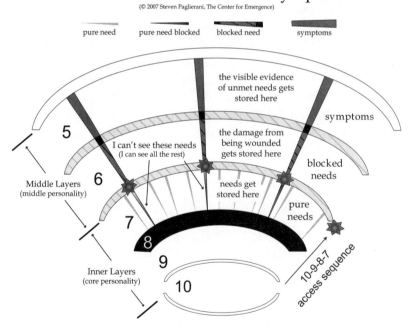

Why Logic Can't Explain Symptoms

Now consider how having blocked needs affects you over time. For instance, say you drive to work on a superhighway. Say too that you go under a lot of overpasses. Now say you have a wound which impairs your ability to see these overpasses. In effect, each time you approach one, your mind empties and you go blank. Here, safely navigating under overpasses would be a blocked need.

Ridiculous, you say? How could someone not see an overpass?

Setting this objection aside for a moment, can you see how zoning out as you approach overpasses would affect you when you drove to and from work? At the very least, you'd feel tense and nervous and not know why. On bad days, you'd arrive worn out for no apparent reason. This tension might even lead you to call in sick a lot. And you'd probably have an accident at some point, most certainly near an overpass. Oh, boy!

Worst of all, because most people see zoning out as nothing important, none of this would make sense to you. In effect, you'd have an overpass phobia. But you'd be unable to make the connection. Indeed, because wounds are like hypnotist's cues in that simply imaging them can put you under, you could experience these symptoms even on roads with no overpasses.

This tendency for wounds to generalize to all places is what makes us turn to logic to explain our fears. Ideas exist in all places and logic explains ideas. Thus if your tendency was to self examine, you might conclude something like, "Maybe I'm just a bad driver. I can't understand why. I try to pay attention. Truly, I do. I just can't keep my mind on my driving."

Alternately you might conclude that you hate your job. Or that you have a bad habit of letting things get to you while you're driving. Then again, if you tend to seek external causes for your problems, you might say something like, "God knows who designs these damn roads. No doubt some pencil-pushing, four-eyed geek who has never driven a day in his life, but who has a lot of letters after his name and gets paid the big bucks."

Whatever you concluded, the more you turned to logic, the further from the truth you'd get. Indeed, the last thing you'd consider would be a fear of overpasses. After all, with no visible evidence, this conclusion would be illogical, wouldn't it? Unless, of course, you knew that being wounded makes you zone out. In which case, you'd stop focusing on what you *can* see—your symptoms—and start looking for something you *can't* see—your visually-blocked needs.

Are you getting why logic fails here? Since logic can't work on problems with missing pieces, it's useless when it comes to locating your wounds. As for what sort of symptoms you might experience if you zoned out near overpasses, it's not hard to imagine. Anxiety, self criticism, self worth problems, insecurities about driving and about cars in general, reluctance to own a car, a phobic fear of driving, physical muscle aches due to the tension you'd feel when you drive, and so on. Worst case, you might even have an accident. Moreover, since there's no way logic could connect these symptoms to overpasses, your best efforts to heal this would fail.

When Wounds Have No Symptoms

Now as if this isn't bad enough, at times your symptoms would just go away. This would happen because, like the tendency of buildings to sustain more damage at the epicenter of an earthquake, the wounding cues at the epicenter of a startle get the most charge. Thus you could encounter one or more of the peripheral cues and experience no symptoms whatsoever. This could then lead you to wrongly rule these things out.

For example, say they were doing construction on the superhighway. Temporarily you might use a road wherein there were no overpasses. Then given your drive to work was long enough, some of your confidence might return. Eventually you might begin to get out and drive more. Your friends might even pat you on the back for having conquered your fears. Until the day the superhighway construction was done, that is. At which point your symptoms, fear and all, would return with a vengeance.

And if you then concluded superhighways were the problem and began to avoid them entirely? All well and good until you drove on a minor road which had an overpass. At which point, your symptoms might again return for no discernible reason. Leading you to conclude, you might as well accept it. You're just a nervous Nelly—a bad driver. Oh, well.

Are you beginning to see why logic fails when it comes to locating wounds? The whole key rests on the one thing no one pays attention to—zoning out. Incredibly, while most people easily follow the logic behind all this, at the same time, they have trouble believing they wouldn't notice themselves zoning out.

To wit, most people, when first introduced to the idea that being startled permanently blocks our ability to see certain needs, find this idea at least conceivable. They can also imagine how, over time, not meeting these needs could lead to symptoms. What they find hard to believe though is how someone could zone out like this and not connect it to the source. For instance, if you had the overpass wound I've been describing, wouldn't you eventually notice you were zoning out near overpasses?

In truth, no, you wouldn't. However, to understand why, we're going to need to take a deeper look at our hypothetical overpass wound.

Why Most Talk Therapy Fails

Okay. Let's say you have this overpass wound. Let's also say that your anxiety has gotten so bad that you've decided to go to a therapist. Now imagine it's your first time in his office and that the two of you have just begun to talk. What kinds of questions might he ask you?

As I've mentioned, most people, including most talk therapists, rely mainly on logic to "fill in the blanks." Thus your therapist might ask you to tell him everything you can about your fear of driving. Logically, this seems sound, yes? He might also ask how you've been sleeping lately, saying, it might be related to that. This too is possible. Or he might ask if you've had a lot on your mind lately. Could worries be distracting you? Maybe that's it?

Then again, perhaps he'd focus on your childhood and ask if your family had gone on long drives when you were a kid. Maybe your parents used to argue on those drives and that made you nervous? Could this be it? Or he might ask how you feel about long drives in general. For instance, he might ask if you get nervous when big trucks come near you on a long drive and perhaps, if you feel more nervous when they pass you? This, too, sounds logically possible.

The problem of course is that while all these things are possible, logic can't tell you which it is. Faced with this, most folks go with the situation which has the most "juice"—the one which elicits the biggest reaction. If it feels big, this must be it, right? The thing is, if wounds "wound" your ability to see your needs—and if your unmet needs cause your symptoms—then these things can't be causing your symptoms. You can picture them.

Now take a moment to consider what I've just said.

If zoning out in certain environments is what causes symptoms—and if you don't zone out when you're being asked these questions—then these situations can't be causing your symptoms. And yes, eliminating them may make you feel better. But in the end, you'll still be just as wounded. Thus while you may temporarily improve, over time, your symptoms will worsen.

Now consider what would happen if your therapist stopped trying to logically explain your symptoms and focused on finding the places wherein you zone out. Here your therapist might even ask you the same questions. However, rather than focusing on whether you could *connect* to any of it—if any of it had juice—he'd look to see if any of it *disconnected* you—if any of it lacked juice.

What then? The next part requires you know a bit about how astrophysicists find black holes. Do you know? In theory, it's easier than you might think. Because even light cannot escape a black hole, black holes are invisible. Like wounds, you can't see them. However, if you look for places wherein the laws of physics break down, you can indirectly define the outer edge of black holes. This area around a black hole—the place wherein things begin to defy the laws of physics—even has a name. It's called the *event horizon*. And if you treat wounds as black holes in your consciousness—and symptoms as event horizons between what's healthy and what's not—you arrive at a useful way to locate the true source of your symptoms; the black holes in your consciousness—your wounds.

The good news is, most therapists already focus on symptoms. Unfortunately, because they treat symptoms as wounds, when they find them, they generally focus on getting rid of them. Doing this is like using a garden hose to find the invisible man and then, when you find him, turning the water off. The minute you turn the water off, you cease to see the invisible man. Getting rid of symptoms does the same thing.

Are you beginning to see why I'm making such a big deal out of zoning out? If it happens suddenly, it can mean only one thing—that you're reliving a wound. Know that if it happens slowly, this indicates you do not have a wound. Times that you might do this are when you're overtired or getting sick, or when you're under pressure to make a big decision.

The point of course is that using logic to locate wounds is like using logic to locate black holes. No matter how hard you try, it can't be done. However, if you treat wounds like black holes and symptoms like event horizons, then symptoms become the best way to locate your wounds.

Want to see this idea in action? Just ask someone to name something they hate. Why something they hate? Let's take a look.

Using Hate to Locate Wounds

In Book III: chapter ten, I'll teach you some good ways to find your wounds. Hating something ordinary is one of these ways. For instance, if you came to me for therapy—and if you had this overpass wound—one thing I'd be listening for would be for you to say something like, "I *hate* driving on superhighways" or "I *hate* hearing tractor trailer horns."

What makes the word *hate* significant? It's referring to something ordinary—to superhighways or tractor trailer horns—and not to something you should hate like child abuse. Here, "hating something ordinary," functions as the event horizon for a wound. I say this because there is nothing wrong with these things per se. They're ordinary. So hating them means that something—a wound—is making the laws of logic and reason break down. Since we all have these kinds of illogical reactions though, we're used to hearing people say they hate ordinary things like certain foods or certain words. So like zoning out, we pay them no mind.

What Makes Us Hate Ordinary Things?

What kind of event could have caused this overpass wound? Certainly, it could have been something like being in a car accident, or getting startled by a mean driving instructor, or witnessing your parents fighting in a car. More likely though, it would come from something far less obvious. For instance, it could easily have come from a time when you were young and got startled while playing near an overpass.

For example, say when you were six years old that your home sat several hundred feet from an overpass. Say also that despite there being a chain link fence bordering this highway, that your parents had forbidden you to play near this overpass—certainly understandable, given your age. Add to this that it was summer and you were watching a butterfly which had just landed near the fence. Then suddenly, you looked up and saw your father's angry face with the overpass right behind him. Certainly, getting caught doing something you weren't supposed to do could have startled you.

Now add to this that in that startling moment, a semi-tractor trailer had noisily barreled by, that the grass had been freshly mowed, that the sky framing your father's head was bright blue with puffy clouds, and that the truck had honked his horn. Do you realize what being startled while all this was going on would have done to you? Everything you were conscious of at the time would have been charged by the startle.

The Significance of the Timing of the Startle

Does this sound unlikely? Illogical? Ridiculous? In truth, even when we get injured by truly violent events, it's never the whole event which gets charged. And yes, we can and often do get wounded in scenes which we can logically connect to our symptoms. But it's the timing of the startle—and not logic—which determines which parts of the event get charged.

The problem, of course, is that we desperately cling to the idea that everything happens for reasons. We then assume things like that the symptoms we experience in a car must be related to cars and driving. After all, wouldn't a car accident better explain feeling tense while in cars, a reluctance to drive, anxiety attacks of superhighways, self criticism and self worth problems stemming from your driving, etc?

The thing is, no logic could account for the serendipitous timing of the startle. Thus if you had this overpass wound, you'd also feel anxious each time you imagined a man's angry face. You might even hate angry men. Or you might feel self critical whenever you thought of breaking a rule. Seeing children break rules might even make you mad. You might also overreact if you saw your own children go near a highway. Perhaps you'd even tell them you hate it when they do that. And you might feel terrified and frozen whenever a tractor trailer passed you on a highway. Did you say you hated big trucks, especially when they honk their horns?

You also might hate summer picnics and the smell of fresh mowed lawns. As well as butterflies and chain link fences, and blue summer skies with puffy clouds. Or you might zone out whenever you were in the presence of these things, all the while never realizing the implications of this blankness.

Does this all sound crazy? After all, we're talking an overpass wound, not a butterfly wound or a father wound? Then again, if you recall how I've defined wounds—as blocked visual abilities which result from being startled—then it's easy to imagine how this one startling incident at age six could cause you to become unable to visualize your father's face angry, unable to imagine tractor trailers honking horns, unable to picture butterflies landing on freshly mowed lawns in summer, and unable to envision highway overpasses, especially when you're feeling guilty.

A Typical Wound: the Parrot Squawk Story

If this all sounds like nonsense, I do understand. However, before you fling this book onto the nearest dung heap, first allow me tell you about something which happened to me some years ago. In this event, I inadvertently bumped into one of these seemingly illogical cues in myself. At the time, I was meeting with a new editor in a Starbucks and was beginning to explain my work to her. Clearly, she was excited and genuinely interested in what I had to say. Within minutes though—and for no apparent reason—I began to hate this woman. Moreover, up to that point, I'd been looking forward to meeting her and had been having a good day.

Illogical? Yes. So what would you guess was causing me to hate her? That I was feeling insecure about my work and desperately needed her approval? That she reminded me of someone, perhaps a mean grade school English teacher or my mother being critical? That she was being disingenuous and disrespectful, but that I'm such a nice guy that I was incapable of admitting this to myself?

All these things would have been logical. But none of them were true. Fortunately, I quickly realized what I was overreacting to. The editor had been acknowledging each point I made with the words, "uh-huh-uh." And each time she did, it set me off and I hated her even more.

Bizarre, right? Good thing I knew to ignore the illogic. Clearly, I was feeling hatred toward an ordinary thing—the sound of her *uh-huh-uh*. Realizing this, I asked for her help, and explained to her that each time I asked, I needed her to say this phrase to me.

She quickly agreed.

At first, each time she said *uh-huh-uh*, my hatred toward her got worse. But as I continued to push myself past this hatred, at some point, I welled up with tears. A moment later, I flashed on a scene from my early childhood. In it, I was about two and a half and was standing in front of my father's friend, Blanche. To my left was my father, also standing and holding my then eighteen month old sister, Teresa, in his arms. Unbeknownst to me, there was also a rather large parrot perched—right above my head—on an open, hanging swing. Somehow, I hadn't noticed the parrot when I entered the room. So when it squawked, *uh-huh-uh*, I got startled.

None of this is hard to imagine. Kids get startled all the time. What's important to pay attention to though is what I was experiencing right before I got startled. At the time, I was looking down. No biggie, right? After all, I was shy. However, this also meant that when the parrot squawked, I was looking at a purple Persian rug.

Almost instantly, my gaze then rose toward the source of the squawk, and as it did, I noticed the tan shorts I was wearing, then my short sleeved white shirt. Finally, my gaze landed on the off-white gossamer, pin dot curtains. It was late spring and they were blowing in by an open window.

Oddly, I cannot remember seeing the parrot, probably because I went blank before my eyes reached it. How can I be so sure? Because as long as I can remember, I have *hated* Persian rugs, especially purple ones—and wearing shorts, especially tan ones—and short sleeve shirts, especially white ones—and off-white, gossamer curtains blowing in the breeze, especially those which use pin dot fabric. I've even hated spring and looking down.

At the same time, I have a vivid memory of my father and Blanche laughing and pointing out the parrot to me. Including that I felt amazed by what I saw. Since then, I have *loved* parrots and any birds which resemble parrots. And any birds on swings, really, especially noisy squawking ones.

Yes, I know. Cute story. But what's the point?

After that incident with my editor, I began buying and wearing shorts—mostly tan ones. I also began buying and wearing short sleeve shirts—some of them white. About six months later, I also bought a new rug for my office. You guessed it. Purple with a Persian pattern. And while I have yet to buy any gossamer curtains, I literally fell in love with a photograph I had taken some twenty five years earlier in which an off-white, pin dot, gossamer curtain is blowing in front of an open window in late spring. Add to this that I probably have far more short sleeved shirts than long sleeved ones at present and you begin to get the idea. All the things this injury caused me to hate became things I love.

How Healing Changes Hate into Love

Can you imagine the things a conventional talk therapist would have done to explain my reaction? Indeed, had I not known the significance of my hatred, I might have turned to logic myself. The thing is, we always blame our suffering on what we can see, when the wound is always what we can't see. Thus prior to that day, I had never considered that a wound might be causing me to hate spring, shorts, Persian rugs, short sleeved shirts, and gossamer curtains. To me, this was nothing more than that I just didn't like these things.

Six months later, a postscript to this story occurred. At the time, I was visiting my sister, Teresa, the one in the story. Being she was there, I wanted to tell her what had happened. Moreover, it all seemed to be going rather well until I got to the part of the story in which I imitated the *uh-huh-uh* sound. At which point, my sister recoiled in pain, then blurted out, "I *hate* that sound."

To this day, I have found no other example of a time wherein a single startling moment implanted the same charged cue in two children. It may even happen a lot. I just haven't seen it. More significant though, is how that realization changed my reaction to that sound. Since that day in the Starbucks—and all the way up to the present moment—I have loved hearing it. And imitating it. I love that sound. Period.

This raises yet one more thing to know about the inadequacy of treating symptoms. When symptoms go away, obviously you feel better. You may also feel relieved, grateful, uplifted, energized, and healthier. However, I've yet to see a single case wherein ridding people of their symptoms has resulted in them loving anything, let alone loving the very things they had been blaming their suffering on. Yet whenever you heal a wound, this is exactly what happens. You end up loving the very things which you previously hated and blamed.

Not sure of what I'm getting at here? Then recall what happened to me in the story I've just told you. Now realize that I not only no longer *hate* spring, tan shorts, short sleeved shirts, purple Persian rugs, parrot squawks, and off-white gossamer curtains. I also now *love* these things. Indeed, each time I think of this story, I feel pleasantly surprised by how I once could have hated these things. Moreover, it's been well over a decade since that day in the Starbucks. Yet I still feel just as surprised by how my feelings changed as I did that day. Given I've literally witnessed thousands of similar stories since then, I feel confident telling you that hating ordinary things always means you have a wound. And that healing these wounds always makes you love the things you previously hated.

A Brief Review of the Medical Layers: 6 and 5

Now let's review what we've said so far about layers 6 and 5.

First, we call them the "middle layers" because they occur between the four inner and four outer layers. Second, we call them the "medical layers" because they contain all the experiences medical people deal with.

What do you store in these layers?

In layer 6, you store your wounds—the scripts of the events which led to your being startled. Each time you relive one of these scripts, you become unable to see the needs you had at the time. And since you can't see these needs, you constantly overlook them.

Over time then, these unmet needs accumulate, resulting in the visible suffering called *symptoms*. You then store your experiences of these symptoms in layer 5.

Why do I call what you store in layer 6, *wounds*?

Being startled puts holes in your visual consciousness. The word *wounds* refers to these holes. Technically, the phrase *blocked needs* is more accurate though, as it refers to the nature of these holes. Here being startled creates a hypnotic script which associates certain life circumstances to the startle response. And whenever you reexperience these circumstances, reliving the startle blocks your ability to see your needs.

This then gives us a better way to define the word *symptoms*.

Since wounds are blocked needs, symptoms become both the signs of—and the often painful compensations for—these blocked, need-meeting abilities. In other words, symptoms are what you see when these chronically unmet needs cause problems. Therefore whenever you see symptoms, it means you have some particular pattern of chronically unmet needs.

Why can't you see these needs? Because abrupt 10-9-8-7 accesses cause visual blankness. These experiences, which we commonly refer to as being startled, are actually a sequence of three events, the dynamics of which resemble whips snapping.

• First, being startled causes you to draw back then hyperfocus, hypnotically connecting you to your immediate environment. This part of your experience gets stored in layers 10 and 9.

• Second, the direction of this hyperfocus suddenly reverses, causing the hypnotic field to deepen, then collapse, abruptly disconnecting you from your immediate environment. This part of your experience gets stored in layer 8.

• Third, as the snap of this disconnection passes, you enter the state medical people commonly call *shock*, a condition characterized by extreme neediness and profound inner blankness. Here you return to a state which resembles your early childhood, including that you feel so needy that you experience a kind of psychospiritual paralysis. And the essence of this psychospiritual paralysis is a gross inability to meet your own needs.

Eventually, you come out of shock, and when you do, you store this third part of the wounding experience in layer 7. At this point, the wounding event is over. However, because you also store a script for the events which led up to being startled in layer 6, from then on, each time you encounter a similar situation, you involuntarily relive this wounding event.

Know these scripts function much like movie plots wherein the same plot can underlie many movies. Wounds are similar in that they often cause symptoms to emerge in seemingly unrelated scenes. Indeed, even imagining this script can cause you to suffer, and this is true even when nothing bad actually happens.

What does this tell you about symptoms? That you can't use logic to diagnose them. This would be like trying to use logic to locate the invisible man. Moreover, since these scripts can affect any situation wherein the plot can apply, most symptoms occur in settings unrelated to the original wounding scene.

How then do you find your wounds? You treat your symptoms like the event horizon of an astronomer's black hole. Here your symptoms are the visible evidence that you have chronically unmet needs, and your wounds are the invisible scripts which make these needs invisible.

Used in this way, symptoms function like squirting water on the invisible man. By using what you can see—your symptoms—you define the outline of what you can't see—your wounds.

Finally, how do you know for sure that you've healed a wound, as opposed to that you've managed to avoid these invisible scripts and so, have become asymptomatic? It's simple. Healing always generates pleasant surprise. To prove you've healed a wound then, you need to ask but one question—do you feel pleasantly surprised in the formerly unpleasant circumstances? If yes, then you have healed this wound. If no, then you haven't. And this question works even when you're asymptomatic.

How does this question work? Healing changes what is stored in layer 6. Thus whenever you heal, the things you used to hate, fear, and avoid now feel surprisingly pleasant. This happens because healing alters the wounding script. The pattern underlying your wounds—hyperawareness, startle, shock—changes into the pattern underlying healing—hyperawareness, startle, amazement.

By the way, has it dawned on you yet how the wounding script explains what makes babies so vulnerable to injury? Babies live in a constant state of hyperawareness. In effect, they live, for the most part, in the first stage of the wounding script. And since you must be in a hyperaware state in order to be startled, this explains why they startle so easily and hence, their vulnerability to being wounded.

Finally, we have the formal definition for the word, *wounds*. Wounds are *recognizable patterns of abrupt 10-9-8-7 accesses which hypnotically associate the startle response to certain environmental cues.*

When Do the Middle Layers Begin to Emerge?

Some of you may have noticed that I've yet to address the question of when the middle layers emerge. Know I've purposely waited until now to do this. Why? Because the outer four layers emerge quite differently from the inner and middle layers. Thus I'd like to contrast and compare the emergence of the outer layers with that of inner and middle layers.

When do the two middle layers emerge and what triggers their emergence?

To begin with, all ten layers exist from the moment of conception on. However like croissants—wherein already existing layers expand as they bake—as life bakes us, meaning, as we accumulate life experience, the layers of personality expand. For instance layers 10 and 9 expand to their full size in the moment of conception. Here we live in a constantly-connected state and this makes us feel loved.

Layers 8 and 7 are similar in that they expand to their full size in the birth separation moment. Here the amount of disconnection (8) and neediness (7) created in that moment require a lot of storage space too.

At this point, the remaining six layers are tightly packed against the outer edge of layer 7. They then expand only as needed. Moreover, since newborns can be both wounded (6) and develop symptoms (5), the two middle layers, 6 and 5, slowly expand from the moment of birth on.

The outer layers (4, 3, 2, 1) are different in that they start to expand only after age seven. Prior to this, these four layers stay tightly nested against layer 5. What makes them change at age seven? Let's see.

What Makes the Outer Layers Expand at Age Seven?

In Book I: chapter four, I told you there are two ways we sense time—the brain in the gut's way, as *one-moment-at-a-time*, and the brain in the head's way, as *time-over-time*. With *one-moment-at-a-time*, we live as if every moment is the only moment we'll have. With *time-over-time*, we know that things can happen later, in essence, that things have a past, present, and future.

What does this have to do with the layers expanding?

Things we sense as single moments get stored in the inner and middle layers. Feeling connected, feeling needy, feeling symptoms—all are here and now events. Whereas, things which occur in sequences get stored in the outer four layers. Planning, learning from mistakes, cause and effect logic—all require a sense of how time unfolds.

The thing is, we don't learn to sense time this way until about age seven. This is why we begin to learn watch, clock, and calendar time at about this age. Before then, we sense time only as individual moments. And without a sense of time-over-time, we can't have outer layer experiences. So the outer layers stay tightly packed against layer 5.

It's our sense of time-over-time then that determines when the outer layers expand. From birth to age seven, we sense time only as single moments. So we store things only in layers 10 through 5. After age seven, we also sense time as sequences of moments. Thus from this age on, we also store experiences in layers 4 through 1.

Please note, I am not dividing these experiences into those we have before and after age seven. Even after age seven, we can, at times, sense things in *one-moment-at-a-time* time. However, before age seven, we sense all things this way. Thus it's not until age seven that we can sense time both ways.

Personality-wise, the thing to take away here is how the timing of when and how fully the ten layers emerge depends entirely on two things—one, on the age at which we begin to acquire content to store in each layer—and two, on the amount of content we need to store in each layer. With layers 10 and 9, we get enough content for these layers to fully expand in the moment of conception. With layers 8 and 7, we get enough content for these layers to expand fully in the birth separation moment. With layers 6 and 5, we can begin to get content from the birth separation moment on and thereafter, these two layers expand slowly, only as needed. And with layers 4 though 1, we begin to get content only at or about age seven, and from this point on these layers expand slowly as well.

How Having After-Age-Seven Time Changes Us

Now take a few minutes to consider how acquiring a sense of *after-age-seven* time changes us. And how significant this change is. Indeed, it's so important, I sometimes call it, "time puberty." As opposed to psychosexual puberty. Moreover, while most folks can easily recognize when children are learning to tell watch, clock, and calender time, few realize the implications.

To wit, because we cannot grasp events as related sequences of moments prior to age seven, we cannot predict how changes will occur. When we learn to sense *after-age-seven* time, however, not only can we now predict *what* may happen, ergo, the empirical wise man's story-telling skills. We also can deduce from these sequences *how* and *why* these things happen—the rationalist wise man's truth.

The downside, of course, is that we lose access to some of the spiritual wise man's truth, and with it our ability to marvel at the same story being told over and over again. This happens because young children have no way to deduce what is coming next. This also explains their blank stares and blurted guesses whenever adults demand explanations from them as to "why" they did something. Without *after-age-seven* time to make sense of life events, children can't comprehend cause and effect. Thus they can't "tell you the story" of what they did, let alone why.

This also explains why children can repeatedly make the same mistakes and have no clue as to why. Without *after-age-seven* time, they have no way to interpret history. Thus, the saying "those who forget the past are doomed to repeat it" very much applies to young children. As well as to adults when they relive wounds and act "childish."

How After-Age-Seven Time Creates Morality and Reason

Now consider how many other skills stem from having a sense of *after-age-seven* time. Morality as in a knowledge of right and wrong, for one. If you can't see how time unfolds, then morality loses its teaching potential and all that's left is a sense that right and wrong means rules.

This explains why young children can, at times, act so crazy and how adults can do impulsive things like overspend and cheat on their spouses. It also explains why jail sentences rarely teach. Most wrongdoings occur while we're experiencing *before-age-seven* time, and to see these things as wrongs, we must see them in *after-age-seven* time. Some people can't.

What puts adults into this state? Meditating, doing sports, dancing, and falling in love can all do this. But becoming extremely needy can also do it, as well reliving early childhood injuries. Whatever the cause, when this happens to us, we lose our ability to see how wrongdoing will affect our future. Moreover, since we can't sense events in both time states at once, when this happens, we can do all kinds of stupid things then later, not understand why. Why? Because when we do something wrong, we do it in *before-age-seven* time. But while processing this event in *after-age-seven* time restores our adult sense of right and wrong, this very feeling makes it hard to believe we ever felt like doing it.

Now consider what this aspect of *after-age-seven* time tells us about the events we store in layers 10 through 5. In these layers, we process everything in *before-age-seven* time. This explains why things like falling in love, feeling hungry, and getting a bargain can feel so intense. And why, when we experience these things, they can feel as if they'll be the only events of their kind—the only love we'll ever have, the only hot-fudge sundae we'll ever eat, the only chance we'll have to talk, the only time we'll get a bargain like this. This is what life feels like in the present moment.

The Benefits of Sensing Life in After-Age-Seven Time

Okay. So let's review this a bit. What do we gain from having a sense of *after-age-seven* time?

First, it's *after-age-seven* time which gives us our sense of what it means to make choices, as well as our ability to recognize and learn from our mistakes. It also gives us our sense of compassion, empathy, and sympathy—as well as our planning skills; money management, time management, anger management, and so on.

Second, it's *after-age-seven* time that gives us our sense of right and wrong, including an awareness of how our actions will affect ourselves and others. For instance, when regressed adults feel urges to cheat on their spouses but don't, it's because they're afraid of things like getting caught or being punished. Healthy adults chose not to cheat because they can see the hurt it will cause, and this allows them to make conscious choices.

Third, it's *after-age-seven* time which gives us the ability to see cause and effect, and this gives us our ability to reason. It also gives us our sense of wonder at how things change over time. How long it took water to create the Grand Canyon. How old amber really is. How puppies and butterflies change as they grow up. How all things, good and bad, pass in time.

Fourth, it's *after-age-seven* time that gives us the ability to be amazed by scientific and technological progress. As well as the ability to learn technical skills like using computers and power tools, playing sports, and mastering languages—skills which must be acquired over time.

Fifth, it's *after-age-seven* time which gives us the ability to credit ourselves for the process as well as the outcome. Sans this ability, our efforts mean nothing except when they net positive results. Here we're talking not only about the effort it takes to achieve our goals. We're also talking about the processes underlying all spiritual endeavors, from becoming more conscious and morally aware to learning to meditate.

Of course, like all wonderful things, there must also be a downside to having *after-age-seven* time. What is it exactly? We're about to find out.

The Downside of After-Age-Seven Time

Having just told you all the marvelous things we gain from knowing about *after-age-seven* time, what I'm about to tell you may come as a bit of a shock. It turns out that having this second sense of time has a heck of downside. For one thing, it potentially colors everything we do with four new flavors of suffering, none of which exist in the inner and middle layers—we'll talk about these four "poisons" a bit later. At the same time, we also gain what amounts to a respite from our suffering—the numbing non-existence of layer 1.

Despite the obvious benefits this numbness can bring however, beneath it all lies the same ambivalence I've been referring to throughout the chapter. On the one hand, we desperately want to find a way to return to paradise. On the other, we want to do everything we can to avoid the hell of layer 8.

In a way then, everything we store in the outer layers—and hence, everything we experience in *after-age-seven* time—has something to do with wanting to find a way to return to paradise, while at the same time, avoiding layer 8. This brings us to one of this personality theory's more important ideas. Indeed, this idea may be one of the more important in the book. The idea? If we successfully avoid layer 8 by not exposing ourselves to love, then how do we deal with the suffering that comes from not feeling loved—in effect, the suffering that comes from being alone?

The answer lies in seeing how the ten layers nest. To wit, *there are only three layers wherein you don't feel alone or fear layer 8*. In layers 10 and 9—the two innermost layers—you don't feel alone or fear layer 8 *because you are not alone*. You are connected. But in layer 1—in the outermost layer—you don't feel alone or fear layer 8 *because you are too numb to care, even though you are alone*.

What does this imply?

Throughout the chapter, I've been telling you that the primary drive in human nature is to avoid suffering. Here, by *suffering*, I mean the pain you feel whenever you disconnect from something or someone. I've also been telling you we have a secondary drive—to escape this aloneness by returning to paradise. Here, by *paradise*, I mean your pre-birth experiences—those wherein you felt perfectly connected to another person (layer 9) and to all things (layer 10).

Now remember that in layer 1, you're too numb to feel alone or fear layer 8. This makes getting to layer 1's numbness our tertiary drive. Moreover, being as layer 1 is on the opposite end of the onion from layers 10 and 9, you now have a way to see what propels us through the ten layers—the relative positions of these layers to each other. And to see how this works, we'll need to look at yet another detail drawing, this one titled, the *Currents of Human Motive.*

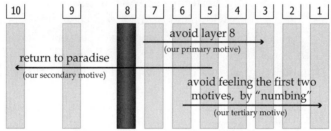

The Currents of Human Motive
(how we attempt to avoid suffering)
(© 2007 Steven Paglierani   The Center for Emergence)

The 10 Layers of Human Nature

The Three Human Motives: Suffering, Love, Numbness

What this drawing represents is a fractal composite of the three motives I've just mentioned, [1] our main motive—to avoid the pain of disconnecting, [2] our secondary motive—to feel connected, and [3] our tertiary motive—to become numb to the ambivalence caused by the first two motives. To forget they exist.

Together, these three motives create the currents underlying everything we think, feel, say, and do. And if you add to this the four perspectives from which we try to make sense of these currents—facts, feelings, stories, and ideas—you begin to see why it can be so hard to find personal truth.

Why isn't connecting our main motive? Because all connections are followed by disconnects. So if we avoid connecting, we avoid disconnecting. At least, much of the time. At the same time, we all do want connections, even if only to our world at large. And this ambivalence causes us to spend much of our lives deciding whether to be alone (suffer no disconnects), seek love (be connected), or numb out (pretend we don't care).

What about the moments wherein we courageously rise above this fear and go for love? Admittedly—and to our credit—many of us do this at times. However, even the most courageous people never do this for long, as inevitably their inner ambivalence undermines their resolve.

Ultimately then, most of us come to resemble the physicists who search for a unified field theory—a theory of everything. Only in our case, we spend our lives searching for what amounts to a unified human motive, a single viewpoint from which to make sense of love and life.

Is there such a theory—a theory of everything about love and life? I admit to wanting there to be one. However, I suspect that even if there is one, our inner ambivalence would prevent us from seeing it. After all, it's one thing to recognize that something exists—another to personally experience it.

In the end then, perhaps the best we can do is to take comfort from knowing that our drive to understand and resolve the multiple forces present in the natural world perfectly parallels our drive to understand and resolve the multiple forces within our nature. Personally, I find reassurance in knowing this. As for how the outer four layers play out in all this, all I can say at this point is that, once again, it's complicated. These four layers literally contain everything we "do" in life. And by the end of this chapter, I hope to have given you a decent overview.

Being (the inner four layers), *hurting* (the middle two layers), *doing* (the outer four layers)—connecting, disconnecting, and numbing out. Is any of this beginning to make sense? If not, don't worry. We've got a lot more to talk about. Including explanations for everything from why you feel urges to analyze and explain yourself to what makes you want to blame and punish people—including authors of long, boring books filled with too much information.

Before we do, we first need to take one more look at the inner and middle layers, specifically at how we react to suffering in these layers.

Wise men? Are you still there? Would you please get the lights?

Suffering in the Inner and Middle Layers

When I was a kid, I remember hearing some guy in a western saying, "hanging's too good for him." Ever since then, when I hear this phrase, something about it makes me chuckle. Certainly, I'm not taking it seriously, let alone picturing it happen. In all likelihood, then, it causes me to make 4-5-6-7-8-9-10 accesses—one of the most intensely funny experiences we can have.

Humor aside, there are a few things I still need to address before we turn our attention to the specifics of the outer layers.

First, I need to describe how suffering changes as we traverse the inner and middle layers. Second, I need to point out that none of this suffering provokes urges in us to blame anyone. Third, I need to point out that none of this suffering involves urges to punish anyone. And fourth, I need to point out that none of this suffering involves urges to restrain ourselves—no urges to do "damage control."

What do I mean by all of this, and how do I define suffering anyway? To see, we'll need to take a quick look at the kinds of suffering which exist in layers 10 through 5. As opposed to the kinds of suffering which exist in layers 4 through 1. As we do, please keep in mind that while there is only one kind of "pure" suffering (the fear of moving into layer 8), this suffering can take on many faces.

This is similar to how there is only one pure drinking alcohol—ethyl alcohol—but many commercial variations, each with it's own taste. What I mean is, with drinking alcohol, the individual tastes of the different drinks comes from what has been added to an essentially tasteless, colorless, and odorless substance—pure alcohol. Similarly, with the layers, the different types of suffering come from what has been added to the abject emptiness of layer 8's pure suffering.

What does this suffering taste like? Let's take a look.

Layers 10 and 9—Suffering Overridden (connections)
To begin with, recall where our experiences of life come from. They come from moving into or between layers. Suffering is just another word for moves which involve disconnects. Thus because all moves into or between layers 10 and 9 involve no disconnects, we feel no suffering during these moves. Here an example would be seeing the glowing, red metal of a hot kitchen-stove grill. Ever stare at this beauty? If you have, you know, the more you look, the more it draws you in.

The point is, whenever you feel this feeling, you are moving into, or between, layers 10 and 9.

Beautiful, isn't it? Ah, ain't love grand.

Layer 8—The Invisible Cause of All Suffering (disconnections)
All this goes to hell from layer 8 on out. Every move into or out of a layer now involves suffering. Moreover, since the root cause of all this suffering is moving into or out of layer 8, this gives us two ways to define layer 8's pure suffering. One, as layer movements. Here pure suffering is *the disconnecting experience of moving into or out of layer 8*. And two, as a reference to the primary motive—resolving aloneness. Here pure suffering is "what happens to us in moments of startling aloneness."

As for what layer 8 is actually like, a good example would be putting your hand on a hot stove grill. Indeed, if you've ever been unfortunate enough to have done this, you know all too well what moving into layer 8 is like. The instant you realize where your hand is, you suddenly freeze. And in that empty, frozen, timeless moment, nothing exists. Including you.

What makes moving into or out of layer 8 feel so bad? To see, you'll need to focus on the timing of what happens right before and right after that frozen moment.

To wit, you move into layer 8 *right before* that frozen moment. And you move into layer 7 *right afterwards*. And since all experience comes from moving into or between layers, while you're in that frozen moment, you aren't moving. Therefore, you can't suffer. Nor can you experience anything else, for that matter. Hence the abject emptiness of layer 8. While you're in it, you and all you know blink out of existence.

This frozen, mid-movement pause even has a name. It's called the *stillpoint moment.* This stillness is the essential nature of layer 8. It's also the closest you can come to dying and not be dead. Thus these moments create the dreaded black hole aspect of layer 8. And our fear of this sudden non existence is where our primary motive comes from.

Layer 7—Disconnections Made Visible (pure needs)

What's it like to escape layer 8 and move into layer 7?

The main thing that happens is that your previously invisible suffering gets a face. By this, I mean that layer 7's "pure need" is *suffering made visible.* Or to voice it theoretically—as a reference to the primary motive—in layer 7, "moments of startling aloneness become visible."

What's it like to move into or out of layer 7? To be honest, it hurts like hell. Indeed, while layer 8's abject emptiness is certainly painful, layer 7's pure need is almost as bad. Thus, while it's surely a good thing to realize you need to take your hand off a hot stove, at the same time, while you're in layer 7, you have yet to move your hand. You still *need* to move it.

This then is what makes layer 7's pure needs so intense. You abruptly realize you have them—but haven't satisfied them yet. In the case of the hot stove, for example, you suddenly realize you need to move your hand. But while you're in layer 7, you haven't moved it yet.

Obviously, in the case of hot stoves, our needs arise abruptly. Know there are also times when they come on slowly—situations which involve slow trips through layer 8. Here a good example would be sitting in a concert or movie wherein the experience is intensely beautiful *but does not change.* Have you ever had this happen? It slowly dawns on you that you *need* to get up and move, or that you *must* get something to eat, or that you *have* to know the time, or that you *can't wait* to go to the ladies room.

This intensely uncomfortable suffering also has a name. We call it, "boredom"—*the urgent need to have experience.* Here the suffering comes from having lingered for too long in layers 10 or 9. This causes us to slowly drift into layer 8. We then enter layer 7 where it dawns on us that we desperately need "a change." A change from what? A change from not changing. A change from making no layer movements.

Finally, while moving into layer 7 always makes your suffering visible, know the opposite is true as well. Moving out of layer 7 and into layer 8—or into layer 6, for that matter—makes your suffering invisible.

Layer 6—Pure Needs Made Invisible (blocked needs)

What's it like to move into layer 6?

Moving into layer 6—either from layer 5 or layer 7—causes you to lose touch with some particular suffering. Your suffering literally becomes invisible to you. Conversely, moving out of layer 6—either into layer 5 or layer 7—makes this suffering reappear. Moreover, because layers 5 and 7 contain different kinds of suffering (symptoms and pure needs), there are two kinds of suffering these movements can make visible or invisible. Moving from layer 7 into layer 6 causes certain pure needs to become invisible. And vice versa. And moving from layer 5 into layer 6 makes the symptoms caused by not meeting these pure needs invisible. And vice versa.

Here again, there are abrupt movements and slow movements in and out of this layer. When you abruptly move from layer 7 into layer 6—such as when your hand comes off a hot stove—the invisible script of a startling event gets stored in layer 6. And when you abruptly move from layer 5 into layer 6, you involuntarily relive one of these scripts, including that you feel like you've been wounded all over again.

In both cases, a good way to refer to what we store in layer 6 is to say they are "recordings of moments of startling aloneness." Thus, we can define this kind of suffering—"blocked needs"—as *permanently stored scripts of abrupt layer 10 to 7 accesses which, when reexperienced, cause a profound inability to respond to specific pure needs.*

Did you just hear the sound of the four wise men hoohahing in the background? Did your mind just go blank again? If so, just breathe. It's perfectly natural. Anytime you try to grasp what is stored in layer 6, your mind will empty. This happens because each time you attempt to experience what is in layer 6, you reexperience your birth separation moment, including the blankness of the stillpoint moment.

All this changes when you move into layer 6 slowly. Slow movements from layer 7 into layer 6 are boredom gone blank, rather than a wounding script getting stored. And slow movements from layer 5 into layer 6 are symptoms gone numb, rather than accessing a wounding script.

This said, can you now see how layer 8 and layer 6 interact? If layer 8 is personality's black hole, then what we store in layer 6 are the stories of all of our trips through this black hole.

The worst part of all, of course, is that because we go blank whenever we move into layer 6, we have no way to visualize these stories, let alone know they even exist. This results in our having "stalled moments of disbelief" whenever we try. Here we're talking about two kinds of disbelief—the kind you feel right after you realize you've touched a hot stove—and the kind you feel when a football seems to hang in mid air in the final throw of the game. Either way, with no way to see where it's coming from, we cannot resolve what we feel.

A good way to describe what it's like to move into layer 6 then is to say that it's sort of like moving into layer 8—except we can still experience something. Here the thing we can still experience is the bit of life which occurred just before we got startled. Unfortunately, being startled hypnotically charges this bit of life with the intense emptiness of layer 8. Thus each time we revisit this scene, we not only go blank. We also experience the pain of moving through layer 8.

Worse yet, because we go blank, we can't see what is causing this pain, let alone the pure needs aligned with this bit of life. Hence moving into layer 6 not only makes us go blind. It also makes us intensely needy.

Layer 5—Blocked Needs Made Visible (symptoms)

Finally we arrive at layer 5, the layer wherein we store the suffering we call *symptoms*. Or stated as a reference to the primary motive, we could say that "reliving moments of startling aloneness cause us to experience the visible evidence of chronically or acutely unmet needs." This makes symptoms *the visible evidence for either chronically, or acutely, unmet needs*. And in the case of the stove burn, we end up with both. We get the acute and immediate suffering of the burn. And we get the tediously chronic suffering which results from an internal battle between two desires—to touch the stove again—and the anticipatory tension caused by knowing that we are free to give in to this desire if we wish.

Know that both experiences involve moving from layer 6 into layer 5. Indeed, so potent are layer 6's wounding scripts that even imagining them can cause us to relive the pain. Moreover, because wounding scripts are fractal—and because fractals always repeat differently—even our symptoms can generalize to other situations, for example, when you fear getting close to the glowing embers of a campfire or a charcoal grill after having burned yourself on hot a stove.

Lastly, know we can also move into layer 5 from layer 4, and these movements result in much the same outcomes. Whether fast or slow, we experience the symptoms of our chronically unmet needs, as well as potentially augmenting these symptoms with similar, imaginary ones.

Following the Stove Burn Through the First Six Layers

Now recall what I said a few sections back about how we sense time in the first six layers as single, individual moments. In large part, this explains why we suffer differently in each of these six layers. What I mean is, because we experience suffering in these layers in *before-age-seven* time, as we change layers, we experience these changes as completely separate moments, each of which feels intensely personal. And intensely painful.

For example, were you to be so unfortunate as to burn yourself on a hot stove—and were you to follow this experience through the first six layers—you'd find a series of events which go something like this:

• a moment of timeless amazement wherein you become hypnotically drawn to the beauty in the glowing, red hot stove grill—layer 10.

• a similarly amazing moment wherein you see yourself seeing this beauty, a moment in which the subjective you observes—and then connects to—the objective you—layer 9.

• a moment in which you get startled by how abruptly both you and this beauty disappear, as you mindlessly reach out and touch this hot stove grill—layer 8.

• a moment in which it painfully dawns on you that this beautiful stove grill is horribly hot and that you urgently need to move your hand—layer 7.

• a moment in which this terrible neediness exceeds your capacity to observe, causing you to tumble into a pit of numbing gray blankness—layer 6.

• a moment in which you become frighteningly hyperaware, as you begin to feel the symptoms of a burn, then urgently start to evaluate the extent of the damage—layer 5.

This is the thing to keep in mind then as we begin to look at the outer layers. There is no way to experientially join this sequence of six moments. Logically, yes, it's obvious, they form a sequence. But because we experience things in these six layers in *before-age-seven* time, to us, these moments remain as separate as if we had lived them in different lives.

All this changes when you move into the outer four layers,. There you experience changes between layers as sequences of inseparable moments. And as you're about to find out, this change radically alters the way you experience life, especially the way you experience suffering. Worse yet, it also impairs the way you seek personal truth. How? Let's see.

Section Three

The Outer Layers
of
Personality:

"Doing"

Shifting Our Focus from What to Why: the Outer Layers

From about age seven on, we can, in theory, sense events in both *before-age-seven* time and in *after-age-seven* time. Those we sense in *before-age-seven* time, we store in the inner and middle layers. And those we sense in *after-age-seven* time, we store in the outer layers.

How much does this change us? More than you might imagine. For instance, as I've previously said, before age seven, we experience life as one long moment. This makes us experience the journey and the outcome as one and the same. But at or about age seven, we become able to experience life as sequences of moments. And whenever we do, we experience the journey and the outcome as two separate states of mind.

The upside of this separation is that it gives us some powerful life skills. But we also incur some terrible losses. In the plus column, we gain the ability to reflect on our mistakes, the ability to plan for the future, and the ability to make commitments. Along with these skills, we also gain an awareness of who we are—a sense of personal history. In the minus column, we begin to lose touch with the present moment, and this shifts our focus from what is happening now to what *was* or *will be*. And each time this happens, we lose the ability to see beauty, the ability to be spontaneous, and the ability to be creative.

The result, of course, is that at or around age seven, we begin to change the way we look for truth. Before this age, we seek truth mainly in the present moment—truth is *what* we see happening now. After this age, we increasingly shift our focus away from *what* is happening now and onto *why* things happen. This makes retrospection—rather than reality—our main truth-seeking tool. From this, we gain a new maturity and an inner wisdom. But we also inherit four new kinds of suffering—each of which impairs our ability to access our personal truth.

The Four Poisons of Adulthood

What kinds of suffering are we talking about? Resentment, blame, punishment, and damage control. All four poisons exist in us only after age seven. Why? Because in order to experience these four things, we must understand cause and effect. And to experience cause and effect, we must be able to see how things change over time. This makes learning to sense *after-age-seven* time much like eating from the tree of knowledge in the Garden of Eden. We gain the ability to understand much about how life unfolds. But we lose touch with our innocence and our natural ability to forgive. We'll talk about why in a moment.

The Four Poisons of Adulthood
(resentment, blame, punishment, damage control)
(© 2007 Steven Paglierani   The Center for Emergence)

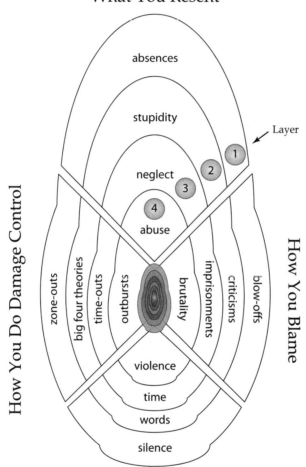

What You Resent

absences

stupidity

Layer

neglect

abuse

How You Do Damage Control

How You Blame

zone-outs · big four theories · time-outs · outbursts · brutality · imprisonments · criticisms · blow-offs

violence

time

words

silence

How You Punish

The Four Poisons of Adulthood
Styles of Resentment (abuse, neglect, stupidity, absences)
Style of Blame (brutality, imprisonments,criticisms, blow-offs)
Styles of Punishment (violence, time, words, silence)
Styles of Damage Control (outbursts, time-outs, big four theories, zone-outs)

Not coincidentally, early in the Twentieth century, the Catholic church acknowledged this very transition when they lowered the age at which children could make First Communion to seven. Their explanation? These children had reached "the age of reason." They could now tell right from wrong. This meant they now met the prerequisites to receive Communion—they could confess their sins (know they'd transgressed and blame themselves). And they could do penance (self administer punishment).

This then is where the four poisons of adulthood come from. They come from our after-age-seven tendency to use cause and effect logic to seek truth. From this tendency we gain the ability to introspect and see ourselves as persons. But we also lose much of our ability to enjoy what we find, including our ability to enjoy the present moment.

Here then are the four things we'll focus on as we explore the outer layers. What is resentment? What is blame? What is punishment? What is damage control? Truly, a lot to learn. Amazingly, a single question holds the key to understanding all four things—as well as the outer four layers in general. The question? How does *after-age-seven* time change the way we suffer. Can you guess how already? Let's see if you're right.

Poison Number One—Resentment

One clue to what makes this change significant is that everything we store in the outer layers gets a time stamp. Like dates on digital photos, this stamp associates individual moments to specific life events. Moreover, because human beings tend to group similar life events together, these time stamps cause us to experience the suffering we store in the outer layers cumulatively—as historical collections of painful moments.

This effectively magnifies the perceived size of all of our suffering. Single instants of pain blend and distort into whole categories of things we hate. This leads to a new, more insidious kind of suffering—the painful iterations we call, *resentments*. Here we not only feel the intensely unpleasant experience of chronically unmet needs. We also feel the hellish pain of repeatedly rehashing whole collections of suffering.

What are resentments anyway?

To resent is *to review a startling moment of aloneness*—in effect, to re-feel a painful event. Here the "re" part means "again," and the "sent" part means "to feel," as in the word, "sentient." Thus to resent a painful moment is to re-feel it, again and again.

This makes resentment the psychophysical equivalent to feedback in an auditorium. When sound systems feedback, the sound they emit keeps getting louder until it begins to distort. If this feedback then continues, the distortion will keep getting worse until we either kill the volume or turn this sound system off. At which point, we'll hear nothing.

Resentment is similar in that it amplifies our symptoms, often to such a degree that we either feel the urge to kill someone or the urge to turn ourselves off. Either way, it's at this point that the other three poisons of adulthood come into play. Here blame is the equivalent of locating the sound system amplifier—punishment, the equivalent of killing the volume—and damage control, the equivalent of turning the volume down, rather than smashing the amplifier into pieces.

How does this work in the real world? Imagine you've burned your hand on a hot stove. Now consider how the feedback of resentment would magnify your suffering. In all likelihood, the instant you felt the burn, you'd pull back your hand, look at it, perhaps curse, then look at it again. At this point, your resentment would be beginning. You might then look at the stove with hate in your eyes, then survey the damage some more. Here your resentment would be building. Finally, at some point, the pain in your hand would begin to subside. But by this time, you'd have revisited this burn many times. This would have effectively turned a single, painful instant into a whole new category of suffering—the collectively resented symptoms of everything which has ever or might ever burn you. Stoves to matches. Soups to soufflés. Hot stuff—bad. Cool stuff—okay.

This feedback loop typifies how resentment magnifies suffering. Collectively re-feeling symptoms amplifies painful experiences. This is why you can sometimes feel like killing people for small offenses—such as when they cut in front of you at the bank teller line, or accidentally spill hot coffee on your new cashmere sweater, or tap your bumper when they're pulling out of a parking lot. You experience the initial suffering, intensely, but only once, in *before-age-seven* time. You then repeatedly revisit this one painful moment in *after-age-seven* time, in effect, turning a single painful moment into many—and making a little thing into a big deal.

This then is the first thing to know about resentment—it magnifies the perceived size of any and all suffering. This happens because whenever we suffer in *after-age-seven* time, we focus more on analyzing the sequence which led to this suffering than on the event itself. To do this, we revisit the event. But because we experience everything in the inner and middle layers in *before-age-seven* time, each time we revisit the pain, we treat this pain as a separate incidence of suffering—e.g. an additional burn. Then when we try to make sense of this pain, we use our *after-age-seven* logic. To do this, we contrast and compare this moment to all similar moments. This then merges these single moments of pain into whole categories of suffering.

Here then is another reason why logic fails when it comes to understanding wounds. Resentment blends all similar events—whether lived, relived, or imagined—into one massive pool of pain. This effectively distorts the size of these events into unknowable amounts, making attempts to determine the magnitude of anything painful as useless as trying to estimate the volume control setting on an amplifier which is feeding back. Feedback distorts an amplifier's volume control setting into an unknowable amount. Resentment does the same thing to our ability to see the size of our suffering.

How Resentment Hides Wounds

Now consider the implications of what I've just said. Most people, including most professionals, assume people's symptoms equate to the size of their wounds, as in, big symptoms—big wounds, and small symptoms—small wounds. However, since resentment magnifies our perceptions of pain, our wounds are almost always smaller than our estimates.

This means resentment not only makes us overreact to others. It also causes us to overestimate the size of our wounds. Or underestimate them, as in, when our symptoms are small, we assume the wound is small. Moreover, since most helping professionals use symptom size to gauge the severity of wounds, this can lead to years of wasted efforts looking for big wounds which, in reality, don't even exist.

Do you doubt this? Then try reading a helping professional's diagnostic manual, the mental health profession's DSM-IV-TR, for instance. In it, you'll find page after page of terrible sounding conditions, none of which come close to describing the true size of the wounds which lead to these conditions. The proof? Beside each condition, you'll find a scale of severity. The severity of what? Well, it's obvious. The severity of symptoms. And since resentment magnifies symptoms (and since symptoms are not wounds), resentment renders these diagnoses next to useless when it comes to identifying wounds. No surprise here.

How Resentment Spawns Professional Nonsense

Obviously, resentment explains a lot about what makes it hard to find wounds. Resentment turns symptoms into a haystack—and wounds into a needle in it. But as if this were not enough, the problems don't stop here. Because resentments affect professionals the same way they do us, we end up hearing—and believing in—some rather strange ideas.

For instance, there are schools who force parents to put their kids on drugs, as if every kid who can't stay focused has ADHD. And television commercials and magazine ads make it sound like we're stupid if we ever feel down. Does everyone who feels unmotivated need antidepressants?

How about men who find their desire waning. Should they all take Viagra? If you judge how lovable you are by the stiffness of your dick, then maybe the ads are correct. And what about eating red meat. This could lead to a heart attack, right? Well, have you ever considered how having a fear of eating meat affects your ability to digest meat?

If symptom size equated to wound size, then all these things would be true. Intuitively, we know there's more to these things, though, no matter what professionals say. Here a theoretical knowledge of how wounding scripts work can go a long way toward seeing through these simple-minded proclamations. But if you add to this the idea that resentment magnifies symptoms, you begin to see why so many good sounding theories fail to offer lasting help. And why so many popular diagnoses more resemble the emperor's new clothes than professional advice.

How Resentment Leads to Procrastination

Do you ever put things off because you expect them to be hard? Yet when you finally do them, you find, they're really small? Here is yet another problem resentment creates. Resentment magnifies suffering, remember? The thing is, these distortions affect a lot more than your symptoms. They also affect everything from your estimates of how difficult your everyday chores will be to your expectations about what therapists, doctors, and spiritual counselors will tell you to do.

For instance, say you're feeling poorly. Resentment can make you worry that you've got six months to live—or lead you to expect to be in therapy for life. Or it may cause you to think you're too dysfunctional to find love—or make you fear you've become allergic to everything, including air.

These expectations can then cause you to put off getting help, allowing your symptoms to worsen. Ironically, if you don't understand resentment, this can easily happen. And while you probably won't die from putting off chores, you never know. Oops, see what I mean. Obviously, you can't die from not doing chores. Damn resentment, at it again. Sorry about that.

How Resentment Impairs Our Ability to Forgive

Now let's look at how resentment affects our ability to forgive as adults, whereas children don't have this problem—they usually get over things quickly. This happens because, before age seven, we don't resent. So while getting hurt can feel like a major catastrophe at that age, once this hurt passes, we just go on with our lives. After age seven however, we experience symptoms in cumulative categories, and with each retelling, the category swells. And the longer this goes on, the harder it is to forgive.

Complicating this further is the idea that, for adults to forgive, they must review what they're trying to forgive. This inevitably stirs up more resentment, swelling this category of suffering even more.

So can adults learn to get over things? In a word, yes. And the key to being able to do this lies in realizing that resentments magnify symptoms. At the same time, just knowing this is not enough. You must also learn to let the full force of your unmet needs hit you head on. And yes, it's a bit more complicated than I'm making it sound. But if you can manage to do these two things, you will be able to heal your wounds.

Obviously, it can take great courage to seriously allow for the possibility that your suffering is smaller than it seems. If you can learn to do this though, two things will happen. One, you will gain access to your pre age-seven ability to forgive. Two, because you are an adult and have a sense of *after-age-seven* time, you'll also gain access to the positive side of being able to resent things. Here we're talking about how reliving a single moment of forgiveness can turn it into a lifelong category of compassion.

Lastly, I need to add that young children can, on occasion, relive a painful experience. This pain may stem from a wound or from the struggles which led to a discovery. Since young children do not store their experiences of suffering collectively though, this reliving does not cause resentment. So even when children do relive painful experiences, they forget this suffering as quickly as it comes.

The Two Kinds of Forgiveness: Temporary & Permanent

Before moving on, there is one last thing to know about resentment—that it creates two kinds of forgiveness. There is the temporary kind of forgiveness I just described—the kind young children feel when a painful moment passes. And there is the permanent kind all people feel when they heal a wound.

What's the difference?

If you can't resent things, you automatically forgive. When suffering passes, you forget it and it's like nothing bad ever happened. But since nothing has healed, this forgiveness is temporary. Thus the next time you relive this wound, you'll feel the suffering all over again.

All this changes when you learn to resent things. Now in order to forgive, you must actually heal. At the same time, when you do heal, you need do it only once, as healing leaves you with an indelible memory of both the suffering and the joy of forgiveness.

In large part, this explains why young children and adults suffer differently. When young children relive a wound, each reliving is an easily forgotten event. Each time it happens, they forget and forgive, until they relive it again. Adults, on the other hand, remember their suffering even after it passes. So in order to forgive, they must heal.

On the other hand, when young children heal, they rarely remember being wounded. So to them, forgiveness is more like the wound never happened. When adults heal though, they remember their suffering. Thus for them, forgiveness is amazing. It not only allows them to see the true size of their wounds. It also ends forever the need to change, punish, or kill whatever led to this suffering, as the pain of the original event gets infused with genuine feelings of love and compassion for the very thing they once wanted to change, punish, or kill.

Can you now see how compassion and love are both byproducts of permanent forgiveness? And in order to gain either, you must learn to heal your wounds? This said, the thing to take away here is how the retrospection which derives from *after-age-seven* time has both an upside and a downside. The upside? You can gain from your suffering, including that you can learn to love and feel compassion. The down side? You can resent things, making it hard to see the true size of your suffering. Thus it's resentment which makes it difficult for adults to forgive. But it's also what makes love and compassion possible.

Poison Number Two—Blame

Now let's look at blame. What is blame anyway? And why is it so hard for us not to do it?

Blame is *the act of deciding who or what caused our suffering*. Here the word to pay attention to is *cause*. Because we assume that symptoms are *caused* by some wrongly done deed or deeds, we believe that knowing who or what caused these wrongdoings will allow us to end this suffering.

Ironically, like resentment, blame is itself a kind of suffering. In other words, when we do it, it hurts. So rather than ending suffering, blame only makes things worse. Indeed, even after we eliminate what we see as the causes, we often continue to feel urges to blame. But because we believe eliminating these causes will end our resentments, we ignore this suffering and do it anyway.

We also blame because it justifies our urges to punish. And we do it to save face and to vent our feelings. Mainly, though, we do it because it keeps us from having to admit that suffering is inevitable. In effect, blame makes us feel our suffering is optional.

This then is the first thing to know about blame. We blame because we believe it will end our suffering. Here blame tells us there is a knowable, logical cause for our symptoms, and that if we find this cause, we can then root it out and so, prevent future suffering.

By the way, can you now see what this means about children younger than age seven? They can't see cause and effect. Thus they can't blame. And yes, they can and often do look like they're blaming—when they get mad and throw tantrums, for instance. But when they do this, they're more pointing to where the suffering first appeared than assigning wrongful cause to this suffering. Thus children younger than seven cannot blame.

Do All Things Happen For Reasons?

Have you ever found yourself saying, "everything happens for reasons?" If you have, then you may be surprised to hear this is actually a common justification for blaming. Thus while most folks hear this saying as a spiritual maxim, in reality, it's a reference to the idea that all suffering stems from causes. Therefore, all suffering is avoidable. As in, if we avoid the cause, then we avoid the suffering.

Does everything happen for reasons? Not according to the four wise men, albeit, they do teach that we can make reasons for everything that happens. Oh, boy, can we! Unfortunately, saying there are reasons for everything that happens—at least when referring to personality—is just a fancy way to say that blame makes sense. Hence, my claim that the saying "everything happens for reasons" is just our way to justify blaming.

How about you? Do you believe all things happen for reasons? Chances are, you probably do, even if you've never thought much about it. Know my reason for bringing this up is to point out that despite our usual take on this phrase—that we say it to spiritually comfort ourselves—the belief underlying this saying is actually where blame comes from. It comes from the assumption that all suffering has causes.

This means whenever we blame, whether knowingly or not, we're assuming things happen for reasons. And vice versa. Every time we say that everything happens for reasons, we're assuming there's someone or something to blame. (Shut up, wise men. It's not funny.)

What Happens When Blaming Doesn't End Our Suffering?

What do we do when blaming doesn't end our suffering? To be blunt, most people just look for new ways to blame. Indeed, most of us spend much of our lives inventing new ways to blame. So when it comes to blaming, we're constantly looking to "self-improve."

This leads some of us to spend years persistently rehashing our suffering, in hopes we'll finally make sense of it. During this time, we may ingest enough self help books to make toilet paper for an army. Others do their best to put it all behind them by taking what is assumed to be another spiritually motivated path—pretending to be the bigger person. Others take what is often seen as THE spiritual path, deciding their suffering must have been the will of God. So they do their best to just turn it over and let it go. Still others drown themselves in distractions—eating five pizzas a day, or shopping 'til they drop—all the while hoping the cause of their symptoms will somehow just evaporate.

Whatever we decide, eventually, we all arrive at more or less the same conclusion—eliminating this person, place, thing, or event does not end our pain. We then conclude that this person, place, thing, or event can't have been the real reason. At which point, many otherwise intelligent people begin to suspect that they, themselves, must have done something to deserve this suffering. If everything happens for reasons—and if you rule everything else out—then it must be you. Right?

Obviously, blaming yourself is not a very attractive prospect. But when all else fails, what the heck—it's easier to blame the wrong thing than to admit you may never know. Then again, maybe you just haven't looked hard enough for something to blame? Or perhaps you just need a larger menu of possible wrongdoers to choose from?

At this point, many folks run down to their nearest B&N, looking for a new self help, miracle book. After all, perhaps you're being punished for wrongdoings you've never considered before? Unfortunately, while most of these books are pretty good at telling us *how* we suffer, common sense also tells us they're mostly nonsense when it comes to explaining *why* we suffer.

This leads many folks to eschew the book path and pick from the list of usual suspects. For instance, maybe it's your karma, or a penance, or perhaps you've been too selfish all your life? Perhaps you've eaten too many Twinkies, or been drinking the wrong water, or been going to the wrong church? Then again, maybe you've been too codependent, or too independent, or maybe, not codependent enough? Or perhaps you've wasted food while children in Africa were starving, or maybe it's a test of your faith? Then too, maybe it's another of those bloody life lessons, something your soul chose before you were born? Could that be it?

For cripes sake, can you believe all the things we consider when we're looking for something to blame? And a lot of them are contradictory besides. For instance, if we're not always positive, we're told this is why we're suffering. But if we can't get to our sadness or anger, we're told this is our fault too.

And what about the food thing. Hell. If we eat the wrong foods and we get fat—or sick—it's our fault. But when we're told that eating fats, sugars, starches, and meats are all bad for us—and that there's DDT on veggies and fruits and mercury in fish, what's left? Lawn grass?

What do we do if all these attempts to blame also fail? What then?

Getting Help From Professional Blamers

I don't know about you, but to me, doing this much blaming can feel more exhausting than a day at the mall. Which is why so many of us seek professional help. The thing is, while professionals do have professional training, they're also human. So they have the same sorts of damaged containers we do.

This means, while most of them sincerely attempt to teach us to stop all this nonsense, more times than not, all they succeed in doing is to help us find new things to blame. Case in point. There are now whole generations who have been taught to blame their quiet, hard working fathers—or their less than perfect teachers. Or their mothers—or their doctors—or whole religious groups. That even therapy, medicine, and spiritual beliefs can lead us to blame each other should tell you just how strong our urges to blame are. And the lengths we'll go to find someone to blame.

Do you doubt this? Then try visiting your nearest library. There you'll find whole sections dedicated to explaining every suffering known to man—why our relationships fail, why we never have enough money, why our children turn out lazy, why our dogs bark too much, why our meat loafs taste like crap, why our orgasms are too infrequent, why our bosses are so stupid, and why our houses fall apart.

In the end, then, even when done with the best intentions, the only thing most professionals do is reinforce our belief in blame. And it's easy to see why. At times, we—and they—can see wrongdoing in others. And notice what preceded this wrongdoing. Things like talk therapies often help us to hone these skills. These new skills then lead us to falsely conclude that if we look hard enough at our life (or if we pay someone to help us look), that eventually, we'll discover what's been causing our suffering and prevent it from happening again.

Unfortunately, since suffering derives not from wrongdoing but rather, from chaotically occurring unmet needs—and since all unmet needs derive from wounds to our ability to see these needs—these efforts are also doomed to fail. After all, how can you find, let alone change, what you cannot see. In reality then, blame exists mainly as a way for us to pretend we understand suffering. By blaming, we assuage our fears and insecurities regarding how unpredictable life is. In this way, blame holds great appeal for most human beings, so much so that it's study and execution could, without exaggeration, be called one of our most beloved sciences. After all, blaming makes us feel like we have some control over our suffering, and ultimately some control over life itself. Moreover, when you realize that the four layers in which we store our memories of doing things (4-1) all contain blame, it's easy to see how blame could cloud the motives of everything we do.

The Four Resentments and the Four Kinds of Blame

Finally, there is the idea that each layer has it's own kind of blame, as well as its own class of resentment.

In layer 4, we resent acts of violence done to us. Here we see the cause of our symptoms as *abuse*. Thus, in layer 4, we respond to resentment with the style of blame known as *brutality*—the idea that we should abuse these abusers by violently pointing the finger at them.

In layer 3, we resent something or someone for not responding to us in a timely manner. Here we see the cause of our symptoms as *neglect*. Thus, in layer 3, we respond to resentment with the style of blame known as *imprisonments*—the idea that we should force wrongdoers to endure long periods of boredom, all the while hoping they're reflecting on what they've done wrong.

In layer 2, we resent someone doing something patently illogical. Here we see the cause of our symptoms as *stupidity*, either intentional or otherwise. Thus, in layer 2, we respond to resentment with a kind of counter-stupidity—*criticisms*—the idea that we should use logic and reason to blame people, followed by some logical excuse for what they've done.

Finally in layer 1, we resent someone not caring whether we have needs or not. Here we see the cause of our symptoms as *absences*. Thus, in layer 1, we respond to resentment with *blow-offs*, the idea that if we ignore people for long enough, they'll get the idea.

Poison Number Three—Punishment

Now let's look at punishment—what it is, and where it comes from.

To begin with, punishment is yet another kind of suffering. Thus like blaming and resenting, it hurts to do it. This time the thing to see is the sequence of poisons that leads us to punish. Symptoms cause resentment. Resentment makes us blame. And blaming gives us urges to punish.

Beneath it all lies the same motive—to end our future suffering. Is suffering optional? Not according to the four wise men. They teach that no matter how much we punish, life will continue to have flaws. Indeed, like many spiritual belief systems, the four wise men teach that suffering is normal. We suffer not because we're broken or bad, but because we're human.

This is not to say we should blindly accept suffering, self-inflicted or otherwise. Doing this would be downright crazy, regardless of how spiritual it might sound. Nor should we blindly plow through our suffering in hopes it will eventually end. Rather, the four wise men teach that when suffering comes, there is something you can do about it—you can vow to not let it to pass without gaining something from it.

Not clear what I'm getting at? Then bring to mind something which has been hurting you. Now try picturing this situation while saying the following sentence to yourself—out loud and with conviction.

I will not let this suffering pass without getting something from it.

Can you say this and really mean it? Yes, I know. It's hard. On the other hand, treating suffering as *the pressure to change*—rather than as something to avoid or get rid of—can give your life purpose and meaning. Thus while some suffering is inevitable, if you take this vow, when it comes, you can gain from it.

For instance, consider the suffering that reading a difficult book like this one can provoke. Seriously. People want easy answers, and books like this make you work for what you get. But if—when you're reading a tough passage—you were to say to yourself, *I will not let this suffering pass without getting something from it,* you'd be amazed by what would happen. What sounded only moments before like gibberish will begin to make sense. Moreover, the more stupid it seems, the more you have to gain.

The point? Suffering is *not* optional. But the gain from suffering is. So chose wisely. And consider taking the vow.

How Resentment and Blame Lead to Punishment

Now let's take a deeper look at the nature of punishment, starting with where it comes from.

Punishment is the third of the four poisons of adulthood, all of which derive from our belief in cause and effect. Moreover, we arrive at this poison in the same way we arrive at most things we do in life—by trying to make sense of our suffering. Here when we suffer from symptoms, resentment is the way we assess this suffering. Thus resentment is *the act of recycling symptoms in order to inventory the damage.* Then, when we think we've sufficiently inventoried this suffering, we use blame to look for its cause.

This makes blame *our attempt to find the causes of our resentments.* We blindly throw darts of blame hoping they'll land on these causes. Then, when we think we've identified these causes, we use punishment to address the problem. Thus punishment is *any action taken to eliminate what blame identifies as the problem.*

How do we punish?

In layer 4, we punish with *violent, permanent endings.* We do this thinking it will keep this particular suffering from ever happening again. After all, if we kill the cause of our symptoms, these symptoms can't harm us again. One can only hope, yes?

In layer 3, we punish with *empty time.* We do this as a way to teach people to not risk provoking our symptoms again. To do this, we use time-outs, which is to say, forced boredom, as in the desperate need for experience. Here we're talking about everything from putting three year olds in corners and confining fourteen year olds to their rooms to sending drunk drivers to prisons and putting embezzlers on probation.

In layer 2, we punish with *words and logic,* in hopes we'll convince these wrongdoers of the error of their ways. All the while, we're hoping we won't have to punish them more severely. So we make excuses like that they didn't know any better. Or that they're mentally ill. Or that their parents were fuklunct and didn't teach them how to behave properly. Or that they're just too stupid to know any better.

Lastly, in layer 1, we punish with *silence,* in hopes, if we wait long enough, our symptoms will just go away. Here some folks turn to old friends—like potato chips with dip and TV—to get them through the waiting. Others turn to spending, or booze, or to drugs, sex, or gambling— legal (the stock market, mutual funds, lotto, bingo) or otherwise (the bookies' ponies, dog races, various get rich quick schemes). Regardless of what people do though, the goal is always the same—to ignore something or someone in hopes we'll wake up and our symptoms will just be gone.

Now restating these four kinds of punishment more formally, we have *uncivilized punishment*—the urge to punish with violence, *time-limited punishment*—the urge to punish with time, *civilized punishment*—the urge to punish with words, and *non-existent punishment*—the urge to punish with silence.

Finally, let me offer you a more formal definition for punishment. Punishment is *anything we feel urges to do which could, in theory, prevent us from seeking causes for our moments of startling aloneness.* Thus punishment is to suffering what solutions are to math problems. Unlike math problems, however, since blame never includes all the numbers, punishments never lead to lasting solutions.

Poison Number Four—Damage Control

This brings us to the fourth and final poison to emerge in the outer layers—our urges to do "damage control." Here we feel torn between using punishment to end our suffering—and doing something to avoid punishing because we may be blamed and punished in return.

So should we always opt for the later—avoidance—and does punishment always make symptoms worse? Let's start by defining damage control. What is *damage control* anyway?

Damage control is yet another kind of suffering and like all suffering, when we do it, it hurts. Moreover, we feel urges to do damage control only when we fear that resentment will make us blame and punish.

This makes damage control our attempt to respond to resentment without having to blame or punish. As such, it can be called, "loving restraint." Or stated more formally, damage control is *anything we do which in theory could restrain, avoid, diminish, or eliminate our urges to blame or punish.*

Know I say "in theory" because in the real world, we can't always stop ourselves from doing these things, albeit, with sincere effort, we can learn to do them less.

Where do these urges to do damage control come from? Two places. One, they come from times wherein we, as adults, process symptoms in *before-age-seven* time. Here we control ourselves because we want to minimize the pain which symptoms inflict. Two, they come from processing symptoms in *after-age-seven* time. Here we delude ourselves into thinking that if we take our time and think things through, that we can avoid suffering by side-stepping our symptoms. Ha! Wouldn't that be nice.

Sadly, these two beliefs are so ingrained in some of us that we mistake damage control for spiritual growth. However, truly spiritual things like moderation and equanimity are never rooted in avoidance. Others see the opposite path—self-inflicted suffering—as the road to spiritual growth. In truth though, if you are human, then learning to face your suffering more honestly, more personally, and with more dignity—while at the same time vowing to not let your suffering pass without gain—is a far more spiritual path.

The Four Kinds of Damage Control: Layer by Layer

Finally, like the other three kinds of outer layer suffering, there are four kinds of damage control as well. In layer 4, we use *outbursts* to minimize our urges to blame and punish—letting off steam, getting plowed, howling at the moon. In layer 3, we use *time-outs* as our means to restrain ourselves. Unlike using time to punish however, here we use it to calm down and regain our composure. Counting to ten. Taking big breaths. Walking away. In layer 2, we turn to *the big four people-ality theories* as a means to do damage control. Here reason, logic, and common sense light our path. Politics. Psychology. Philosophy. And religion. And in layer 1, we look to *zone-outs* to manage our urges to blame and punish. Here we look for ways to forestall our urges to lash out, howl, or silently ignore.

Suffering Can't Be Destroyed—It Can Only Change in Form

Having introduced you to the four poisons of adulthood, we now arrive at what may be the most important thing of all to know about suffering—the idea that like all energies, suffering can neither be created nor destroyed. It can only change in form. Here again, we see a psychophysical parallel between the nature of our world and our own nature—the idea that the law of conservation of energy and matter also applies to personality. And specifically, to suffering.

Know that Freud himself based much of what he theorized on this belief, including that he used it as a proof for that we have a dynamic unconscious replete with invisible defense mechanisms.

This begs the question, is damage control a defense mechanism? The answer? We certainly perceive it as such. However being as there is no real defense against suffering, in reality, all four poisons are but variations on the same theme—the pain of layer 8's disconnections. Only by the time we engage in them, we feel them less personally, leading us to mistake the detachment we feel in the outer layers for having decreased our suffering.

Ironically, were you to pay close attention to the times wherein you resent, blame, punish, and do damage control, you'd find that each time you do these things, you feel painfully alone. Moreover, to see this for yourself, just try punishing someone, for instance, by yelling at them, while at the same time preventing your gut from tensing. Try it. You'll quickly realize that you can't do it. Why not? Because just as the wise men of old taught, what we do to others, we simultaneously do to ourselves. In other words, whenever you punish with words, you'll be hit in the gut by your own punishing words.

Finally there is the idea that some folks can punish and not feel bad. How can this be? It's simple. If you punish someone and while you're doing it, you occasionally do not suffer, then you are reliving an injury and this has made you temporarily mentally ill. On the other hand, if you can punish people and never feel bad, then you are the rare person who is truly mentally ill—the kind of person therapists call a sociopath.

Likely no such person would ever risk reading a book like this.

Breathe now. You're not a sociopath.

Does Being Blamed Make You Responsible?

In a moment, we'll move on to the specifics of the outer layers. Before we do, I need to address one more thing—the question of whether being blamed for suffering makes you responsible for fixing this suffering. Remember, we've defined punishment as what we do to fix the causes blame finds. Thus punishment and blame are indelibly intertwined with responsibility.

The thing is, if blame points to who is responsible, we need to address yet another thing about blame—the idea that there are two kinds of actions commonly referred to as blame. The first kind is the normal kind—*evaluations*. Here *we decide who or what caused our suffering.* The second is the counterintuitive kind—*observations.* Here *we point to the place where the suffering first appeared.*

Why make this distinction?

To most folks, the first kind of blame is the one which makes the most sense. After all, it's the second poison of adulthood we're talking about here. So it's just part of our nature. Here we assume there are knowable causes for our suffering and that whomever caused this suffering is responsible to fix it. Thus with first kind of blame, responsibility is based on *after-age-seven* time—and a belief in cause and effect.

On the other hand, the second kind of blame feels weird to many folks. Considering it contradicts our nature, this is not surprising, at least in adulthood. Here people focus entirely on the origin point of their suffering—rather than on the cause of it—as they see this cause either as unknowable or unimportant. So whomever witnesses the suffering is responsible to try to fix it. Thus with the second kind of blame, responsibility occurs in *before-age-seven* time—and is based on the belief that shit just happens.

Now add to this that philosophers have made it even harder to understand blame by associating it with ideas like intent, free will, and circumstances. As if resentment wasn't enough. Here, by intent, we're talking about whether someone understood what they were doing and intentionally caused suffering—by free will, whether someone voluntarily caused suffering or was forced to do it—and by circumstances, whether being in special circumstances justifies inflicting suffering.

So does being blamed make you responsible? Again, it's complicated.

The Four Wise Men's Take on Responsibility

What do the four wise men have to say about responsibility?

As usual, we find no shortage of spokespersons willing to present the four wise men's arguments. Let's start with the empirical wise man's current choice of representative—Aristotle. What did he believe?

Aristotle tied blame to intent and volition—that to be at fault, you need to have known what you were doing and have done it willingly. To him, ignorance—or being forced—equate to innocence. Thus, Aristotle believed that *the story of what happened* is what determines responsibility.

The Utilitarians, such as John Stuart Mill and Jeremy Bentham, agree about the voluntary part. But they do this from the materialist wise man's position—that even when ultimately proven incorrect, the one-two punch of blame and punishment has therapeutic (healing; teaching) and deterrent (damage control) properties. Thus, they say you should blame whenever actions do not turn out well, in hopes, this will teach people to do better next time. Here *the measure of future outcomes* is what determines responsibility.

Then we have folks like Immanual Kant and P. F. Strawson, who together represent the rationalist wise man's position, what has come to be known as the "desert" theory. Here, Kant sees responsibility as being built into whatever a person does—if an action causes suffering, the person deserves to be held responsible; if not, then he should not. Or as twentieth century philosopher, P. F. Strawson, might have said it, responsibility is the natural outcome of our expectations of self and others (*Resentment and Freedom*, Oxford University Press, 1972). Thus, *a logical assessment of the source of the suffering* is what determines responsibility.

Finally, presenting the spiritual wise man's position, we have Socrates who taught that no one would cause suffering if they knew what they were doing—that we cause suffering only out of ignorance. Here we see a position which strangely presages the four wise men's concept of wounds—that being startled blinds us to the true nature of our suffering, as well as to certain needs, our own and others. Thus, to Socrates and to the spiritual wise man, *no one is truly at fault* for our suffering. How much more spiritual can you get?

What's your opinion? Do you think people should be held responsible based on blame—as defined by cause and effect, intent, free will, and circumstances? Or do you believe witnessing someone suffering makes us responsible?

The answer, of course, lies in that all these positions are true—but only in their own realms. Yet another example of how personal truth requires input from all four wise men. We'll talk more about this later.

A Brief Review of the Four Poisons of Adulthood

Now we're finally ready to explore the four outer layers. As we do, please keep in mind the order in which the four poisons occur.

• One—in the outer layers, all suffering focuses more on reprocessing things which have already happened than on things which may happen, or are happening. Thus each time we enter an outer layer, the first thing we do is resent our suffering.

• Two—the next thing we feel is urges to find a cause for this suffering, in effect, we look to blame someone or something for this suffering.

• Three—we then feel urges to punish someone or something for this suffering, in hopes we'll end or at least discourage this suffering.

• Finally, four—we then feel urges to restrain these cravings to blame and punish, the desire to do some kind of "damage control."

The main thing to keep in mind, of course, is that all four poisons are watered down versions of the primary suffering—disconnection. We do them rather than face the dreadful emptiness of layer 8. At the same time, at best, they only temporarily allay our pain. So eventually, our symptoms resurface. At which point, we again feel urges to cycle through the four poisons of adulthood.

By the way, have I told you why they're called "poisons?" It's easy enough to see. Poisons do something to otherwise good things which destroys our ability to use them. This is what the four poisons do. They don't break anything. They don't take anything. They just ruin otherwise good things—like religion, politics, psychology, and philosophy.

Layer 4: Temporal non Existence (eternal punishments)

Now let's look at how all this applies to layer 4. We'll start by naming the six must know things about Layer 4—the overall character of this layer—how this character affects each of the four poisons of adulthood—and your goal for engaging in these four poisons.

The Four Sub Layers of Layer 4
(abuse, brutality, violence, outbursts)
(© 2007 Steven Paglierani The Center for Emergence)

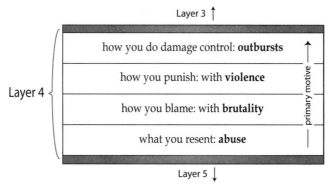

What are we talking about here?

• The overall character of layer 4: *uncivilized experiences*
• What you resent: being *abused*
• How you blame: with *brutality*
• How you punish: with *violence*
• What you use for damage control: *outbursts*
• Your primary goal: to permanently *destroy* the cause of your symptoms, thus ending your suffering forever.

So what is it like to move into layer 4?

If you remember where layer 4 is in relation to layer 8, you'll have a good idea. Here the outer layer closest to layer 8 is layer 4. Thus whenever we move things into layer 4, we feel urges to send someone to hell—or to kill something or someone.

Whom do we wish to send to hell? Generally whomever or whatever is right in front of us at the time. Often, this is just some unfortunate soul who did nothing wrong per se but just happened to be in the wrong place at the wrong time. The face-licking dog. The adventurous cat. The friend who asks, at a bad moment, if we need help.

For example, say you've just burned yourself on a hot stove—or have been trying to deal with your kid's malfunctioning PlayStation 3. In layer 4, you'd feel urges to smash both these things into oblivion. And if someone burned you in a bad deal—for example, the unfortunate soul who sold you the defective PlayStation? Then you might feel urges to smash him—and his freakin' game—into oblivion. And burn down his house to boot.

These urges to punish might then be followed by urges to scream at the stove, or yell at the salesman. After which, you'd likely start cooling off. At which point, you'd move into layer 3.

What Do We Store in Layer 4?

What kinds of events do we store in layer 4? Anything from being cut off in traffic—or having a ball hit you in the face—to wanting to kill your doctor, veterinarian, or spiritual advisor for making your loved one feel even worse. Your goal here? To permanently rid the world of this heartless bastard or worthless hunk of junk. Think the death penalty and nuclear wars. Think blind rage and road rage. Think ruining someone's career or wrecking someone's marriage. Think poking people's eyes out with pencils and inserting pointy objects where the sun don't shine.

"If you were any kind of a real doctor (therapist, teacher, minister, politician), you would have been able to save my child (mend my marriage, comfort my mother, keep my kid out of the army). I'd like to make you sit on it and rotate."

"Anyone who does that to old people (kindergartners, whales, sacred relics, the ozone layer) should have a red hot poker shoved up their ass."

"People who act like that in public (hit their kids, abuse their friends, mistreat animals, fart in elevators without remorse) should be shot, hung, stoned, stabbed, burned at the stake, and drawn and quartered. And perhaps, also have a pinecone vigorously inserted into their rectums."

"Whoever makes this kind of worthless crap (useless shit, lousy junk, disgusting rubbish) should have it shoved up their bum."

Why all the remarks about bums and what comes out of them? This is layer 4 we're moving into, remember? Or to paraphrase Paddy Chayefsky, we're mad as hell and we're not going to take any more shit.

What are we going to do about it? Something "criminal." Or to voice this urge as a function of the primary motive—resolving aloneness—we've repeatedly relived moments of startling aloneness. Now it's time to commit criminal acts against the perpetrators.

The Nature of Suffering in Layer 4

Obviously, despite these threats and urges, most of us don't do any of this stuff. Thus the suffering we feel in layer 4 comes not so much from our symptoms—or from what we do about these symptoms—but more from what we'd like to do, but can't let ourselves do. For instance, if you burn yourself *once* on a hot stove, you may feel urges to kill the stove. If you burn yourself *twice* on a hot stove, you may feel urges to kill your hand.

Or the person who left the stove on. And if you burn yourself a *third time*, you may feel urges to destroy the whole freakin' kitchen. Or the whole darn world. But even if you burned yourself a *fourth time*, you probably wouldn't do any of these things. Thus you'd likely suffer more from being caught between your urges to retaliate and your urges to restrain yourself than from anything you actually did.

Recapping Layer 4

Now before we look at layer 3, let's briefly recap what we've discussed about layer 4. To begin with, like all the outer layers, there are four qualities which define layer 4—urges to revisit our symptoms, urges to blame, urges to punish, and urges to do damage control. Here the suffering comes from *repeatedly reliving moments of startling aloneness* (revisiting symptoms)—the urges to blame from making first glance assumptions about the source of these symptoms—the urges to punish from our desire to permanently destroy the causes of these symptoms—and the urges to do damage control from the concern that we'll either destroy something we value or be destroyed in the process. Or to state these ideas in more formal terms, in layer 4, we feel four *uncivilized* experiences:

• *Uncivilized Resentment*—the urgent need to immediately discover the nature of how you were abused. You resent *being abused*.

• *Uncivilized Blame*—the urgent need to brutalize people, places, and things into "admitting" they are the cause of your symptoms. You blame with *brutality*.

• *Uncivilized Punishment*—the urgent need to use violence to punish people, places and things into oblivion—in effect, permanently ending your suffering through abuse. You punish with *violence*. Destruction is your goal.

• *Uncivilized Damage Control*—the urgent need to restrain these urges in order to prevent criminal retaliation or personal loss—but only after violating this person, place, or thing with threats. You diffuse your violent urges with sudden *outbursts*.

How is layer 3 different? Let's look.

Layer 3: Temporal Duality (time-limited punishments)

Again, let's start by naming the six must know qualities of this layer, the overall character of this layer—how this character affects each of the four poisons of adulthood—and your goal for engaging in these four poisons.

What are we talking about this time?

The Four Sub Layers of Layer 3
(neglect, imprisionment, time, time-outs)
(© 2007 Steven Paglierani   The Center for Emergence)

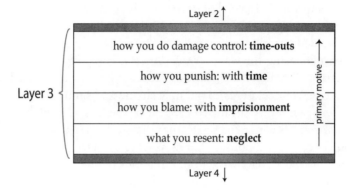

- The overall character of layer 3: *time-limited experiences*
- What you resent: being *neglected*
- How you blame: with *imprisonments*
- How you punish: with *time*
- What you use for damage control: giving yourself *time-outs*
- Your primary goal: to *teach* whomever or whatever is causing your symptoms to think twice before ever doing this to you again.

So what is it like to move into layer 3?

In layer 4, you were red hot and out for blood. Burning your hand on the freaking stove hurt like hell, and whomever left the blasted stove on was going to pay. But by the time you enter layer 3, both you and the stove have cooled down a bit. Thus your urges to dole out layer 4's permanent punishments have given way to layer 3's urges to give temporary ones. No need to give these folks the death penalty. Just have them serve "time." And yes, you still want retribution, just like you did in layer 4. But you also don't want to permanently damage anything or anyone you might need later. Thus your goal in punishing this offending person, place, or thing is not to eliminate them forever. Rather, it's to teach this salesperson, dog, corporation, or town government to never ever dream of hurting you or yours again.

How Layer 3 Changes Your Attitude

In large part, then, what changes when you move from layer 4 to layer 3 is your attitude. What does this change in your attitude look like?

Say you catch your thirteen year old smoking pot with her friends for the tenth time. Rather than feeling urges to smash her new PlayStation 3 into a million pieces, you lecture her for ten minutes, then banish her to her room for a month. Or say your three year old is being mouthy for the umpteenth time. Instead of destructively screaming back and risking permanent damage, perhaps you give him a deadly look and few slashes of the dreaded wagging finger, followed by three long minutes of sitting in the corner, facing the wall. Or say someone cuts in front of you in the supermarket line. Instead of urges to repeatedly ram their head into a cash register, you feel urges to publicly shame and humiliate them, then make them penitently shuffle to the rear of the line. Or say some white collar crook steals your pension. Rather than following the time honored tradition of cutting off both his hands, you take him to court in hopes he'll get fifteen years in a cell with a rambunctious fellow named bubba.

In each of these situations, the thing to see is that your means for punishing focuses on time rather than on destruction. This leads us to have thoughts like the following:

"I think all road-ragers should get six months in a yellow jump suit cleaning roadsides with a pointy stick."

"All child molesters should have to meet bubba. And his friends. And have to spend some time in the shower getting real close and personal."

"If it was up to me, I'd take the terrorists and suspend them from the ceiling of the Siberian tiger's cage. At lunchtime. Before the cat ate."

"If I ran the world, I'd make every abusive parent sit in the corner for a few months while Ann Coulter poured verbal gasoline on them."

Whatever the punishment, the thing to see is that, in every case, the punishment revolves around time. Thus layer 3 is to purgatory what layer 4 is to hell. And in layer 3, some type of temporary suffering is meant to lead to permanent redemption. Hence the title, *temporal duality*. Duality, as in, me good—you bad. And temporal, as in, I'm going to punish you with time.

What makes us want to use time as a punishment?

In part, this comes from what we resent. In the case of the stove, we feel someone should have anticipated the problem—but they just didn't care enough to take the time. Hence, we feel they neglected us.

Then there's the idea that we deserved "more." More consideration. More concern for our safety. More time taken to be sure we'd be okay. So another part of what drives us to blame and punish in layer 3 is the idea that we suffered because they didn't take enough time. They should have taken more.

This brings up a second kind of time-related resentment—the suffering we endure from waiting in general. Here we're talking not about anything individuals do to us per se. Rather we're talking about things like the time you spend paying dues to advance at a job—how many years have you been there? Or the amount of time you invest in twelve step meetings—how much time do you have? Or the years you spend waiting for retirement—how much time do you have left? Or the time it takes to get a degree—how long until you graduate?

In each case, we see layer 3's version of the primary motive at work. Long periods of repeatedly reliving moments of startling aloneness make us feel like life is just one long wait for the suffering to end.

Recapping Layer 3

Now let's briefly summarize layer 3. Remember, layer 3, like all the outer layers, has a character which slants everything we store in this layer, including the four poisons of adulthood—urges to revisit our symptoms, urges to blame, urges to punish, and urges to do damage control.

In layer 3, this slant comes from *long periods of repeatedly reliving moments of startling aloneness*—the urges to blame from enduring the pain of waiting for our symptoms to end—the urges to punish from our desire to teach people to never, ever think of making us wait again—and the urges to do damage control from the concern that we'll lose something that will take a long time to replace.

Now, stating these ideas in more formal terms, in layer 3, we feel four *time-limited experiences*:

• *Time-limited Resentment*—the strong need to immerse yourself in a comprehensive review of how neglect led to your symptoms. You resent *having been neglected*.

• *Time-limited Blame*—the strong need to force people, places, and things to learn how they neglected you, by making them think about what they did to you. You blame with *imprisonments*.

• *Time-limited Punishment*—the strong need to punish people, places and things by neglecting them in return, in hopes they will learn what it feels like and never treat you like this again. You punish with *time*.

• *Time-limited Damage Control*—the strong need to limit or restrain these urges until we are sure we have it right, but only after neglecting this person, place, or thing into feeling remorse. You control yourself with *time-outs*, such as counting to ten or taking walks.

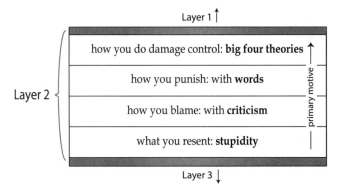

The Four Sub Layers of Layer 2
(stupidity, criticism, words, big-four theories)
(© 2007 Steven Paglierani The Center for Emergence)

Layer 2: Impersonal non Existence (punishing words)

Now let's address what may be the most complex layer of all—layer 2. In this layer, we store everything related to the four big classes of people-ality theories—philosophy, religion, politics, and psychology. We also store everything else we associate with being civilized—theories to therapies, war strategies to wampum making skills. And to see this in action, let's again start by listing the six must know qualities of this layer.

- The overall character of layer 2: *civilizing experiences*
- What you resent: *stupidity*
- How you blame: with *criticism*
- How you punish: with *words*
- What you use for damage control: *the big four theories*
- Your primary goal: to *correct* the errors which led to your symptoms, by making people, places, and things more civil.

So what is it like to move into layer 2? Let's start by recalling the two names for this layer, the formal one—*impersonal non existence*, and the informal one—"punishing questions, excuses, and explanations for not punishing." And yes, this name is indeed a mouthful. But if you take it slowly, one idea at a time, it's not too bad.

Let's start with the formal name. Why call this layer *impersonal non existence?*

The reason we refer to layer 2 as *impersonal non existence* is because whenever we move into this layer, we disappear into one or more big groups. By doing this, we hurt less, as we no longer exist as individuals. In effect, by joining a big group, we swap being a person for being a group member.

And doing this waters down our pain. But we also lose our individuality, and with it our ability to find personal truth.

For example, say we're talking about the four examples I used in layer 3—paying dues at a job, acquiring time in a twelve step group, counting the years until retirement, and waiting to graduate. In each case, it's the waiting that cause us to suffer. And in layer 2, this waiting still hurts. But by the time we enter layer 2, we've resigned ourselves to the waiting. Or we've managed to logically justify it.

Either way, in layer 2, our strategy for dealing with symptoms changes from neglecting people into submission to finding solace and comfort by associating ourselves with big groups of similar sufferers. To do this, we turn to the four big categories of people-ality theories—philosophy, religion, politics, and psychology. In all four cases, these categories of experience arise out of our need to get more comfortable while we wait for our symptoms to end. And by joining groups, we divide our suffering amongst like-minded sufferers. Moreover, the more people there are in our group, the less we exist as individuals—and the less we suffer.

In layer 2 then, we join groups in order to cease to exist as individuals. By doing this, we comfort ourselves with assurances we're not alone. We also further distance ourselves from our symptoms, as well as from our fear of layer 8. But we also continue to move further and further away from our personal truth.

How Being in Groups Changes Us

What exactly do we do in these groups? Basically, we use logic and reason to shift the blame for our symptoms off ourselves and our group and onto the folks in rival groups. Nothing personal, mind you. It's just the way things are done. Thus one of our goals in layer 2 is to join the biggest group—Christians (2 billion) versus Buddhists (1.5 billion), for instance. Another is to join the more powerful group—the rich folks in the US (the top 5% have 59% of the wealth) versus the poor folks in US (80% of people have 16% of the wealth), perhaps.

Another goal is to claim a birthright membership—for example, China (1,337,722,000) versus US (306,294,000). And another goal is to align ourselves with the winners—athletic folks versus couch potatoes. And yet another goal is to align ourselves with the more popular group—e.g., women, children, and minority rights versus men (men have rights?).

Realize, a big part of why we join these groups is to have a place in which to openly resent and blame. How? We do this in two stages actually. In stage one—*the punishing questions stage*—we use cause and effect reasoning to logically associate our symptoms to whomever or whatever we wish to blame. And in stage two—the *excuses, and explanations for not punishing stage*—we use this same kind of reasoning and logic to let people off the hook.

What does this look like in the real world? Let's start by looking at a few examples. We'll start with stage one.

"Do you know why kids today (parents under thirty, people in the armed forces, utility workers) goof off so much? Because no one holds them accountable."

"Can you see why we have global warming? It's because the only thing big corporations (the federal government, the oil companies, labor unions) care about is how much money they make."

"You know how our country got so in debt? Because those stupid Republicans (those dumb-ass Democrats, all those soft-hearted liberals, all the jerks who didn't vote) prefer to sit on their fat asses all day long."

Please notice that in stage one, our punishing remarks imply intent, volition, and a clear lack of extenuating circumstances. Know that when we reach stage two, we suddenly reverse our position. Here, in *the excuses, and explanations for not punishing stage*, we've so exhausted our venom that we lose interest in punishing. So we begin to look for ways to let people off the hook—while at the same time, not losing face.

In effect, after we're done punishing people with words, we make excuses for what we think they've done wrong. This allows us to punish people while at the same time, be seen as kind, compassionate, civilized, and healthy. For instance, in the following examples, people are first punished with words, then let off the hook with excuses for their faults or wrongdoings:

"Sure, all black people (Jews, tree huggers, white trash, corporate executives) are lazy a-holes. But they've usually had bad childhoods."

"I saw a study the other day which proved, conclusively, that teenagers (fourth grade teachers, under-age-twenty New Yorkers, blue-eyed whores, seniors who keep more than five cats) have lower IQ's than the rest of us. That's why they're so screwed up. They're just too stupid to know better."

"My boss (sister, neighbor, teacher, doctor) is so dumb, she couldn't even explain what she meant. She made a heck of an effort though."

"Our country (my kid's high school, your county government, their daughter's day care) is so screwed up, they should all be taken out and shot. Then again, what do you expect. Look who they hire."

By Whose Authority Do We Say These Things?

By whose authority do we say these things? The authority of our group. Here rather than actually doing anything about what we're complaining about, we restrict our responses to our group's officially sanctioned punishing words, then follow this with some lame excuses for not doing more. Moreover, since everyone in our group feels and acts the same way, we feel entitled—and empowered—to voice these poisonous remarks, knowing full well we can hide behind the skirts of the group if need be.

Here then is the dark side of every big group—religious extremists to conservative universities, aggressive military to controlling PTAs. Each, in their own way, seeks to blame, punish, and ridicule those in the opposing groups. And when we join in, we have moved into layer 2.

In Layer 2, It's All Damage Control

Overall, the thing to see this time is that, despite these poisonous remarks, in layer 2, we're trying to curb our urges to dole out even worse punishments. In effect, we're trying to be civil to our enemies. Thus everything we feel urges to do in layer 2 is infused with elements of damage control—the resentments, the blame, and the punishments.

Our goal, of course, is to try to reason ourselves—and our group—out of punishing people with weapons of mass destruction (layer 4) or heartless neglect (layer 3). Instead, we try to use more civilized punishments, such as making destructive comments and using heartless words. This makes the punishments we dole out in layer 2 among the most insidious of all, in that we dress them up in concern and restraint.

In the end, this turns seemingly well-motivated efforts like, "we have to talk" into thinly masked prefaces to revenge. This ruins any chance we have to find personal truth. Here we replace the threat of war with lie-filled political negotiations, all the while, both sides knowing this is more charade than honest effort. Moreover, when I refer to "political" negotiations, I'm not just referring to countries. This same painful bait and switch goes on in almost all relationships—from marital conversations which seek revenge and business negotiations which look to win—to talks with teens wherein we try to shame them into changing and talks with ourselves wherein we justify cheating on our tax returns.

Layer 2 sure is tough, eh? And as I said, it's complicated.

Masking Blame and Punishment with Disclaimers

Am I making layer 2 sound rather bleak? Sorry for the bad news. In my experience, this is more often the case than not. At the same time, we're not talking about something which stems from injury or indifference. Rather, we're referring to something we all do—something which is just part of human nature.

Ironically, all these negatives derive from sources which, in theory, hold great beauty. Politics, religion, psychology, philosophy. Used wisely—and as a means to find truth—these four things are among the best things ever invented. But perverted into excuses for hurting people, they justify some of the worst abominations we do.

Thus like all things in our world, layer 2 holds equal parts good and bad, black and white, beauty and ugliness. And what we do with logic and reason is up to us. We can use it to justify hurting people. Or we can use it to better ourselves and our world.

How can you tell if people in layer 2 have gone over to the dark side? It's easy. They make mean spirited, shrew-like comments—and give patronizing lectures, prefaced with disclaimers like the following:

"I'm not blaming you. But you could have gone back to school (spoken up when you had the chance, left him the first time he spoke to you like that, been more firm with her when she was little)."

"I know it wasn't your fault. But you didn't have to call her back (send your daughter to that school, move into that neighborhood, buy it at that store)."

"I can see your point. But at the same time, how could you have been so dumb (said nothing, taken his crap, let her get away with treating you like that)."

"I understand. You couldn't help it. Still, can you see how easy it would have been to just step aside (walk out, stop shouting, ignore the bastard)."

Here the thing to notice is how these folks have prefaced their blaming remarks with statements which disavow their desire to blame. But then they go ahead and blame anyway. And if confronted, they just refer back to the preface.

This creates a painful feedback loop which can, at times, magnify the punishing nature of their remarks even more. And the only defense against these kinds of attacks is to keep in mind that saying something—no matter how seemingly logical—doesn't necessarily make it so.

How Founders Differ From Their Philosophies

As I've said, in addition to the negatives we store in layer 2, we also store great beauty there, especially in and around the four people-ality theories. In other words, while it's obvious that human beings often use what they find in layer 2 to justify mistreating each other, at the same time, there is much good to be found in this layer.

The problem, of course, lies in knowing how to access this good. And essentially, this comes down to seeing the great beings who author these theories and belief systems as separate from the crimes done in their names.

For example, take Jesus. Despite the fact that I am not a Christian, Jesus is one of my heroes. In truth, I have probably read more books on Jesus—and on Christianity in general—than on any other single topic. At the same time, similar to Nietzsche, I separate my sense of Jesus, the person, from the horrors done in his name. Or to say this in the language of the four wise men, I separate Jesus—the "founder" of Christianity—from the philosophies that some Christians use to justify hurting others.

Founders. Philosophies. What's the difference?

The founders live in the inner layers, whereas their philosophies exist in the outer layers. Thus, in reality, these two things exist separately whether we believe this or not. Moreover, by seeing these folks as living beings rather than as mere propounders of certain philosophies, we get to see the true greatness in people like Mohammed, Gandhi, and Buddha.

We also get to see the single thread which connects these great beings—they all aspire to live blameless lives. And largely do. This reveals the real meaning of sayings like "do unto others" and "turn the other cheek." And "don't judge them until you've walked a mile in their shoes." They're not saying allow folks to abuse you. They're saying we're all more alike than not.

Of course, despite the obvious beauty in these philosophical truths, it is one thing to be familiar with these words, another to know how to live them. Indeed, this difficulty is the problem inherent in all things layer 2. Here the Tao Te Ching may say it best when it says, *The Tao that can be told is not the eternal Tao*. Thus what really separates founders from their philosophies is that no matter how hard we try to put their blamelessness into words, there are no words which can truly express this blamelessness, as to be human is to have blocked needs—and to have blocked needs is to blame.

This means, even if these great beings did state their teachings perfectly, we could not hear these teachings perfectly. We filter everything through the distorted lens of personality, including each and every one of these great teachings. Something to keep in mind then about layer 2 is that everything in it is imperfectly stated. Add this to how imperfectly we hear and you realize that, at best, layer 2 gives us beautiful theoretical horizons to aspire to, while at worst it gives us justifications for wrongdoing. This includes every theory ever conceived, every spiritual practice in existence, and every well meant shred of medical and psychological advice. Thus while none of these things are inherently blaming, used wrongly, some of the best things in life become some of the worst.

The Illogic of Layer 2's Punishing Logic

Speaking of turning good into bad, one of layer 2's more insidious aspects derives from those times wherein we use the beauty in logic as a weapon. For example, take the belief that the unconscious functions logically. In other words, that we make *decisions* we aren't aware of.

We believe this because we can reduce the content of the unconscious mind to logical presuppositions. We then assume that because these assertions sound logical, they must be true. As we've discussed throughout the book however, logic alone doesn't make something true, no matter how beautifully stated (sorry, rationalist wise man). Nor does this logic in any way prove there are no illogical contents in the unconscious mind.

Why make such a big deal out of this? Well, let me ask you. How many times have you used logic and reasoning to blame and explain why bad things happen? A thousand? A million? A billion? Uncountable times? Now realize that each of these efforts was based on a lie—that because choices exist on paper, that we—or someone else—could have, and should have, chosen to take them.

Think alcoholics drinking. They're stupid, right? They could just choose not to drink. Or think verbally abusive spouses shouting. They could just suck up their anger and walk away, yes? What about empty-headed women drivers. They could pay more attention to how they're driving, couldn't they? Or how about accident-prone teenagers. They could just look where they're going and everything would be fine? Don't you think?

In truth, the minute you realize what having a blank mind means, you realize these assertions are more excuses to blame—and justifications to punish—than anything based in reality. Moreover, once you understand how needs get blocked, you realize you can't blame people for having blank spots in their minds. So yes, good choices almost always do exist on paper. And to others, these choices can seem easy to take. But no matter how you package this up in logic, you cannot choose what you cannot see.

So am I saying that no one should be held responsible for their wrongdoings? As I told you before, no, I'm not. However, like many before me, I see responsibility as being separate from blame. This means, in theory, responsibility lies both with the suffering person and with everyone who witnesses this suffering. What kind of responsibility? To, in some way, help unblock the suffering person's blocked needs.

An Example of Healthy Responsibility: A Class Divided

What would taking this kind of responsibility look like? Consider what Jane Elliot did with her Riceville, Iowa, third-grade class, the day following Martin Luther King's murder in Memphis in 1968. In the words of ABC news producer, William Peters, she "assumed the risks of even temporary trauma to her students—and of stated or unstated resentment on the part of parents and fellow teachers." How? She divided her class by eye color, then had each group of children spend a day feeling more privileged than the other. First brown eyes were superior to blue eyes, then blue eyes to brown. Afterwards, they all talked about what it was like. Amazingly, not only did this two day exercise permanently change how these children felt about discrimination. It also, in two days, improved the classroom performance of some of these children. It caused a measurable increase in their ability to learn. A permanent improvement.

Two years later, Peters filmed Jane Elliot as she did this with a third third-grade class, with similar results. Then fourteen years later, Peters filmed a class reunion in which eleven of those sixteen third-graders returned. Amazingly, what this film shows is that what had happened to these children stayed with them, including that they all reported how this one exercise had changed their lives.

Have you read Peter's book documenting what happened in that classroom (A Class Divided, Then and Now, 1987)? To be honest, I cannot read it without being brought to tears. Nor can I find the words to describe the honesty—and beauty—with which these children described the suffering inherent in discrimination. Talk about personal truth.

More important, according to everyone involved, what occurred in those two days opened the minds and hearts of each and every child in that class *permanently*. Indeed, Peters himself states this quite clearly in the preface to his book when he writes that "what was notable about this social experiment was that the positive influence on these children was not temporary."

Are you getting what happened here? Two days of "walking in their shoes" instilled compassionate attitudes and raised the consciousness of all those third-graders. Amazing. Add to this that this change was permanent and it becomes even more incredible. All this from one courageous woman who allowed her personal truth to guide a single decision.

More amazing still were their permanent increases in love and compassion. Indeed, this is a good example of what emerging from blocked needs looks like.

So who is responsible for helping people to emerge from their blocked needs? We all are. And lest you think children should be exempted from this burden, consider this. How many lives do you think that first group of third-graders affected over the course of their lives? And the second? And the third? In truth, there's no counting. Peter's book detailed quite a few instances wherein what these kids said afterwards changed the lives of the adults around them. Moreover, while these children did indeed come to this only after having been subjected to suffering, the idea that two days of personal discomfort could permanently alter a person's attitudes toward prejudice more than qualifies their struggles.

Recapping Layer 2

To begin with, like all the outer layers, there is a character to layer 2 that slants the four qualities which define it—urges to revisit symptoms, urges to blame, urges to punish, and damage control. Here the suffering comes from *trying to make sense of long periods of repeatedly reliving moments of startling aloneness*—the blame from making logical cause and effect assumptions about the source of this suffering—the urges to punish from our desire to reason this suffering out of existence—and the damage control from the belief that our membership in groups, and the protection they offer, depends on what we look like to the rest of the group. And to the world at large.

Stated more formally, in layer 2, we get four *civilizing experiences*.

• *Civilizing Resentment*—the need to search for cause and effect reasoning which explains your symptoms. You resent *stupidity* and feel, these explanations keep you from appearing stupid.

• *Civilizing Blame*—the need to use logic and reason to cause people, places, and things to "admit" how their wrongs led to your symptoms. You blame people with *criticisms*. In essence, you critique their stupidity.

• *Civilizing Punishment*—the need to use words to threaten people, places, and things to the point wherein they no longer act stupid—in effect, permanently ending your suffering through the use of philosophy, religion, politics, and/or psychology. You punish people with *words*.

• *Civilizing Damage Control*—the need to limit or restrain these urges until you have given this person, place, or thing a chance to logically reconsider. You use the *four people-ality theories* to do damage control.

The Four Sub Layers of Layer 1
(absences, blow offs, silence, zone outs)
(© 2007 Steven Paglierani The Center for Emergence)

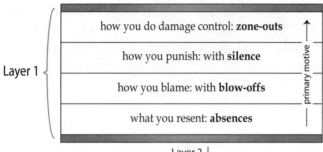

Layer 2 ↓

Layer 1: Personal non Existence (connections to nothing)

Finally, we come to the coldest layer of all—layer 1. Out here, we've arrived at the last known outpost in personality—the Pluto of the personality planets. Moreover, having just made a long arduous trip to escape the gravity of layer 8, we're freakin' tired. Thus the only thing we want to do is to throw ourselves onto the proverbial couch and become a couch potato.

What are the six must know qualities of this layer?

• The overall character of layer 1: *personally non Existent experiences*
• What you resent: *absences*
• How you blame: with *blow-offs*
• How you punish: with *silence*
• What you use for damage control: *zone-outs*
• Your primary goal: to *avoid* the cause of your symptoms in hopes it will all just go away.

How do we end up in layer 1?

For one thing, this is where the primary current in human nature carries us. If we don't resist, we drift here. No effort necessary on our part. Why don't we resist? Because while we're in layer 1, we feel no fear of layer 8. Nor of anything else for that matter. Life just goes on, blank minute by blank minute, as we watch from the sidelines quietly zoned out.

In a way then, layer 1 is where we go when we have our off duty sign lit. And while we're there, we may appear to be doing our best to participate, while in reality, we're far away. For instance, were we to engage in a conversation about what should happen to murderers while we're in layer 1, we'd likely offer nothing but empty words, idle chatter, and pass the dip and chips please.

Burned hand? Hey honey, can you bring me some more ice? Daughter smoking pot again? What the heck. At least she isn't doing intravenous heroin. Mouthy three year old? Hey, just calm down, will you. Can't you see I'm taking a nap? PlayStation broken again? If you let me finish watching the game, I'll buy you a new one later.

Layer 1 as Avoidance

Does this all sound like avoidance? In many ways, it is. However, we avoid these same things in all four outer layers. Thus, it's only our strategy which changes layer to layer.

So what's different about how we avoid things in layer 1?

In the prior three layers, rather than facing our suffering, we actively focus on doing something to ourselves or to others. In layer 4, we violate people—in layer 3, we control people—and in layer 2, we find fault with people. But in layer 1, we seek to avoid our suffering entirely, by disappearing into the wallpaper and becoming distantly passive and vaguely compliant. Thus rather than criticize, violate, or imprison, we distance ourselves from the whole mess.

Realize, we can also appear passive and compliant in the other three outer layers as well. Despite what this may look like though, inside, we're alive and buzzing with resentments, urges to blame, and urges to punish. By the time we reach layer 1 however, we're no longer interested in any of this, as we more just want to get it over with than find personal truth.

This makes layer 1 more resemble the exhaustion you feel after having just fought a fifteen round prize fight than the vengeful go out and get 'em attitude you feel in layers 4 through 2. And in a way, we could say that, as we enter layer 1, we surrender our membership in the human race. In doing so, we gain the ultimate excuse for not responding to suffering—we cease to exist. So when suffering happens, we say things like, no biggie. I'm fine. No harm done. No reason to take it personally. And because we no longer exist to ourselves as persons, these things seem to make perfect sense.

Realize that as bad as this may sound, passively avoiding things has its upside as well. Rest and relaxation require us to temporarily let go of our struggles against suffering. Who wants to always be on duty anyway.

Problems arise only when we fail to return to life. And the longer our stay in layer 1, the more we come to see exchanging the beauty in life for the absence of fear as a worthwhile trade.

Recapping Layer 1

Restating what we've just said about layer 1 more formally, we can say that in layer 1, we get four *Personally non Existent experiences*. We get:

• *non Existent Resentment*—the vague desire to understand why you haven't had your needs tended to yet. You resent *absences*.

• *non Existent Blame*—the vague desire to blow-off the whole world and by doing so, forget your symptoms. You blame with *blow-offs*.

• *non Existent Punishment*—the vague desire to use silence to get people to notice you're not exactly happy with what's happened. You punish with *silences*.

• *non Existent Damage Control*—the vague desire to disappear into the woodwork, or get lost in mindless activity. You use *zone-outs* to do damage control.

The Hot Stove Injury Through All Ten Layers

Now let's take a quick look at an event as it progresses through all ten layers. Please note, the example I've chosen—burning your hand on a red hot stove grill—involves being wounded. So it's not normal. Know I'm using this example not so much because it is representative of all layer movements. Rather, I've used it more because most people can vividly imagine it. Indeed, the overwhelming majority of movements though the layers do not involve wounds. Which is why they are so much less noticeable.

So what is it like to wound yourself by touching a hot stove?

Moving From Layer 10 to Layer 1

Seeing a red hot stove grill causes you to be mesmerized by, and connect to, the beauty you see (you move into or between layers 10 and 9).

Touching a red hot stove grill abruptly disconnects you from the beauty you see, causing you to suddenly lose all sense of yourself (you move from layer 9 into layer 8).

The sudden realization that you've just touched a red hot stove causes you to feel intensely needy (you move from layer 8 into layer 7).

You go blank. As you do, your feelings of intense neediness disappear and you unconsciously store the wounding script in layer 6 (you move from layer 7 into layer 6).

The symptoms of a burn begin to be visible (you move from layer 6 into layer 5).

You feel an intense desire to find someone or something to blame and punish for your burn. You feel a powerful need to violently avenge yourself (you move from layer 5 into layer 4).

You feel a strong desire to force someone to admit that their negligence caused you to burn yourself. Your need to violate people disappears (you move from layer 4 into layer 3).

You feel urges to punish people with patronizing explanations and logical criticisms, all of which tie your symptoms to people's shortcomings (you move from layer 3 into layer 2).

You feel the desire to just get everyone to leave you alone. You tell them you'll ask for their help if you need it. Now just please go away (you move from layer 2 into layer 1).

Moving From Layer 1 to Layer 10

Your desire to just have the pain go away fades, as you begin to feel the need to understand how this burn happened (you move from layer 1 into layer 2).

The desire to explain why you burned your hand changes to the need to hold people hostage until they vow to never let this happen again (you move from layer 2 into layer 3).

You begin to believe that hostage taking will not get the job done. The desire to violently punish someone resurfaces. The desire to kill them for not preventing this burn returns (you move from layer 3 into layer 4).

As your focus shifts from punishing people to examining your symptoms, the desire to kill something or someone for burning yourself on a hot stove disappears (you move from layer 4 into layer 5).

You go blank. As you do, the symptoms caused by your inability to avoid touching a red hot stove grill become invisible (you move from layer 5 into layer 6).

The neediness you felt when you first realized you'd touched a hot stove grill resurfaces (you move from layer 6 into layer 7).

All things, including the suffering caused by touching the red hot stove grill, become invisible again. But you fall into an incredibly empty state wherein everything you know, including yourself, ceases to exist (you move from layer 7 into layer 8).

You notice once more how beautiful the glowing red-hot stove grill is, this despite the fact that your hand is still burned (you move from layer 8 into layers 9 and 10).

Access Sequences as the Source of All Experience

Although I've mentioned these ideas many times already, I feel the need to underscore them even further. The ideas? For one thing, that you experience life *only* when you move things into—or between—layers. For another, that the closer you get to layer 10, the more alive you feel. Also, the closer you get to layer 1, the more you detach from life. And the closer you get to layer 8 without entering it, the more intense everything feels.

The thing to keep in mind then is that we treat *sensation* as something which happens to us—and *experience* as something we do. Yet if we set aside our preconceived notions as to what these two words mean, we find they both refer to the same thing—change—only seen from the opposite perspective. Here sensation is change as seen from the observer's perspective, and experience is change as seen from the participant's perspective.

Why raise the idea of change?

Like all things in our world, personality is knowable only through the observation of change. This is true because, whenever we become unable to witness change, we lose our ability to connect to life. Moreover, whether we witness this change (sense it) or reprocess this change (experience it), either way, it all boils down to access sequences. Thus the key to understanding ourselves—and ultimately to finding our personal truth—is to focus on learning to see these access sequences.

Finally, beneath these ideas lie three key concepts.

• One—all experience arises from movements into or out of layers (or as we'll find in the next chapter—into or out of sublayers). These movements *are* what we refer to as experience.

• Two—just as you can't skip layers in an onion, you can't skip layers in personality.

• And three—if these movements equate to experience, then the kind of movements we make equates to the kind of experiences we have. Specific movements equate to specific experiences.

Access Sequences as the Key to Understanding This Theory

Containers and content. Layers and access sequences. The five big questions. The four big people-ality theories. Know I'm well aware that I've introduced you to a shitload of new concepts in this chapter, some of which can seem extremely complex. In reality though, the key to learning the four wise men's personality theory is simple—learn the access sequences. They explain the patterns underlying much of human experience, and in ways which even lay people can grasp. With this in mind, let's review a few of the access sequences I've introduced you to so far.

Moving into layer 10 is being in love. We dissolve into the warm, caring wonder and awe of creation.

Moving into layer 9 is falling in love with another person or person-like being (i.e. a personified object, like a car or boat). We connect to another being, either a literal being or a personified object. Or both.

Making abrupt 10-9-8-7 accesses wound us. We then store the scripts of these movements in layer 6. Sans the Layer 6 storage step, this is the birth separation moment sequence.

Making slow 10-9-8-7 accesses cause boredom.

Making smooth 7-8-9-10 accesses permanently heal our wounds. And make us more conscious—teach us about life—and expand our ability to love. Here pleasant surprise is the only acceptable proof for this having happened. Hence, knowledge alone in never enough.

Moving from layer 7 to layer 6 makes certain pure needs disappear. And because we can't see these needs, we cannot meet them.

Moving from layer 6 to layer 7 makes certain pure needs visible. Their sudden appearance makes us feel very needy. And very young. This is what therapist's call, "regression."

Moving from layer 6 to layer 5 makes certain symptoms visible. This gets our attention, but can throw us off track. Symptoms aren't wounds, remember? Thus eliminating them does not heal wounds.

Moving abruptly from layer 5 to layer 6 makes a wounding script run, causing us to relive an already existing wound. We don't see it coming.

Moving from layer 5 to layer 4 makes us want to permanently end the source of our suffering, by killing someone. Criminal urges appear.

Moving from layer 4 to layer 5 takes our focus away from our criminal urges and onto our symptoms. This moves us one step closer to healing the blocked needs which cause these symptoms and criminal urges.

Moving from layer 4 to layer 3 makes us want to neglect someone into promising not to hurt us again. This imprisons us within a jail of our own device, as we become the blamed-person's jailer.

Moving from layer 3 to layer 4 makes us feel homicidal urges again. We've given people enough chances—now they'll have to pay.

Moving from layer 3 to layer 2 makes us want to punish someone with words, then use excuses or explanations to let them off the hook. Here joining groups of similar sufferers gives us anonymity and authority.

Moving from layer 2 to layer 3 makes us feel that time is against us. This turns our sense of the good in the journey into the pain of waiting for this good. Urges to take hostages surface.

Moving from layer 2 to layer 1 makes us forget about our fear of layer 8 and all it's painful incarnations. But in the process, we cease to exist.

Moving from layer 1 to layer 2 makes us think about who and where we are. And we gain a group identity, and the support of the group authority. But we exist sans a sense of our personal voice.

Finally, making slow 4-5-6-7-8-9-10 accesses make us laugh. And see the absurdity beneath our struggles. Otherwise known as "graveyard humor."

What's Next? A Deeper Look at Layer 7

Alrighty, now. You've made it. You're halfway through the book. Lord knows this was one heck of a long ass chapter. Even so, here you are, reading the chapter closing. Bravo!

So what's next? And when do we get to the useful stuff?

Do you like personality tests? Have you ever taken one which changed your life? You will in the next chapter. You see, as it turns out, if you know what's in a person's layer 7, you can predict how this person will behave in almost all situations, everything from marital arguments and personal decisions to friendships and romance in general.

How hard is it to learn this stuff?

Actually, it's surprisingly easy. Moreover, you're not only going to know how these tests work. You're also going to know how to make your own tests. Imagine that?

Unlike other personality tests, then—wherein most of what's behind the questions makes no sense—this time, you're going to know how the questions work. Indeed, by the time you've finished this next chapter, you're going to have answers to some of the most interesting how-people-work questions ever devised. How romantic attraction overrides your logical mind. What makes you feel safe around your friends. How some people can so easily understand you—while others haven't a clue. Why some teachers favored you—and some just didn't connect.

What determines who you'll be attracted to anyway, and how can you know if you'll like a career? Where do your special interests come from, and where do your talents lie? Layer 7's personality tests reveal all this and more. Sound interesting? Once again, you have no idea.

The Four Poisons Through the Outer Layers
(resentment, blame, punishment, damage control)
(© 2007 Steven Paglierani   The Center for Emergence)

Layer 1	damage control: **zone-outs**
	punishment: **silence**
	blame: **blow-offs**
	resentment: **absences**
Layer 2	damage control: **big four theories**
	punishment: **words**
	blame: **criticism**
	resentment: **stupidity**
Layer 3	damage control: **time-outs**
	punishment: **time**
	blame: **imprisionment**
	resentment: **neglect**
Layer 4	damage control: **outbursts**
	punishment: **violence**
	blame: **brutality**
	resentment: **abuse**

the direction of the the primary motive - to avoid suffering

Notes Written in the Margins of Chapter Five

On the Idea That Fractals Are *Stochastically Self-similar*

In the next chapter, we're going to look at how the four wise men's personality theory is *stochastically* self-similar. As opposed to being *deterministically* self-similar. Realize that understanding this difference is critical when it comes to finding personal truth. In a nutshell, this difference defines what you can and cannot predict. And since we roughly equate predictability with proof that something is true, being able to predict what will repeat is a crucial element when it comes to personal truth.

Know that the entire key to grasping this difference lies in knowing how these two words—stochastic and deterministic—change the meaning of the phrase "self-similarity." What is self-similarity, and to what degree can we predict it? Here again, while the answer is simple, it's not easy to understand.

In the real world, fractals are *stochastically* self-similar (recognizable patterns that always repeat differently), never *deterministically* self-similar (recognizable patterns which always repeat identically). However, in theory, they can be either. Here a good example is the difference between quantum physics—which is stochastic, and classical physics—which is deterministic. In classical physics, we assume that if we know all the starting points—and the way these things behave—we can, with certainty, predict what they will do over time. But in quantum physics, we assume that we can never know these two things completely—moreover, that the very act of measuring things affects the outcome.

The thing to keep in mind then is that neither stochastic self-similarity nor deterministic self-similarity are false. Moreover, in the right venue, both ideas serve us well. Indeed, in reality, we can know truth only by simultaneously considering them both. But since sums never fully describe anything in the real world, we must also keep in mind that our sense of personal truth will always be less than deterministic. Or per quantum theory, that at best, we can know only 50% of any truth.

On the Idea That, in Theory, All Fractals Exist in Layers

Something I realize I failed to explain properly during this chapter is how the layers themselves come into being. Yes, I told you that as they begin to fill with content, they expand and become active. But I failed to tell you the nature of their origin. Where do these layers come from?

To see, you'd need to explore the work of three scientists— mathematician Steven Smale, chemist Otto Rössler, and astrophysicist Michel Hénon. Each, in their own way, came up with an explanation as to how fractals develop in layers. Moreover, each of their explanations in some way resembles the processes by which pastry chefs and toffee pullers create layered pastries and toffees—by stretching and folding.

Can you picture this? Can you imagine what a croissant is like? Flaky layers, layer after layer, each one a nested copy of the one before?

The point is, the layers of personality described in this chapter are representative of how things in chaotic systems organize around strange attractors (Hénon attractors, Rössler attractors, Lorenz attractors, Tamari attractors). Thus the fact that all ten layers of personality exist right from conception is perfectly normal for fractal systems. And as life bakes our personalities, they puff out just like pastries. Hopefully, they end up being tasty ones.

On the Roman Catholic Idea of Seven as the Age of Reason

I have always found it odd how a few life events stick in your mind while most fade forever. Making First Communion when I was seven is one of those events. In part, this was due to that my mother somehow managed to dress me in a double-breasted, off-white linen suit—certainly an amazing accomplishment for a family always struggling to pay their bills. In part, it was the beautiful spring flowers and the incredible church—a miniature stone cathedral. And in part, it was what it felt like to wait outside that church that day—standing in line by the carp pond, alternately fascinated by the church architecture and the colored fish.

Somehow though, the thing my mind latched onto most was what I had been told right before that wait—that I had reached the age at which I was expected to have wrongdoings to confess—that I had reached the "age of reason." That was in 1953. Not surprisingly, some Catholic churches had found this decree too harsh. So in 1977, Cardinals James Knox and John Wright issued the following clarification from the Vatican. It was intended to reinforce prior Vatican decrees stating that age seven was indeed the age at which a child could receive the sacrament of "penance."

The age of discretion both for confession and for communion is the age in which the child begins to reason, i.e. around the seventh year, either before or after. From that time begins the obligation of satisfying both the precept of confession and of communion.

The thing to see here is how seven year olds were considered able to tell right from wrong. And required not only to fabricate wrongdoings to confess to but also, to punish themselves for these transgressions, fabricated or otherwise. So while it's obvious that doing this to seven year olds is pretty screwed up, the idea that it perfectly matches the developmental timing of what happens in the outer layers does not surprise me.

Resources for Chapter Five—Who We Are

Obviously this chapter is quite long. However, because the theory I've presented here strays so far from the norm, for obvious reasons, I've included very few references.

On Hypnosis

I've been hypnotized by—and have studied hypnosis with—a number of people. Of these, Brian Weiss M.D. was especially helpful. Obviously though you cannot learn hypnosis from books alone. Rather, to learn hypnosis, you must learn it by doing it and by having it done to you. This said, the following books raise some interesting points as to the nature of hypnosis.

Brown, Donald C. (2009). *Advances in Hypnosis for Medicine, Dentistry and Pain Prevention/Management*. Bethel, CT: Crown House Publishing.

Hunter, Marlene E. (2007). *Healing Scripts: Using Hypnosis to Treat Trauma and Stress*. Bethel, CT: Crown House Publishing.

Kroger, William S. & Michael D. Yapko. (2008). *Clinical and Experimental Hypnosis*. Rev. 2nd Ed. Baltimore, MD: Lippincott Williams & Wilkins.

Neill, Kweethai PhD. (2008). *Hypnotherapy*. Bloomington, IN: Xlibris Corporation.

Lynn, Steven Jay & Irving Kirsch. (2006). *Essentials of Clinical Hypnosis: An Evidence-Based Approach*. Washington, DC: American Psychological Association.

Wheeler, Jeremy. (2007). *Insights and Confessions of an English Hypnotist*. 2nd. Edition. UK: Mystics. (Okay. He's a stage hypnotist. But what he has to say adds color to the dry, clinically-oriented volumes previously mentioned.)

Woolger, Roger J. Ph.D. (1988). *Other Lives, Other Selves, A Jungian Psychotherapist Discovers Past Lives*. New York: Bantam. (When I first read this book years ago, it changed my life, both by correcting my misconceptions about the meaning of Karma and by giving me the courage to be a therapist who follows his heart regardless of whether I have theories to back it up. Ironically, this led me to write my own theory. Thank you, Dr. Woolger, for your courage.)

On Layered Fractals

The idea that fractals form in layers around strange attractors has been understood for decades. Since the wise men's personality theory is based on this design, I've included a few resources for this idea.

Hénon, M. (1976). *A Two-dimensional Mapping with a Strange Attractor*. Communications in Mathematical Physics 50: 69–77. Springer-Verlag.

Smale, Stephen. (1976). *Differentiable Dynamical Systems*. Bulletin of the American Mathematical Society 73: 747–817. Springer-Verlag.

Rössler, Otto E. (1998). *Endophysics: The World of an Internal Observer*. River Edge, NJ: World Scientific Publishing Company.

Strogatz, Steven H. (2008). *Chaos*. Chantilly, VA: The Teaching Company.

Strogatz, Steven H. (2001). *Nonlinear Dynamics and Chaos*. New York, NY: Perseus Publishing.

On Responsibility

Were I to attempt anything like a comprehensive list of writings on this topic, I'd fill an entire book. Confusing, to say the least. This said, the following are a few of those I referred to during the writing of this chapter.

Delany, Joseph. (1907). *Age of Reason*. The Catholic Encyclopedia. Vol. 1. New York: Robert Appleton Company.

Hume, David. (1975, 1777, 1748). *Enquiries Concerning Human Understanding*. 3rd edition, Selby-Bidgge, L.A., and P. N. Nidditch (eds.). Oxford: Clarendon Press.

Peters, William. (1987, 1971). *A Class Divided: Then and Now*. New Haven, CT: Yale University Press.

Strawson, P.F. (1974/1982). *Freedom and Resentment*. Reprinted in G. Watson (ed.) Free Will. Oxford: Oxford University Press. The original essay was published in the Proceedings of the British Academy, Vol 48, (1960), 1-25.

On the Startle Response

We'll talk a lot about the startle response in Book III, in the chapter on wounds and healing. For anyone interested in some clinical background including the most up-to-date research, the following are a good place to start.

Blumenthal, Terry D. & Joseph C. Franklin. (2009). *The Startle Eyeblink Response* (chapter 6 in *Methods in Social Neuroscience*, Harmon-Jones, Eddie & Jennifer S. Beer, ed.). New York: Guilford Press. (This whole book is excellent, as are Guilford Press's books in general. A tough read for a non technical person, but well worth the effort.)

Landis, Carney & William A. Hunt. (1939). *The Startle Pattern*. New York: Farrar & Rinehart, Inc. (In part, a little known look into the misguided efforts carried on in mental hospitals—deliberately startling people just to see what it would do to them. Shades of John Watson's "little Albert" all over again. Cripes, ain't science grand.)

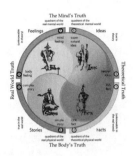

Chapter 6

Discovering the Real You (Your Core Personality)

The Idea of Personality Tests

Have you ever taken a personality test? Has doing this ever changed your life? In this chapter, you'll use what you learned in the last chapter to do just that. You'll learn how to use a series of simple personality tests to permanently change your life. These tests enable you to describe the part of you which is measurably unique with just five words. Thus they hold the power to predict the nature of everything you'll ever think, feel, say, and do. And lest you hear this as the kind of gratuitous nonsense pop psychology tabloids spew, know this. By chapter's end, you will not only be able to describe and predict a good portion of how you think, feel, and act in almost all normal situations. You'll also be able to do this for everyone around you, all this with no need to spend years painfully ingesting—and trying to understand—mountains of psychobabble and statistical fecal matter.

How can I possibly be so cocky about pulling this off?

In the last chapter, I introduced you to something which turns out to be the pivotal ingredient in defining personality—the idea that everything about personality can be divided into two piles—what is the same in all of us and what is different. What is the same, I called the *container* for personality. What is different, I called the *content* of personality.

I also told you that the container for personality is best visualized as an onion with ten nested layers (the naturally occurring, real world version of the container)—or as a Russian matryoshka doll with ten nested dolls (the man-made, theoretical version of the container). Here because the ten layers are fractal, these patterns are easily recognizable in all people, this despite the fact that they can manifest in an infinite variety of ways. This is similar to our bodies which, despite being infinitely different, are all based on the same design. Likewise, our personalities, which are also based on infinite variations of a single design.

The point is, we use our knowledge of the human body to improve our lives, to heal our wounds, and to plan for the future. Indeed, the more we know our bodies, the better our choices become. Similarly, knowing the design of human personality can help us to do the same thing. But only if we can make this design as visible and predictable as the design of our bodies.

This is what personality tests are supposed to do. By enabling you to visualize and predict who you are and what you will do, they are supposed to improve your life. After all, you cannot change what you cannot see. At least, not purposely. Unfortunately, since personality is an idea and therefore not physical, you can't normally see your personality. And here is where the idea of dividing who you are into the container and content comes in.

All personality tests must deal with the container and the content, regardless of whether they acknowledge this division. However, most personality tests make a fatal mistake. They focus on trying to make the content visible. This is like trying to describe the particles of a rain cloud as it crosses the sky. The more you focus on these particles, the more data you see, and within seconds the amount of data has exceeded the capacity of any known supercomputer to track and describe. The thing is, any seven year old with crayons and paper can draw this rain cloud with enough literal accuracy for an adult to know that it's a good day to carry an umbrella and that the picnic might be cancelled. How can seven year olds do what a supercomputer can't? They ignore the content and focus on the container. Likewise, personality tests which do this. They make personality—and everyday life—as understandable and predictable as the rain cloud drawings seven year olds make with paper and crayons.

The Inner Structure of Layer 7
(this plus your mind body type equal your core personality)
(© 2007 Steven Paglierani The Center for Emergence)

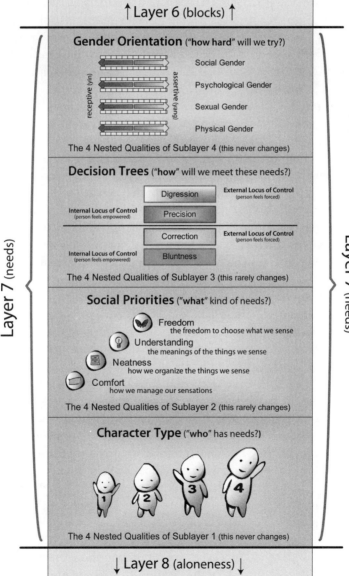

The Two Kinds of Tests: Psychophysical & Psychological

The upshot of all this is that there are actually two classes of personality tests, both of which are supposed to make personality visible. There are psychophysical personality tests, and there are psychological personality tests. What's the difference?

Psychophysical personality tests ask us to make observations, whereas psychological personality tests ask us to make interpretations. Here by *observations*, I'm referring to the outcome of questions which ask us to describe *what we see* in ourselves. Literally. And by *interpretations*, I'm referring to the outcome of questions which ask us to explain *why we see what we see* in ourselves.

For example, if I asked you which you prefer, chocolate cake or chocolate cream pie, I'd be asking you for an observation. But if I asked you why chocolate cakes taste better than chocolate cream pies, I'd be asking you for an interpretation. And if I asked you whether you prefer getting up early or sleeping in, I'd be asking you to make an observation. Whereas if I asked you whether you thought it was better to get up early or to sleep in, I'd be asking you to make an interpretation.

Of course, sometimes the distinction between these two kinds of questions can be hard to discern. For instance, say you banged your thumb with a hammer and I asked you how this happened. Your answer could go either way. You could offer observations, like that this was the first time you used a hammer or that you were distracted at the time. Or you could offer interpretations, such as that you are bad with tools, or that you are a klutz or a moron, or that the hammer was made poorly.

The problem here of course is the same one we have with personality in general. Because interpretations are ideas, they aren't physical. Therefore they aren't visible. Whereas observations are ODE facts. Thus they refer to definite visible events. So while you can observe someone using a hammer for the first time and someone being distracted while using a hammer, you cannot actually see someone who is "bad with tools" or someone who is a "klutz" or a "moron." You can only interpret what you see this way.

Then there's the problem we spoke about back in Book I: chapter one, wherein a word or phrase can have multiple meanings. When this happens on personality tests, we must interpret this word or phrase before we can answer the question. For instance, if we're asked to observe chocolate cakes, there is no interpretation required. All chocolate cakes are chocolate cakes. But if we're asked if chocolate cakes are better than chocolate chip cookies, what exactly does the word "better" mean? That one is more chocolaty? Less sweet? More moist? Less fattening?

Similarly, questions asking us to observe ourselves using a hammer for the first time. There can be only one meaning to this. But the words "bad," "klutz," "moron," and "poorly" can mean many things to many people. How do you know what you're being asked?

If you now apply all this to personality tests, it's easy to see why interpreting who we are, in and of itself, doesn't help us much when it comes to making personality visible. Whereas the observations we make can accurately communicate, even centuries later, truths as fresh as the day they were made. For instance, take the cave paintings at Lascaux. Have you ever seen them? These amazing paintings are said to be over 17,000 years old. Yet anyone seeing even reproductions of these paintings can almost hear the stags, bison, and ibex running from the hunters. Why? Because these paintings function much like children's drawings in that they consist entirely of observations—and posit no interpretations whatsoever.

This then is the flaw in psychological personality tests. They ask you to explain why you are seeing what you are seeing and pretty much ignore what you've observed. The thing is, while most seven year olds can do a pretty good job if asked what things look like, knowing why they look like this is beyond the reach of even the most powerful supercomputer. Moreover, because interpretations can vary as widely as the content of rain clouds, describing personality this way rarely leads to the kind of lasting insights we all long for.

Not getting this? Then let me ask you. Can you see how, by focusing on what you physically see, you make personality as accessible as children's rain cloud drawings? This works because the fractal patterns in what you can physically observe are easily described, including every aspect of personality. Think facial expressions. Think body language. Think tone of voice and so on. And lest you think personality tests based only on these kinds observations would lack sophistication, consider this. The cave paintings at Lascaux contain not a single nod to either the spoken or the written word. Nor to numbers of any kind. Yet even without using words or numbers, they so manage to describe complex aspects of the way those human beings lived that even millennia later, these paintings speak to us in ways no words could ever speak. All this because they focus on making observations—not interpretations.

While the Tests Shouldn't Interpret Life, the Test Results Must

Okay. So personality test questions must ask us to make observations, not interpretations, because observations are tangible whereas interpretations are not. Thus to get valid test results, we must use psychophysical tests (observation-based tests) rather than psychological tests (interpretation-based tests). But what about the answers to these questions? If we don't interpret the results of these tests, then how can they change our lives? In and of themselves, observations have no meaning—and meaning is what we use to guide our choices.

As it turns out, the solution to this problem is surprisingly simple. However, before I can tell you what it is, I first need to briefly clarify what I've told you so far about what makes something part of personality. As opposed to what makes something not part of personality, something incidental to personality.

To wit, in the last chapter, I defined *personality* as the sum of all the recognizable patterns of human experience and behavior which always repeat differently. Obviously, this definition is an idea. Thus to make it visible, I used two metaphors to clothe this idea in something physical. I used the onion metaphor—a metaphor based on a naturally occurring object, and I used the nesting dolls metaphor—a metaphor based on a man-made object.

I also told you that I chose these two metaphors because personality is where we store our life experiences. Hence my calling the sum of all these recognizable patterns, the *container*—as in the layers of an onion contain the onion, and the nested dolls contain the parts of an imaginary self.

This makes *personality* and *the container* equivalents in that they both refer to the same thing—the place where we store our life experiences. As opposed to what we store in this container, which is not part of personality.

I then went on to define what we store in our personality—the content of our personality—as the sum of all human experience and behavior in which the patterns are either unrecognizable or linear. Once again, because this definition is an idea, it is by nature invisible. Therefore, I needed to make this idea visible. I did so by making references to a number of real life examples, all of which could be called *life experiences*. This makes *life experience* and *the content* of personality equivalents as well, in that they too both refer to the same thing—in this case, to what we store in our personality.

Why go to such great lengths to point out that personality and life experience are separate? Because it turns out that the solution to the interpretation problem lies in realizing that personality tests are only supposed to evaluate personality, not life experiences. And this is fortunate. You see, while even a supercomputer cannot track let alone interpret your life experiences (the content of your personality), you yourself can track *and* interpret the part of you that contains these life experiences, the part of you I've been referring to as your personality.

How exactly does this play out when we're talking about real people? It turns out that once we observe who we are, there are two ways in which we can interpret the test results—one drawn directly from our reactions to what we see, and the other based on explaining why these reactions occur. How are they different? Let's see.

The Two Ways to Interpret Who We Are
native (container based) vs. **synthetic** (content based)
(© 2007 Steven Paglierani The Center for Emergence)

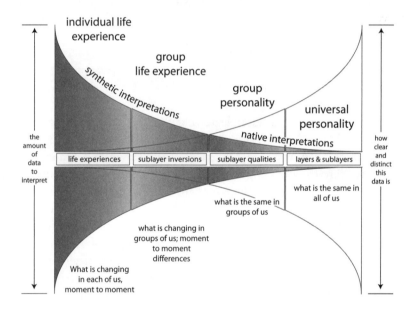

The First Way to Interpret Test Results: Native Interpretations

To begin with, I'm going to call the interpretations we draw directly from our reactions to what we see, *native interpretations,* and those which attempt to explain why we have these reactions, *synthetic interpretations.* What's the difference?

Native interpretations stem from our natural reactions to observing fractal patterns. These patterns—and our reactions to them—are what underlie our interpretations of children's rain cloud drawings and the cave paintings at Lascaux. Here we experience levels of meaning no supercomputer could ever hope to discern. And no words could ever fully capture. Complex meanings. Transcendent meanings. Poetic meanings. Transpersonal meanings. All this and at the same time, deeply personal meanings.

These meanings are the true core of your personal truth. They are the direct result of your visual interactions with life. I say "visual" because all fractals are, by nature, visual. And I say "direct" because this type of pattern recognition requires little to no effort other than to direct your attention to what is right in front of you.

Indeed, from the moment you were born, you began to make these kinds of personal observations—and will continue to make them throughout your life. This includes looking for what I call *metafractal story lines* in these observations. Here I'm referring to the way we tend to stitch together sequences of fractal patterns to create even larger fractal patterns—then look for the kind of underlying patterns we sometimes refer to as story lines. Indeed, taken to the upper limits of visual reductionism, these metafractal story lines become the kind of patterns upon which proper personality theories are based.

For example, young children learn that a setting sun heralds the onset of night, while a rising sun signals the onset of day. And that a candle flame is hot and can burn you, while a frosty-freeze is cold and can hurt your head. Here the meaning of what these children see is inextricably intertwined with how seeing these sequences of fractal events affect them and those around them. A sunset normally presages being sent to bed, and a sunrise usually means you'll be told to get up soon. I hold my finger in the flame too long—my finger hurts and my mother yells. I suck down the frosty freeze too quickly—I get a brain freeze and my brother laughs.

The thing to notice of course is that none of these interpretations include psychological references as to why we responded this way—only that we did. Thus whenever we make native interpretations, we use metafractal story lines to plug directly into the web of life. Indeed, reacting to these kinds of visual observations is what makes Rumi's poems profound and Monet's paintings dreamy. As well as being what makes us sit up and take notice when young children boldly proclaim things like that God made rainbows and that the puppies are being silly again.

In a way then, when you make native interpretations, you're making the same kinds of observations the nineteenth century physicists made— the kind which describe the visual "personality" of what you see. Here rather than arising out of logic and reasoning, your interpretations arise directly out of what you see. Indeed, it may be that what I'm calling native interpretations should be referred to as "secondary observations"—in that all native interpretations can themselves be visually observed.

For example, consider what happened to Einstein when he imagined what riding on a beam of light would be like and discovered relativity. This amazing realization arose directly out of the native interpretations he made about what he saw. Similarly, toddlers do this when they head toward the stairs, then think, if I go any further, mommy will freak out. Prior experiments have revealed this metafractal story line to them. And so on, and so forth.

Here again, we can visualize both our initial observations and our reactions to these observations. Literally, both can be physically observed. Thus native interpretations achieve the primary goal of all personality tests, in that they make personality more visible.

Of course, like learning to observe these kinds of naturally occurring, visual sequences when you study physics, learning to access your native interpretations can take a bit of effort, as we tend to rely more on making synthetic interpretations. Here rather than looking for naturally occurring sequences of personal reactions to visual observations, your focus is on finding universal causal explanations which explain these reactions.

What are "universal causal explanations?" Let's look.

The Second Way to Interpret Test Results: Synthetic Interpretations

What are synthetic interpretations then?

Synthetic interpretations are the meanings we arrive at when we employ logical reductionism to make sense of why things happen. For instance, if a friend falls in love with a little yellow sports car and then buys it—and if someone then says he bought it because he was compensating for having a small penis—this is a synthetic interpretation. As opposed to saying, he bought it simply because he fell in love with what it felt like to drive it—which is a native interpretation. You can see a man falling in love with driving a little yellow sports car. You cannot see "compensating."

Or say your four year old knocks over the knock-off ming vase again and you think to yourself that he did this because he never pays attention to other people's things. This is a synthetic interpretation. As opposed to saying he is four and was immersed in playing tag with his cousin, which is a native interpretation. Again, you can see a four year old playing tag with his cousin. You cannot see a child "never paying attention."

A third example involves something I saw happen at my friend Ed's office yesterday. A very bubbly woman waiting in his waiting room smiled at Ed as he opened his office door. Ed is handsome.

A synthetic interpretation would be that she was buttering him up, or hitting on him, or trying to get something from him. A native interpretation would be that she was simply being friendly.

A moment later, she commented on how nice his office chair was. And it is. Here the same synthetic interpretations I mentioned a moment ago could all apply—while a native interpretation would be that she genuinely liked what she saw. Plain and simple.

The first thing to see about synthetic interpretations then is that they posit psychological explanations as to why things work the way they do—as if all things are planned and intentional. Moreover, unlike native interpretations which derive entirely from visual reductionism, these conclusions derive entirely from logical reductionism. This results in judgmental conclusions such as that all male friends need penis compensation devices (don't they?), and all four year olds should be put in restraints (ah, were it only so easy). As opposed to the simple observations native interpretations might make—such as that your friend loves little yellow sports cars, and your four year old gets excited when he's playing with his cousin.

Said in other words, synthetic interpretations are pretentious attempts to explain the universal essence of what is causing people's interactions with life. In effect, we seek universal causal explanations with which we can stereotype all visually similar things. We do this in hopes we'll be able to use these stereotypes to predict and control the future. Then, when we find them, we treat these things as if all similar people share the same universal personality—leading us to believe in prejudices such as that all men are potential rapists and all women are harpy bitches, and all gay men are pedophiles, and all black men have foot-long penises.

The problem is, some things in personality can be universally observed. All human personalities do indeed share the same underlying design—the same ten fractal layers in the same nested order. But in the real world, there are an infinite number of obvious, discernible differences between your version of the ten layers of personality and the personalities of everyone else. This includes how you move between these ten layers, how much these layers have expanded, how wounds impair your access to these layers, and how you arrange what you store in these layers.

At the same time, it's important to see that both types of interpretations can contain truth. For instance, cultural stereotypes can celebrate groups of people—their foods, their music and dance, and their art and architecture. Thus while these stereotypes do indeed stem from synthetic interpretations, used wisely, they can open your mind to the beauty in things which at first may appear strange and off-putting.

The thing to realize then is that if we plug these two kinds of interpretations into the wise men's map, we find that both types of interpretations represent truth but only in their own realms. Here native interpretations are real world reactions to real world observations. As such, they are knowable in the real world but unknowable in theory. Whereas synthetic interpretations are theoretical reactions to theoretical observations. As such, they are knowable in theory but unknowable in the real world.

Stated as alliances to the wise men, both the empirical and spiritual wise men favor native interpretations and tend to shun synthetic interpretations—while the materialist and rationalist wise men favor synthetic interpretations and tend to demean native interpretations.

Know we'll have lots more to discuss regarding synthetic interpretations as this chapter unfolds, including how they can lead people to falsely conclude they have healed their wounds. For now, the thing to keep in mind is that native interpretations are connected patterns of ODEs. Thus they meet the stated goal for personality tests—they make personality more visible. Whereas synthetic interpretations are non-visual explanations based on logic and reasons. Thus they fail to meet this goal, as these ideas more times than not make personality less visible.

A Brief Summary of What I've Told You So Far

Now let's review what I've told you so far about the nature of personality tests, beginning with what I told you at the beginning of the chapter—that to make lasting personal changes, we must have a clear and distinct method by which to make visible what we want to change. This is the purpose of personality tests. They are supposed to enable you to visualize—and in a general sense, predict—who you are and what you may want to change. This means there are four things to keep in mind as we continue to discuss how personality tests can lead to personal change. One, that you cannot change what you cannot see. Two, that personality is invisible. Three, that personality tests exist primarily to make your personality visible. And four, that for this to happen, they must do two things. They must accurately observe you—psychophysically—and they must interpret what they observe in a personally meaningful way, by making native interpretations.

You should also keep in mind what I told you about how personality tests should limit what they attempt to measure. Obviously, like measuring the content of rain clouds, no personality test can measure all of you. Thus to address this concern, I've divided what we can observe about people into two piles—personality and life experience.

I then told you that because personality is fractal, we need only measure your personality, as even without accounting for every event in your life, these fractals can give you clear and distinct visual baselines from which to know yourself.

So exactly how much of your personality must you measure in order to do this? In truth, you need measure only a small amount—enough for a baseline measurement. The problem, of course, is that like all natural fractals, much of personality is in constant flux—the data in the rain cloud problem. However, there is one part of personality which remains relatively stable for most of our lives. And as we're about to see, if we limit our assessments to this part of personality, we end up with an excellent way to know who we are—something I call our "core personality."

The Idea of an Indestructible "Core Personality"

Now we come to the two ideas around which everything in this chapter revolve—first, the idea that each of us has a core personality which makes us measurably unique and yet, recognizably human—and second, the idea that personality tests which limit their focus to measuring this core personality will succeed in pragmatically defining us as individuals.

What exactly is a core personality?

If I voice it as part of the wise men's personality theory, it's pretty simple actually. Your core personality is your mind body orientation plus the ordering of the qualities in layer 7's four sublayers. Or stated as a reference to that we can be wounded, your core personality is the part of your personality which determines how you'd experience needs—both your own and the needs of those around you—given you had no wounds.

The good news is, none of your wounds actually damage your personality. Moreover, as confusing as this claim may sound—especially after all the remarks I've made about wounds being "damage to your container"—in truth, the damage I've been referring to is more like a poorly maintained dresser with drawers that stick and don't shut properly than a dresser with gouges or burn marks or anything like permanent damage.

How then does being wounded affect your personality?

To see this, you'll need to picture the onion of personality and how layer 7 nests inside layer 6.

Now picture layer 6 as an invisible, bulletproof-glass wall which surrounds—and protects—layer 7.

So what happens when we get wounded? Something akin to getting dirt on this glass. Here layer 6 is the layer which incurs the "damage," while 7 remains untouched.

Know when I say, "damage," I mean a wounding script gets stored in layer 6. This script then acts like the dirt I mentioned a moment ago. To wit, whenever this script runs, your mind involuntarily goes blank. This blankness then temporarily impairs your ability to see what's happening in layer 7—your pure needs.

This then is why I say wounds do not damage your personality. Because layer 6 protects layer 7, nothing in layer 7 gets damaged. Only your access to some part of it gets blocked. And yes, you can't very well meet a need you can't see—so these blocked needs don't get met. And eventually, they cause symptoms. But symptoms are not damage. They are signs of unmet needs. Moreover, used properly, they can point to what we need to heal.

What makes us think that personality can get damaged then? Your mind going blank each time these scripts run is what creates this impression. This blankness keeps you from seeing what's actually causing your symptoms. So logic leads you to conclude that your personality must have been damaged.

This then is what you'll be learning to measure in this chapter—the indestructible part of you which defines who you are—the inner structure of layer 7. Moreover, since this part of your personality doesn't change much after age four, once you measure it, you truly know who you are. Given you had no wounds, that is.

Imagine knowing yourself this intimately?

One last thing. Some may ask how this core personality can define you as an individual, since obviously there are people in the world who have the same core personality as you. The answer? Since no one gets wounded in exactly the same way, even folks who have the same core personality never experience it in exactly the same way.

What Is Your Core Personality Like?

What does the structure of your core personality look like? To be honest, it may seem pretty complicated at first. This said, if you go to the composite diagram at the beginning of this chapter—the one titled, *The Inner Structure of Layer 7*—you'll get a good idea of what it looks like. Here you'll find layer 7's four sublayers—your character type, social priorities, decision tree, and gender orientation—along with the sixteen sublayer-qualities which nest within these sublayers. And if you add to these sublayers your mind body orientation, you have it all—the entire structure of your core personality.

Now look more closely at this drawing. In it, you'll find unfolding one of the qualities which defines all naturally occurring fractals—self-similarity at different scales—the same patterns repeating again and again.

For instance, take how layer 7 is self-similar to the four outer layers.

To begin with, both layer 7 and the outer layers are boundary "layers." Layer 7 is the outermost layer of the four inner layers—10 through 7. Thus it is the fourth layer from the center—and the boundary layer for the inner layers. Whereas the four outer layers—4 though 1—are the outermost layers in personality. Thus together, they are the boundary "layer" for all of personality.

Then we have the total subdivisions. Within layer 7, there are sixteen subdivisions—four sublayers, each of which have four sublayer-qualities. Whereas the four outer layers also have sixteen subdivisions—again, four sublayers, each of which has four sublayer-qualities.

Then there is the way the outer layer sublayers are self-similar—each layer has a sublayer of resentment, a sublayer of blame, and so on. At the same time, each layer's sublayers have entirely different sublayer-qualities, as in there are four kinds of resentment, four kinds of blame, and so on.

Yet another self-similarity lies in the way everything in personality is based on nested subdivisions. Here personality has ten nested layers, and exactly half of these layers—10, 9, 8, 6, and 5—have no sublayers, while the other half—7, 4, 3, 2, and 1—each have four nested sublayers.

In addition, if you total the nested fractals in the inner layers—four layers, plus four sublayers, plus sixteen sublayer-qualities—you get twenty-four. Whereas if you total the nested fractals in the outer layers—four layers, plus four sublayers, plus sixteen sublayer-qualities—you also get twenty-four.

Why mention these similarities?

Because any time you see multiple layers of naturally-occurring self-similarity, you see statistically significant evidence for there being an intelligent design. Moreover, if this design then tests out in the real world as similarly intelligent—as in, real world data that reflect these same patterns—then you can be reasonably certain this theory presents an accurate picture of life.

In part, this self-similarity is what allows me to represent all of personality in a single composite drawing. And because the structure of Layer 7 is self-similar to the structure of your entire personality, discerning your core personality requires only that you answer to a few simple questions about yourself.

So, are you beginning to see what this chapter is about? To find your personal truth, you must start with a clear and distinct sense of who you are. Luckily, there is a portion of your personality which can give you this sense of yourself—your core personality. Here we're talking about the part of your personality which makes you measurably unique. Just how unique are we talking about? To see, we'll need to do a bit more math.

To What Degree Can a Core Personality Be Measured?

Before we delve into the specifics of your core personality, a good thing to know would be, to what degree can we measure someone's core personality? Just how many clear and distinct core personalities can these tests measure anyway?

Start with that there are two possible mind body orientations, four possible character types, and twenty-four possible social priorities. This gives us 2 times 4 times 24 possibilities—192 possibilities. If you then multiply this by the four possible decision trees, this becomes 768 possibilities. And if you then multiply this by the 65,536 theoretical gender orientations, the discernible possibilities balloon out to 50,331,648 core personalities.

Now as if this is not enough precision, there is also the idea that life events can *temporarily* alter—in predictable ways—both your mind body orientation and the order of the sublayer-qualities contained within the first two sublayers. Here the two possible mind body orientations become four (two normal, and two inverted)—the four possible character types become eight (4 upright, and 4 inverted)—and the twenty-four possible social priorities become ninety-six (4 upright, 4 stressed, 4 inverted, and 4 righting). This gives us 805,306,368 clearly discernible variations of our core personality (4 x 8 x 96 x 4 x 65,536), a bold number, to be sure.

Compare this to the only other solidly pragmatic personality tests to be based *directly* on a personality theory typology—the Katharine Cook Briggs and Isabel Briggs Myers variation of Carl Jung's personality typology. Here there are 16 clearly discernible types. Very useful types, at that. But when you compare this to the over fifty million possible core personalities contained within the four wise men's system, you begin to see the power of the personality tests you're about to see. And lest you worry that it will be hard to know which of these fifty million plus core personalities best describes you, know this. By the end of this chapter, you'll know, at minimum, the four most fundamental qualities which define you as a person—which of the 192 possible *basic* core personalities best describes you. As opposed to the 50,331,456 discernible *extended* core personalities, all of which serve to further clarify your basic core personality.

Finally there's one more thing I need to mention. While your character type and gender orientation remain the same after age seven, your social priorities and decision tree can—in rare cases—change. Thus, like the way hurricanes sometimes change the patterns of high and low tides, severe life traumas can—in rare cases—*permanently* alter the order of some of the qualities contained within layer 7's sublayers.

This said, are you beginning to see the possibilities yet? I'm saying there are over fifty-million measurable core personalities, surely an amazing amount of quantifiable discernment. At the same time, I hope it's obvious, even at this point, that it would be close to impossible to invent a personality theory which could have this number of self-similar qualities and discernible differences and yet still test as true in the real world.

At the same time, I'm well aware that unless I can make this theory accessible to you, that it will be of no value no matter how true it is. Fortunately, the personality tests I'm about to introduce make your individual personality as easy to recognize as a child's rain cloud drawing. Thus you'll soon have a baseline from which to find your personal truth.

Of course, it's one thing to brag about complexity, another to offer usable tests which can actually discern your individuality. With this in mind, we need to speak a bit about what makes your personality measurably unique—as opposed to the parts of you we all have in common, and the parts of you which are impossible to measure.

What Do the Wise Men's Tests Measure?

I spent the entire last chapter describing the container for personality, including that all people's containers are based on the same design. This universality is what allows us to define what it means to be human—these patterns are present in all people. However I also said that what is never the same in any of us, and therefore not part of personality, is the part of us which is constantly changing—the part of us we refer to as our life experience. Here we can never hope to accurately measure even a single second of this content, as it is far too chaotic and unpredictably complex.

But if the container—the part of us we can measure—is the same in all of us, and the content—the part we can never hope to measure—is changing minute to minute, then how can we account for our individual differences? What exactly can we measure? Obviously the answer to this question is what allows us to describe the personality of individual human beings, as opposed to all human beings. In order to define what this is though, we first need to explore how the continuum from personality to life experience is actually a continuum of four things—our Universal

Personality, our Group Personality, our Group Life Experience, and our Individual Life Experience.

Let's start with the subdivision I'm calling our Universal Personality. What is a Universal Personality?

What Makes Us Each Measurably Unique?
(our core personality defined)
(© 2007 Steven Paglierani   The Center for Emergence)

← real world measurements   theoretical measurements →

Core Personality
(what is measurably unique in each of us)

Individual Life Experience	Group Life Experience	Group Personality	Universal Personality
(what is different in all of us; moment to moment changes)	(what is different in groups of us)	(what is the same in groups of us)	(what is the same in all of us)
your specific life experiences	your layer 7 sublayer inversions, plus your mind body counter preferences	the normal order of your layer 7 sublayer qualities, plus your mind body orientation	the ten layers, the sublayers, and the sublayer qualities, plus that you have a separate mind and body

Universal Personality: You Will Not Be Measuring This

Our Universal Personality is the part of us which is the same in *all* human beings. Thus personality tests need not measure this, as none of it makes us unique. Moreover, most of it we've already discussed in detail in the prior chapter, albeit not as Universal Personality. Here we're referring to the four major theoretical subsets of personality, in all, 63 discernible parts (1+10+20+32). They are:

- your mind body orientation.
- the ten nested layers of your personality.
- the twenty nested sublayers which exist within layers 7, 4, 3, 2, and 1.
- the thirty-two nested sublayer-qualities which exist within these twenty sublayers.

I introduced you to the first of these subsets—your mind body orientation—back in Book I: chapter four. There I told you we experience many dualities in life, even if we pay them no mind. As the mind and body, they're the foundation of everything we sense. And as energy and matter, they're the underlying basis for everything in our world, including us. Thus your mind body orientation is the primary experience from which your whole personality emerges.

Then in this book, in chapter five, I introduced you to the ten nested layers of personality. There I said, we all have the same ten layers nested in the same order. For instance, we all have a layer 6 where we store the scripts of our wounds. And we all have a layer 7 wherein we store our pure needs.

Next we have the five sets of four sublayers—twenty in all—of which sixteen were introduced to you back in chapter five as well. Here I'm referring to that each of our outer layers has nested within it the same 4 sublayers—a sublayer of resentment, a sublayer of blame, a sublayer of punishment, and a sublayer of damage control. Moreover, these four sublayers always nest within their particular layer in the same order. Thus blame always precedes punishment, and resentment, blame.

This leaves one set of sublayers—the one I previously mentioned but haven't describe—the 4 sublayers of layer 7. Here we're talking about the sublayers of character type, social priorities, decision trees, and gender orientation. Know that defining these four sublayers will be our main focus in this chapter, as the order of these sublayers—and the qualities contained within them—largely define your core personality.

Finally we come to the last part of our Universal Personality, the thirty-two sublayer-qualities. Here again, I introduced you to some of these sublayers back in chapter five as well, in this case, to the sixteen outer layer sublayer-qualities I cumulatively titled, the four poisons of adulthood—the four kinds of resentment, the four kinds of blame, the four kinds of punishment, and the four kinds of damage control. For example, in layer 4, we associate the sublayer of resentment with the sublayer quality of abuse, while in layer 2, we associate the sublayer of resentment with the sublayer quality of stupidity. And in layer 3, we associate the sublayer of punishment with the sublayer quality of time, while in layer 1, we associate the sublayer of punishment with the sublayer quality of silence.

This leaves us with the sixteen sublayer-qualities which exist in layer 7. These I'll introduce you to shortly as well. Unlike the sublayer-qualities contained within the outer sublayers though, this time, each sublayer has multiple sublayer-qualities. For instance layer 7's third sublayer—the decision tree sublayer—has four sublayer-qualities: precision, correction, digression, and bluntness. And layer 7's first sublayer—character type—also has four sublayer-qualities: character types one, two, three, and four.

Is your brain about to burst? Are you ready to smash this book into the wall? Believe it or not, I have a hard time remembering all this myself. At the same time, can you imagine what it's been like trying to figure all this out? In part, this difficulty is what's been motivating me to write this book—I want to give you a method by which you can figure out things like this for yourself. And if I'm diligent—and if you try your best—by the end of Book III, you too will be able to explore things just as complex. I, for one, can't wait to see what you discover.

As for having to retain these ideas, please don't feel concerned. In truth, taken one at a time, they're all simple—once you've learned how to picture them. Once again, without pictures, these ideas mean nothing. However, were you to take a moment to redraw the composite diagrams which represent what I've just told you about personality—the onion, for instance, or the nesting dolls—you'd be well prepared to learn these new ideas. Likewise, if you redraw the composite drawings from this chapter as you go along, you'll make learning these new ideas even easier.

Universal Personality: a Brief Summary

So now, let's sum this up. What is your Universal Personality?

Overall, the thing to remember is that your Universal Personality is like having a ten drawer dresser. In it, you store everything which makes you you, including the three subdivisions I'm about to describe—your Group Personality, your Group Life Experience, and your Individual Life Experience. Indeed, were you to keep this metaphor in mind, you'd have a good way to understand these three subdivisions. To wit, if your Universal Personality is your ten drawer dresser, then your Group Personality is the style of separators you use in these drawers—your Group Life Experience is how you arrange these separators—and your Individual Life Experience is what you put into these separations.

Now let's look at these three subdivisions in a bit more detail, starting with your Group Personality. What kind of separators come pre-installed in your ten drawer dresser—the standard equipment? Let's find out.

Group Personality: You Will Be Measuring This

Our Group Personality is the part of us which is the same in *groups* of us—as opposed to our Universal Personality, which is the part of us which is the same in *all* of us. Thus our Group Personality is sort of like being Republican or vegan or Greek or on the national honor role. Only in this case, we're talking about things like having the same character type or the same decision tree.

Know that your Group Personality is much simpler than your Universal Personality, as here we're only referring to two things. First, we're referring to your normal mind body orientation. Either you are mind first or body first. And second, we're referring to the usual order of your sixteen, layer 7 sublayer-qualities.

For example, one of these four sublayers contains your social priorities, and within this sublayer there are four sublayer-qualities. This means there are twenty-four possible normal sequences in which your social priorities can occur (the permutation of 4 things taken 4 at a time—4 x 3 x 2 x 1). Here for one group of folks, the sequence in which these social priorities normally occur is understanding, freedom, neatness, and comfort—while for another, the normal sequence is comfort, freedom, neatness, and understanding.

Similarly the sublayer containing your decision tree, which also has four sublayer-qualities. Here the normal decision tree sequence for one group of folks is precision, correction, digression, and bluntness (the "AS" sequence)—whereas for another group, it's digression, bluntness, precision, correction (the "ADHD" sequence).

Realize, when I say "normal sequence," I mean the order of your layer 7 sublayer-qualities can change. Normal refers to a normal state of mind, e.g. not reliving a wound. Thus while the order of these sublayer-qualities varies from person to person, there are presently over six billion people on planet Earth and only 4 x 24 x 4 x 65,536 = 25,165,824 possible normal sublayer-qualities orders. Moreover, if you multiply this number by the two mind body orientations, you end up with the 50,331,648 possible core personalities I mentioned earlier.

Now divide this number into the world population. The result? In theory, if you know your Group Personality, you know which group of 120 out of 6 billion people you belong to. Can you imagine! This is what makes knowing your Group Personality so powerful—and important—as once you know which group you belong to, you have a way to know yourself. And everyone else. All six billion of us.

Group Life Experience: You Will Need to Be Aware of This

So if our Group Personality—the part of us which is the *same* in groups of us—is the focus of the wise men's personality tests, then what is our Group Life Experience and why do we need to know about it?

Our Group Life Experience is what is *different* in groups of us. This is sort of like the idea that five people can be Republicans, but no two Republicans are ever the same. Similarly vegans, and Greeks, and national honor role students. Only here we're talking about how the two parts of your Group Personality can vary. One, we're talking about how your mind body orientation can switch on occasion—something called having mind body *counter-preferences*. And two, we're talking about how the order of your sixteen layer 7 sublayer-qualities can change under stress—something called *inversions*.

So for instance, with regard to the first kind of Group Life Experience—mind body orientation changes—say your normal orientation is body first. However, when you want to improve how you eat, you put most of your effort into eating healthy foods, cutting down on carbs, and never over indulging on fattening desserts. The thing is, none of these things derive from physical urges. Thus they're all ideas. So if this is you, then it's likely that whenever you eat, your mind body orientation switches from body first to mind first.

This change is a good example of a mind body counter-preference. You normally trust your gut more than your head. But whenever you eat, this switches, and you trust your mind more than your gut. Literally. In essence, these changes resemble right handed folks when they do things left handed. Only with mind body counter-preferences, we're talking about changing from a person who makes choices based on what your body tells you to a person who makes choices based on what your mind tells you, and vice versa.

What about the second kind of variations in Group Life Experience?

Here an example would be when your character type inverts. So for instance, I'm a character type two. Thus I normally feel gentle urges to give. But when my character type inverts, I feel compelled to give. I must give. And my friend, Ed, who is a three, normally feels gentle urges to get people to give to him. But when his character type inverts, like me, he feels compelled to give to others.

We'll talk a lot about counter-preferences and inversions as we progress though the four layer 7 sublayers. For now, the thing to keep in mind is this. It's your Group Personality which describes how you feel under normal circumstances, whereas it's your Group Life Experience which describes those times wherein you remain within the scope of your Group Personality—but vary as far as the order and intensity of your mind body orientation and or your layer 7 sublayer-qualities.

Individual Life Experience: You Cannot Measure This

So what's left to discuss? Just one division. Our Individual Life Experience. This time we're referring to everything which is constantly changing in us, moment to moment—the things which make each of us truly unique. Not sure what I'm referring to? Then try following your thoughts for a few minutes. Now try predicting your next thought. Or try watching your body for a few minutes. Now try predicting your next sensation.

Know this part of us includes two kinds of experiences—those which are truly non linear and thus, unpredictable—and those which are close to linear and so, are somewhat predictable, but only as far as *what* will occur, never *when*.

With the non linear stuff, there are no set patterns and never will be. Thus these parts of us are impossible to measure let alone predict. And with the close to linear stuff, wounds program us with fixed patterns of thinking and behavior. Here we're talking about the often uncomfortably predictable parts of us which cannot be considered to be part of our true nature—the arguments we repeat, the faults we can't seem to change, the things we avoid at all costs, and the words we don't intend to say.

Realize that coming to accept that we have these kinds of faults can take a bit of time. How can we behave in predictable ways and yet, be unable to prevent this behavior? But if you picture something you hate—seeing your husband track mud onto your newly waxed kitchen floor, for instance, or your teenage daughter failing to clean up her mess after cooking, or having your five year old repeatedly fail to respond to requests to listen to you, or your neighbor's dog leaving steamy brown loaves in the snow on your front lawn again—then you'll have a good idea of the kinds of things I'm talking about here.

Now consider how unpredictable it is as to whether you'll explode about this stuff or not. Sometimes, you'll resemble the Dalai Lama. Sometimes, you'll resemble Genghis Khan. But you'll never be able to predict with certainty which it will be. At the same time, even though you won't be able to predict *when* you'll behave like this, you will be able to predict *what it will look* like if you do lose it.

In this way, wounds are the all-too-predictable part of ourselves. Hence my saying they're close to linear. Thus even within our Individual Life Experience, we see the wise men's map unfolding, in that a continuum extends from the things which are predictable in theory to those which are unpredictable in the real world. Yet one more example of the self-similarity present in the wise men's personality theory.

So What is a Core Personality?

Finally we arrive at the theoretical definition of a core personality—the distinctly individual part of us which the wise men's personality tests measure. Very simply stated, your core personality is your Group Personality plus your Group Life Experience as seen through your Mind Body orientation. And this makes sense. There would be no value in having personality tests account for what is the same in *all* of us. Nor for what is different in *all* of us. The first thing would be measurable but would tell us nothing distinctive—and the second would be immeasurable.

Realize, this means we can never quantify our individual identity. Only our group identity. Thus we each remain immeasurably unique. At the same time, being able to discern over fifty million distinct group identities means the four wise men's personality tests have more than enough resolution to enable you to know yourself—and certainly more than enough to significantly improve your life.

Now consider how these four parts of us fit together.

Start with the entire continuum from Universal Personality to Individual Life Experience. This continuum represents the entirety of human nature. Thus everything we human beings think, feel, say, and do can be represented somewhere on this continuum.

Now divide this entire continuum into two halves. The right half is the continuum of personality, and the left half, the continuum of life experience. Here personality is the theoretical continuum extending from Universal Personality to Group Personality, and life experience is the real world continuum extending from Individual Life Experience to Group Life Experience.

Did you follow this? By dividing the entire continuum of human nature in half, we get two self-similar continuums. The first—personality—is a theoretical continuum. The second—life experience—is a real world continuum. And doing this gives us a clear way to discern between personality and life experience, while at the same time, maintaining the integrity of the whole.

Finally we have the last continuum, the group continuum. In this case, we're talking about the continuum which gets created by joining the two inner groups, Group Personality and Group Life Experience. Here again we see a fractally self-similar subset of the entire continuum of human nature. Moreover, this continuum is also the closest we can come to pragmatically measuring an individual personality. Thus the wise men's personality tests focus on this particular continuum.

A Typical Core-Personality Test Result

Obviously, I've got a lot of explaining to do before any of this can make sense. However, if I were to now offer you a typical example of the outcome of these tests, even at this point, I'm guessing, you would get at least the gist of what I'm saying. For instance, take me. I am a *Mind First Two* with *Understanding Freedom* as my first two social priorities. So do these five words mean anything to you yet? Honestly, they shouldn't. But just so you have some idea of what I'm about to introduce you to, let me give you the five cent tour of what I've just said.

We all have a default speed at which we feel comfortable taking in and broadcasting our experiences of life—either mercurial—as in the quick-witted mental experiences of a Mind First person—or suave—as in the smoothly paced physical experiences of a Body First person. I am the former. Indeed, I am always ready to think, but rarely suave.

I am also a character type Two which means, I'm a natural giver but suck at receiving from others. Don't give me a compliment three times in a row. I might take your head off or at least, get really quiet.

Finally, my first two social priorities are understanding then freedom. In a way, this makes me a free thinker—I'm always looking to understand what's around me. At the same time, I never want to impinge on anyone's freedom in the process. Let alone pressure you to agree with me.

What do these four qualities tell you about me?

That my most fundamental urges are to *give others* (character type 2) *mental* (mind first) *understanding* (1st social priority) *freely* (2nd social priority). Translated into everyday language, this means that, in general, I focus on the needs of others and feel urges to offer them words which I hope will help them to better understand themselves, while at the same time, never wanting to force these words on them. Does this at all sound like the sort of man who is writing this book? Duh. And lest this sound like the kind of empty generalizations newspaper astrologists make, remember what I told you about how many core personalities there are. Over fifty million. Even so, by the time you finish reading this chapter, you will likely have learned so much about yourself, and about the people you are close to you, that you may feel similar feelings to how I think of personality—I never tire of learning about it.

Still feel challenged by what I'm saying? Know I welcome this skepticism. After all, if something is true, it should withstand your scrutiny. And the scrutiny of skeptical but open-minded professionals.

So, are you ready to put me and the wise men to the test?

Here we go.

Section One

Character Type: Your Core Personality—Part One

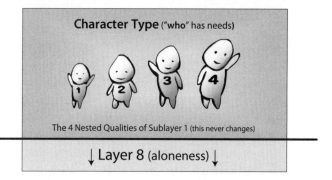

Character Type ("who" has needs)

The 4 Nested Qualities of Sublayer 1 (this never changes)

↓ Layer 8 (aloneness) ↓

Character Type: Who Has Needs?

As I've mentioned, Layer 7 has four sublayers—each a part of our strategy for getting our pure needs met. The four sublayers are—the Character Type sublayer—the Social Priorities sublayer—the Decision Tree sublayer—and the Gender Orientation sublayer. Here our character type dictates whose needs we are focused on—our social priorities, the style in which we would like these needs to be met—our decision tree, the path by which we will decide how to respond to these urges—and our gender orientation, the degree of force, or lack thereof, with which this response is to be delivered.

Overall, the thing to keep in mind this time is this.

You experience these four sublayers in many ways similarly to how you would experience waves in a pond were you to be swimming in this pond. If a rock was thrown into the water near you, the first wave of experience to hit you would be your character type, the second, your social priorities, and so on.

Can you picture this? The first thing you do when an experience hits you is to look to see whose needs have been affected—and who is responsible to meet these needs. Thus your character type biases how you perceive every life experience. Indeed, next to your mind body orientation, your character type is the most significant thing to know about yourself. So even if your character type was the only thing you learned from this book, your ability to discern personal truth would still improve significantly.

What do these four character types look like? Before we can talk about this, we'll first need to look at the two states from which all four character types derive—the "Me" state, and the "You" state. And if you consider that these two states are the experiential raw material for the whole rest of your core personality, you begin to see what makes your character type so important.

Character State

Me!

The First Character State: the "Me" State

Like everything else in the inner layers, the first sublayer of your core personality—your character type—begins in the birth separation moment. Here you emerge from your arrival trauma already in the first character state. This, in fact, is the entire meaning underlying your first complaints. "Me," you cry, as you arrive. "What about ME!"

Know that while babies are in this state, the only needs they can experience are their own—and this is a good thing. If a six month old baby girl were to be suffocating in a twisted-up baby blanket—and if she had to worry about whether 3 AM was a good time to wake her parents—she might die, if not the first time this happened, then not long afterwards. The point? We all arrive programmed to alternate between the self-centeredness of the Me state and the connected bliss of layers 9 and 10. Moreover, this interplay is how we all spend our first year alive.

Amazingly, during this first year, we feel no guilt or shame about being this needy. Thus we have no qualms about demanding attention any time we feel the urge. Moreover, since our very existence depends on being able to get others to meet these demands, surely, this makes sense, as without this lack of inhibition, we would not survive.

Can you imagine how this must have felt? No matter what you wanted, you asked for it without hesitation. Indeed, the minute you felt the need for something, you expected someone to give it to you. And if they didn't give it to you fast enough, you let them know.

What if these folks had needs of their own? Then, oh well. Since "getting" was all you cared about, giving to them wasn't even a thought. Thus as far as needs, the first year of life much resembles the royal "we" once reserved for kings and queens. Every being you come in contact with exists only to serve you. Indeed, there isn't a doubt in your mind as to whether you should get your needs met—let alone a concern as to how these demands will affect others. All that matters is getting someone to meet your needs. And again and again you cry, Me! What about Me!

Character State

The Second Character State: the "You" State

Somewhere toward the end of the first year of life, about seventy-five percent of all babies begin to experience the second character state. Why not all babies? We'll address this in a bit when we talk about how the four character types come into being. For now the thing to know is that the second character state is the polar opposite of the first. Here if the Me state is the yang experience of neediness, then the You state is the yin experience of neediness.

In other words, while babies in a Me state focus entirely on themselves and their own needs, babies in a You state focus entirely away from themselves and on the needs of others. At least in the moments wherein they're aware that others exist.

What does this look like? Here a story is in order.

Years ago, when my friend Lauren's first son, Jacob, was about ten months old, Lauren and I were sitting in her living room when we noticed it was too quiet. Noting this, she and I tiptoed over to her dining room doorway to see what Jacob was doing, only to find that he had hoisted himself up on the potted fig-tree container and was eating dirt. So much for thinking the room was child-proof. The thing is, at the point wherein we interrupted Jacob, he was already eating the first mouthful and had the next mouthful in his hand. However, as he saw us standing in the doorway—and before he could eat the next handful—he looked over at us. Then at his hand. Then at us again. Then at his hand.

Can you picture what this must have looked like and how different this is from how first year of life babies normally behave? In Jacob's case, I had been witnessing his insistent demands and uninhibited explorations for the entire time he was alive. Not once in that prior ten months had he considered anything other than just taking what he wanted. Indeed, whenever he had a need, it was as if no one else existed. Yet here he was, at ten months old, wordlessly looking over at us as if to ask, "Is this okay?"

He also had a guilty look on his face, something I hadn't seen him do before. Prior to this, he appeared incapable of feeling guilt when he asked for things. Now, it seemed, his whole character had changed, and in fact, it had. He had gone from being totally unaware that others can have needs—to having an acute awareness that they can have needs.

Over the next few weeks, Jacob's new awareness seemed to come and go, after which he settled into a new pattern. Whenever he had a need, he would first look to others to see what they thought, then, if there were no protests—and sometimes even when there were—he'd do what it was he had set out to do. Of course, this pattern wasn't absolute. He was still, after all, a baby. But whenever he had a need—*and when he was aware that others were present*—he looked first at them to see what they thought before proceeding.

About a year later, just before Jacob turned two, this pattern changed yet again. In effect, what happened to him this time was that he remembered how good it felt to be the little king, always demanding and the center of everyone's attention. Me, me! What about ME! However, unlike his first year of life wherein he had been unable to see the needs of others, at this point, he had learned that other people can have needs. Thus his tantrums were directly affected by—and in many ways keyed to—how people did and did not respond to his demands.

For example, if Jacob had a need which his mother wasn't going to meet, she had to contrive an alternate need which she could substitute for the need he wasn't going to get. Most mothers see doing this as distracting a baby—and in many ways, it is. However, the nature of these distractions is always that you must get the baby to substitute one need for another. And indeed, the success of these negotiations—or lack thereof—hinges entirely on how well you can get the baby to need the new thing.

In addition, whenever Jacob had a tantrum, his self-centered neediness would eventually be followed by remorse. Admittedly, this remorse was subtle and if you didn't know what to look for, you could have easily missed it. The point is, during these tantrums, Jacob's sense of who had needs would encompass both character states—first the Me state (I am the only one with needs), then the You state (you are the only one with needs). And he always experienced these two character states in this order—first the Me state—then the You state.

Finally, you should know that this was the last time Jacob's character states changed. More than ten years later, he is still a "Me then You."

Will he ever become anything other than a Me then You? No. And in the next subsection, we'll talk about why.

Why All the Talk About Character States?

Why tell you all this? Because all four character types derive from some combination of these two character states—the Me state and the You state. They also derive their names from the year of life in which this particular sequence of character states emerges.

Here first year of life people—those whose character type is entirely composed of Me states—are called Ones. Second year of life people—those whose character type is entirely composed of You states—are called Twos. Third year of life people—those whose character type is entirely composed of Me then You states—are called Threes. And fourth year of life people—those whose character type is entirely composed of You then Me states—are called Fours.

Finally, if you keep in mind that character type describes how babies deal with their needs in one of the first four years of life, you'll have a good way to remember what each character type is like. Moreover, if you set aside the idea that some people are Mind First people and some are Body First, then character type is the most useful thing to know about a person.

In other words, while mind body orientation is important in that it's the broadcast frequency on which we send and receive experience—character type is equally important in that it's the primary filter through which every wave of life experience passes. Here we begin to process these experiences by asking the following two questions—whose needs am I feeling, mine or yours, and what do I need to do, *get* (do I need to get you to give to me?), or *give* (do I need to give to you?).

How does this decision process play out in the real world? Let's see.

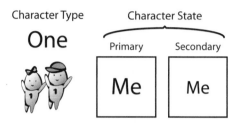

Character Type One: "Me" People

What is a character type One like?

Other than their acquired life skills, there is little difference between people with character type One and babies in their first year of life. Thus a One is a person who is either connected to someone or in a Me state—but with additional language skills, physical mastery, and a general sense of socialization.

Likewise, whenever Ones have a need, they act as if others exist solely to meet this need. And their enhanced life skills only improve their abilities to communicate these demands.

Conversely, when you're connected to a One, it feels as wonderful as being connected to a baby. Thus Ones are often very charismatic people. Moreover, this dichotomy—between feeling totally connected and feeling totally unseen—is the hallmark of being around Ones. You either feel so connected to them that it's like you've died and gone to heaven. Or you feel so totally invisible that it's like you've fallen from grace into hell.

How does someone become a One?

The simple answer is, they finish baking in the first year of life. Here by "baking," I'm referring to the stress they experience during their first year of life. In their case, the stress in their home is so high that it permanently programs them to focus solely on their own needs, while at the same time ignoring the needs of others.

This does not mean they cannot, at times, see and care about the needs of others. However, they can do this only after all their needs have been met. Moreover, even when they do perceive others have needs, rarely can they accurately see these needs, and this holds true even when other people clearly and distinctly state these needs.

Why does this happen? Because ones are simply incapable of putting themselves in another person's place, at least when it comes to their needs. So when they sense that others have needs, at best, they perceive these needs as what they themselves might need. Even then, what they perceive is more an intellectual imitation of genuine care.

What happens when you do not accede to a One's requests?

Very quickly, all hell breaks loose. They kick and scream—lie, holler and demand—and tell you you're always being selfish. That they often tell this to the most generous, caring people of all matters not. When Ones have a need, all they live for is getting this need met. And they'll torture and punish you until you meet this need. Or until you threaten to leave them and they realize you may actually follow through.

And after this need is met?

Amazingly, Ones feel no remorse for what they put you through. Again, no matter how mean, threatening, or punishing they've been—they are simply incapable of feeling bad for what they do to others. What they can feel, however, is regret for what they themselves have just been through. After all, according to them, if you'd only have listened to them in the first place, none of this pain would have been necessary. Indeed, if you'd just given them what they wanted, *everyone* would have been happy.

Does it sound like I am exaggerating their self-centeredness? I'm not at all. In fact, I, myself, have been on the butt end of this self-centered logic many times. For instance, I was once engaged to a One named Lisa who told me this very thing. She said she knew a couple wherein the woman's fiancé did everything for her and that I should be more like this man. And when I asked her what he got from doing this, she told me—with a straight face—that he got her happy! Can you imagine? What he got for himself was that he got "her happy."

Here then are two of the characteristics which define Ones. First, they believe that if they are happy, then everyone else will be happy. And second, while Ones can feel regret for how they have been affected by the struggle to get their needs met, they are incapable of feeling remorse for how they might have hurt others during this struggle. Here I'm defining *regret* as feeling bad about how what you've done has affected you—and *remorse* as feeling bad about how what you've done has affected others.

Are you finding this hard to believe—that these folks are incapable of feeling remorse for hurting others? Here again, this makes sense only if you can picture how babies behave in their first year of life, at least with regard to getting their needs met. Moreover, if you still find this hard to believe, then just think back to the last time you were in the presence of an inconsolable six month old. Holy cow! Talk about someone who cares only about their own needs—and doesn't give two hoots as to how these demands affect others.

This, then, is how Ones react whenever they feel needy. Meet their needs quickly enough and they'll beam at you. Fail to meet these needs and they'll act like first year of life babies. Angry. Demanding. And relentless. So am I making it sound like being a One is a fate worse than death? To people other than Ones, it certainly can feel like this at times. Then again, Ones themselves don't usually feel too bad about being Ones. Moreover, along with the obvious negative aspects, Ones can have many positive qualities.

If intellectually capable, Ones can make great leaders. Their ability to focus entirely on what they need people to do for them is largely unmatched by any other character type. Here their lack of insight as to the personal needs of others becomes an asset, especially in times wherein difficult decisions must be made, such as those which by their nature involve harming others—during wars or medical emergencies, for instance, or after natural disasters. No surprise then that many military leaders, doctors, policemen, politicians, and corporate executives are Ones, as well as most religious fanatics, mega-movie and sports superstars.

Ones can also be among the warmest, most complimentary, and charismatic people you'll ever meet, at least in those times wherein they feel connected to you. In these moments, to them, you are the "one," their soul mate and confidant. And time and again, they generously say this to you as you bask in the light of their infant-like adoration.

Finally, a good way to remember what a One is like is to recall that character type is first and foremost about just two things—determining who has needs, and determining who should meet these needs. Ones are incapable of personally experiencing anyone else's needs, including the need to treat others with respect. Thus the key to understanding Ones is to realize that for them, witnessing someone else with needs can feel quite threatening. Worse yet, when Ones witness people expressing their needs, they often feel personally offended, as if these folks are being incredibly selfish and insensitive. To wit, in the presence of a needy person, Ones commonly switch the focus away from the needy person and onto themselves by saying things like, "What about me! Why does everything always have to focus on you?" And, "You're always being so selfish! Can't you see how this is affecting me!"

For example, during the time I was engaged to the Lisa I mentioned earlier, I once received a call that my then thirteen year old daughter had run away from the rehab she was in and needed to be picked up from the police station near this rehab. Being this was in the middle of my work day—and that she was three and a half hours away—I was understandably upset. However, when I called Lisa to tell her this and that I wouldn't be home on time, she immediately got angry and yelled at me saying I should never call and upset her at work. Thus not only did she not offer me sympathy nor express any concern whatsoever. She yelled at me on top of this for upsetting her.

Lisa never did apologize for being this cold and callous. Nor did I ever try to get her to understand my hurt. Why not? Because back then, I had no idea the wise men existed let alone that I am a Two—a second year of life person. Meaning what exactly? Let's look.

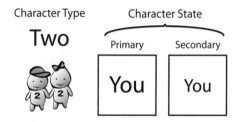

Character Type Two: "You" People

What is it like to be a character type Two? This time, I can speak from personal experience. I am a Two. So is my closest friend, Brit. So was my father. So was my seventh grade teacher, Mr. Branch.

What are Twos like? To paraphrase an old Alanon saying, "when a Two is drowning, her spouse's needs pass before her eyes." Here again, the thing to notice is where these folks focus when in the presence of needs. Twos focus entirely on the needs of others—and barely notice their own needs. For instance, years ago, I worked in management at a large corporation. At the time, this company was considered by some to have been one of the more demanding employers, certainly as far as how many hours you were expected to work. This meant you were expected to show up for work and stay at work, even if you were sick. Yet I once had a boss send me home because he said I was too sick to work. Can you imagine? I myself hadn't even realized I was sick. Yet in truth, I was so sick—and so didn't know it—that my boss sent me home for fear I'd infect the whole department, this in a place wherein they expected you to work, sick or not.

This kind of thing happens frequently to people who finish baking in their second year of life. More times than not they fail to see their own needs, no matter how extreme. At the same time, they rarely miss seeing a need in others, no matter how small. Indeed, sometimes Twos are so intuitive, they can see the needs of others in ways these folks can't see for themselves. However, this sensitivity also has a down side. Twos can sometimes feel so much compassion for others that they exaggerate other people's needs—or see needs that aren't actually there.

Know this focus on the needs of others begins for Twos in their second year of life. What are babies like in their second year of life?

For the most part, they behave like Jacob did in the eating dirt story I told you a few pages back. Whenever they have a need—and whenever they are aware you exist—they first look to you to see how you'll react to them getting this need met. They also look more to themselves to meet this need than babies in their first year of life. Not always, of course. They are still babies. But far more than previously. Thus the upside to this change is their growing independence and self reliance, while the downside is that they frequently underestimate their needs and overestimate their ability to meet these needs.

No surprise then that, as adults, Twos can be among the most generous folks on the planet. Because they can, they frequently befriend—and at times—fall in love with Ones. However, while spending time around Ones can feel quite good to a perpetual giver, whenever a Two spends a lot of time around a One, the Two inevitably feels drained, exhausted, and empty. After all, Ones can't see other people's needs—and Twos can't see their own needs. So in a One-Two relationship, the Two's needs largely go unmet.

This persistent need to give to others can even cause others to feel uncomfortable at times. Twos frequently offer people unsolicited advice and help, even when they cannot deliver. This is especially true when they try to offer help to other Twos, as most Twos don't like it when people even suggest they might need help.

In truth, when Twos push unsolicited help onto people, most healthy people feel uncomfortable. Most adults don't like it when others assume they're helpless or in need. On the other hand, if you actually do need this help, these offers can feel really good. And in these cases—if asked—Twos are typically the most generous with their help.

As for regret and remorse, Twos are the complementary opposite of Ones. Twos can too easily feel remorse—but rarely feel regret for more than brief moments. Indeed, Twos often feel remorse for things they had nothing to do with—folks dying of AIDS in Africa, for instance, or families in the news in disasters. This can even generate urges in Twos to go to great lengths to offer help to total strangers. And in extreme cases, these strangers may feel like their privacy is being invaded or worse, that they're being stalked or patronized.

Conversely, nothing is more annoying than trying to offer help to a Two. Indeed, Twos hate to impose on people and many times refuse help even when they desperately need it. When they do accept help, though, they're extremely grateful, overdoing even this thanks at times. However, when this help is done behind their back—and presented as no big deal—they often feel incredibly touched and offer thanks again and again.

Contrasting Ones to Twos then, we could say that if Ones are the prototypical narcissists, then Twos are the prototypical neurotics. As such, Ones frequently deny wrongdoings they've obviously done, while Twos frequently apologize for things they had nothing to do with. Indeed, even mildly suggesting to a Two that he or she might have done something which hurt someone can often cause this person to painfully self-examine—leading many Twos to make entirely false admissions.

The upside to all this of course is that Twos can gain from their suffering like no other character type. They are also among the most kind, thoughtful, and considerate people you'll ever meet. Given they understand your needs correctly, that is. They're also usually hard workers and can be good self-starters. And their capacity to be a good friend and listener is unequalled in any other character type.

Overall then, the thing to remember about Twos is that, whenever they sense needs, they focus entirely away from themselves and onto the needs of others. And while they are good at owning their wrongdoings and being there for other people—they usually suck at receiving help, holding others accountable, and managing people in general.

It Takes Two Character States to Make a Character Type

In a moment, we're going to look at what Threes are like. Before we do, I need to introduce you to one of the easier aspects of character types—the idea that all character types are made up of a sequence of two character states—a primary state and a secondary state. Here the primary state is like the rising part of the wave of character state experience. Thus it's usually stronger and more intense. Whereas the secondary state is like the falling part of the wave of character state experience. Thus it's usually slower and more laid back.

Now if you look back over the two character type drawings we've looked at so far, you'll find they each have two character states. With Ones, both states are Me states. And with Twos, both states are You states.

With Threes and Fours, however, their primary and secondary states are complementary. For Threes, the primary state is a Me state and the secondary state is a You state. And with Fours, the primary state is a You state and the secondary state is a Me state.

In addition, besides having two character states, each character type also has an identifiable rhythm. This is similar to how we each have an identifiable heartbeat. Only here we're referring to the rhythm of how human beings give and receive. Moreover, because the strength of all giving and receiving is dictated by the strength of these two character states—and because a character type's primary character state is normally stronger than its secondary character state—this rhythm usually begins with more force and finishes with less.

This means, for Ones, a strong Me state is most times followed by a milder Me state. For Twos, a strong You state is usually followed by a milder You state. For Threes, a strong Me state is generally followed by a mild You state. And for Fours, a strong You state is normally followed by a mild Me state.

Now let's look at the first of the two bistate character types—Threes. By this, I mean that Threes have one of each character state—a Me and a You. What are Threes like? We're about to find out.

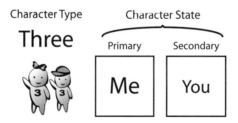

Character Type Three: "Me then You" People

What are character type Three people like? Two of my closest friends, Ed and Lauren, are Threes. Yet when I first met them, they were each quite different in that Lauren's character type was still in the oven, as in, she was what I call a "big Me, little You" Three. Whereas Ed's character type was inverted, meaning, instead of being a normal three—a Me then You—the order of his character states was reversed and intensified, as in he was a "forced to give to YOU, little Me" Three.

Is your head spinning again? If so, just keep breathing and set your questions aside for now. Know we'll address all this stuff about being half-baked and how character types can invert in a bit.

For now, let's just stick to normal Threes. What are they like? In some ways, they're like softer, gentler Ones. Thus occasionally, they do become unable to see other people's needs—especially when they feel mad or hurt or especially needy. On the other hand, Threes can—and most times do—have a good sense of other people's needs. And unlike Ones, they are entirely capable of putting themselves in other people's shoes.

Specifically, Threes have an emphasized Me followed by a weaker You, and this sequence is especially visible in times wherein they make demands on others. In other words, when Threes feel needy, at first, all that matters is getting someone to meet their demands. But once these needs are met, they then feel mild urges to give the person who met these needs something in return.

This makes Threes great folks to work for in that they tend to recognize—and reward—effort, as well as success. They also make good business owners—easily able to ask for what they need and good at negotiating. At the same time, if a boss is giving them what for, expect them to pass this heat on to you without a thought. And if you get into an argument with a three, make sure you're prepared to duck. Three's can blame like no other character type—smart but mean.

As far as regret and remorse, Threes are capable of feeling both. Moreover, under normal circumstances, they always feel these two things in the same order—first regret, then remorse. There are two exceptions. The first is when they are like my friend Lauren was years ago—a half-baked Three. These folks strongly resemble Ones in that they experience the Me part of their character type as powerfully as Ones do and only rarely feel the You part. The second exception is when they are like my friend Ed when I first met him—an inverted Three. These folks begin confrontations feeling intensely remorseful. Then they feel mildly regretful.

To wit, at first, full blown Threes feel bad only about how what they've done has affected them. Then they only feel bad about how what they've done has affected others. That they can feel this way even when they or the other person weren't actually hurt is one of the hallmarks of all four character types. Here I'm referring to how the belief that someone else is feeling needy can sometimes generate false feelings of need in people.

How do these false feelings play out in the four character types?

Ones often feel bad for themselves—even when nothing has happened to them other than that they've witnessed someone else feel needy. Twos often feel bad for the suffering of others even when they're told there was no suffering. Threes can feel similarly bad, but only as a mild, secondary reaction. And Fours can feel bad for others who haven't suffered—then feel bad for themselves for having witnessed this non-existent suffering.

This brings us to our final character type—Fours. Can you guess what they're like? In many ways, they are the inverse of Threes. Even so, like all character types, Fours have their own unique style. Which is what exactly? Let's look.

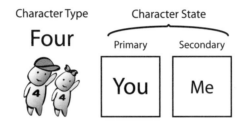

Character Type Four: "You then Me" People

So what are character type Four people like? As you can see from the drawing, a Four is a "You then Me." Fours are similar to Twos then, in that when they're in their primary character state, they experience only other people's needs. However, unlike Twos, when Fours move into their secondary character state, they feel gentle urges to get paid back.

This makes Fours great second-in-command folks. They're understanding and compassionate, but less likely to be taken advantage of than Twos. They also make good first-line to mid-level managers, great high school teachers and college professors, and can be excellent therapists, writers, and classical musicians.

Using Remorse and Regret to Tell the Character Types Apart

Admittedly, telling Fours from Twos can be difficult at times. Because both character types start out in a You state, they can look very much alike. The difference lies primarily in that Twos have a very hard time feeling regret—whereas Fours can easily feel it. Thus like Threes, Fours are capable of feeling both regret and remorse. Only Fours feel these two things in the reverse order from Threes. In other words, while Threes normally feel regret then remorse, Fours feel normally remorse then regret.

This points to yet another way to tell the four character types apart. Because each character type has a recognizable pattern of regret and remorse, asking people questions about situations wherein they might feel these two things is one of the best ways to test for character type. Moreover, if asked without judgment, these questions can reveal a clear distinction between Ones, Twos, Threes, and Fours. Here the four patterns are easy to remember. Ones can feel regret but not remorse. Twos can feel remorse but not regret. Threes can feel both, but they usually feel regret before remorse. And Fours can also feel both, but generally feel remorse before regret.

Of course, the trick to being able to do these tests lies in knowing how to discern between regret and remorse. Know that learning to do this can take more effort than you might at first imagine. Even so, if you keep in mind a few simple ideas, you'll do fine. First and foremost, you need to remember that character type is primarily about giving and getting. Specifically, it's about whose needs people focus on when they themselves feel needy. When people are in a Me state, they focus entirely on their own needs—and cannot experience anyone else's needs. And when people are in a You state, they focus entirely on other people's needs—and cannot experience their own needs.

Now realize that regret and remorse are both mental states which describe how these efforts to give or receive turn out. Here by "mental states," I mean they are both feelings and ideas. Thus regret is a mental state wherein people feel bad about how something they've done has adversely affected their ability to meet their own needs. Whereas remorse is a mental state wherein people feel bad about how something they've done has adversely effected other people's ability to meet their needs.

Even knowing all this, it can be hard at times to tell whose needs a person is focusing on. For example, for the first few years following my discovery of character types, I thought my father was a One. At the time, this made no sense to me as I was certain that to be romantically attracted to someone, the two people's character types had to begin in opposite character states—and my mother was a One. Even so, for years I and everyone in my family had been complaining about how self-centered my father was. Until one Christmas when I flew down to visit him and realized that like my friend Lauren when I first met her, he too had a "half-baked" character type.

What does this mean? Before I tell you, I first need to expand on what I mean by character types "baking." Specifically, I need to address a very important question—how you get your character type?

Where Does Your Character Type Come From?

Back in the dark ages of my late twenties and early thirties, I worked as a UPS driver. At some point, I became friends with a man named Jerry who owned a pizza parlor on my route. Jerry was perhaps a few years older than I was, so we were both still somewhat young. And like young men have been doing for as long as there have been young men, we often exchanged "wisdom stories."

One day our topic turned to—of all things—pizza. Jerry had heard a radio show that morning wherein they were discussing what made the best pizza. He told me they listed the water—as in New York water—and the ingredients—as in the best flour, cheese, and tomatoes. But they also talked about the temperature of the pizza oven. Jerry then expounded on this idea by telling me that in his opinion, the best pizza was cooked longer but at a lower temperature. To him, twenty minute pizza was the best.

What does this have to do with how we get our character type?

Stress equates to the pizza oven temperature. Here I define "stress" as *the experience of adapting to change*. Thus to adults, getting a raise—or moving into a bigger home—is a good thing. But to a baby, these kinds of changes turn up the heat in the home regardless of whether they are good or bad. Not coincidently, one of the assessment tools listed in the psychologist's diagnostic manual reflects this very idea. Here I'm referring to something called, the Global Assessment of Functioning Scale. What's significant about this scale is that some of the examples it gives for highly stressful events are things we would categorize as being good.

For instance, having a baby and having a baby die are both listed as highly stressful events. As are buying a new home and losing a home—and getting a better job and losing a job—and getting married and getting divorced.

What is important to notice then is that stress is more related to the amount of adaptation we're required to make than to any perception of good or bad. This is especially true for babies, as well as for any child who has yet to develop a sense of after-age-seven time.

This means change—rather than goodness or badness—is what determines the temperature of a baby's home. Moreover, once baked, a baby's character type can no more change by being put back in the oven than pizza. Once three minute pizza is baked, it's three minute pizza for life.

Ergo, Ones are like three minute pizza—extremely crispy on the outside, but almost raw on the inside. Babies who become Ones experience a very high degree of stress in their first year of life. Twos are like six minute pizza—not too crispy on the outside, but still pretty soft on the inside. They experience the same amount of stress as babies who become Ones, but it takes them almost two years to accumulate this amount of stress.

Threes are like twelve minute pizza. They experience the same amount of stress as Ones and Twos. However, it takes them almost three years to accumulate this stress. Here Threes are usually cooked more on the outside than on the inside, but pretty well done on the inside. Whereas Fours are like twenty minute pizza. They experience a rather low level of stress throughout their first four years alive. Thus they're cooked pretty evenly all the way through.

Know that in many ways, this idea of how character types bake resembles the classic idea of temperament. Here Fours are normally the most even tempered—and Ones, the most volatile. Unlike temperament though, character type refers only to people's internal urges to give and get. Moreover, while many factors ultimately contribute to how we actually behave, all these behaviors begin with our deciding who—if anyone—has needs, and who should meet these needs. A person's character type determines how these decisions are made.

The Four Half-Baked Character Types

So what is a half-baked character type? Simply put, it's a character type wherein the baking process ended abruptly—so the person's character type never fully developed. Here there are four possibilities—a big Me One, a Me-for-You Two, a big Me-little You Three, and a big You-little Me Four.

Of these four yet-to-finish-baking character types, the easiest to identify is a half-baked One—a One who is basically one big long Me. Like all Ones, everything is always about them. Only in the case of big Me Ones, their self-centeredness is more dramatic—and burdensome—as their entire existence literally revolves around getting people to meet their ever-present and seemingly insatiable needs.

Describing half-baked Twos is a bit more complicated and here a story is in order. This is the story wherein I discovered that people can have as yet unfinished character types. At the time, most of my immediate family lived in Charleston, SC—and as I live in New York, I would normally fly down to visit over the holidays.

Know this visit usually generated a lot of stress in me. Being as I am a Two, deciding on the correct gifts to give people was always hard. To circumvent some of this stress, I had gotten into the habit of taking the whole family out to dinner at one of the city's better restaurants. It felt nice to have everyone together—and it was easier for me to pick up the check than to try to guess what gifts I might give each of them.

Even so, being a Two meant it was hard for me to know which restaurant to take them to. Everyone had their favorite kinds of food, and Charleston has a number of great restaurants. No coincidence, my realization about my father being a half-baked Two came out of my asking him which restaurant he thought we should go to that year.

I knew my stepmother liked seafood. So I suggested a restaurant known for that. But when I asked my father where he thought we should go, he told me to his favorite steakhouse. And when I countered with that his wife preferred seafood, he just lost his words and got quiet.

A few days passed. Again, I asked him which restaurant he thought would be best. Again, he said the steakhouse. I then reminded him that his wife preferred seafood. Whereupon he became rather insistent that we go to the steakhouse—and I lost my words and got quiet.

Long story short, we somehow ended up going to the seafood restaurant. Not because I forced it either. I hadn't brought it up again. And as we waited for the menus, I sat there trying to talk myself past my annoyance at what I was certain was yet another instance of my father's self-centeredness. A moment later though, I leaned over and politely asked him why he had been so insistent that we go to the steakhouse. At which point, my whole sense of who my father was changed. He leaned over and said to me, "because you're on that Atkins diet."

The whole time, my father—a body-first man who had always struggled to find his words—had been focused on my needs over his wife's. Yet all I could see at the time was that he was focused on getting what he wanted. And this was true. He *was* only focused on getting what he wanted. But what he wanted was for me to get what I wanted. Thus he wasn't focused on getting his own needs met. He was focused on me getting my needs met. But because I and everyone else in the family had interpreted his ever-present urgent insistences to mean he had been wanting things for himself, I had totally misread his intentions.

From that night on, I repeatedly observed how he would always focus on the needs of one other person—all the while denying his needs at all costs. Moreover, during the time wherein he was focused on meeting this person's needs, he was oblivious to the needs of all others, including himself.

This is why I sometimes call half-baked Twos, "Me-for-You" Twos. Here the *Me* in Me-for-You refers to how these Twos resemble Ones to all people other than to their currently designated needy person. In other words, any time you are a half-baked Two's currently designated needy person, you will be the recipient of all their giving. But if you are not this person, then you might as well be invisible as far as they're concerned. To them, you simply do not exist as a person who can have needs.

And half-baked Threes? What are they like? As I've told you, I call them "big Me-little You" Threes. Thus like Me-for-You Twos, these folks also bear a strong resemblance to Ones much of the time.

The Four Forms of the Four Character Types
(half-baked, fully baked, inverted, progressed)

(© 2007 Steven Paglierani   The Center for Emergence)

---

a half-baked One:	a big Me One
a One:	a Me (then Me)
an inverted One:	a tyrannical One
a Progressed One:	a Me with a Choice

a half-baked Two:	a Me-for-You Two
a Two:	a You (then You)
an inverted Two:	a self-centered Two
a Progressed Two:	a You with a Choice

a half-baked Three:	a big Me-little You Three
a Three:	a Me then You
an inverted Three:	a forced-to-give-to-You Three
a Progressed Three:	a Me / You with a Choice

a half-baked Four:	a big You-little Me Four
a Four:	a You then Me
an inverted Four:	an urgently Me Four
a Progressed Four:	a You / Me with a Choice

The thing is, even at their worst, their self-centeredness is punctuated by brief instants wherein they momentarily do notice other people's needs. Not that they have any interest in meeting these needs. But still, because even half-baked Threes can at times be aware that other people have needs, it's far less stressful to be around them than to be around Ones.

Finally, we have half-baked Fours—"big You-little Me" Fours. Like half-baked Threes, these folks also—in many ways—resemble Me-for-You Twos. At least until you hear them politely ask, "what about me." This raises yet another way in which to distinguish between the four character types, including the half-baked variety. You look at the strength with which someone asks for their needs. To wit, here are a few brief descriptions of the typical intensities with which the various character types ask for their needs.

• Ones boldly ask for attention and can get angry when you don't respond. Whereas half-baked Ones forcefully demand attention—and will outright punish you if you don't instantly give them what they want.

• Twos go to great lengths to discourage people from giving them attention, getting mad at or even punishing those who offer them help. Half-baked Twos forcefully demand that others give attention to the person they designate as being needy—while loudly insisting that they, themselves, have no needs, moreover, that you're being selfish if you claim you do.

• Threes confidently request that others give them attention—and get upset when these others don't respond. Whereas half-baked Threes boldly insist that others give them attention—and will persist with ever-increasing force until you either give in or they punish you into submission.

• Fours, like Twos, dislike receiving attention—but can occasionally confuse others by suddenly insisting on it. Whereas half-baked Fours, like half-baked Twos, forcefully demand that you give your full attention to their currently designated needy person—while at the same time, getting insulted if someone suggests they too have needs.

How Knowing About Character Types Can Benefit You

How does knowing a person's character type benefit you?

For one thing, it redefines both selfishness and selflessness.

Ordinarily, these two words are moral judgments as to whether people act wrongly or rightly with regard to giving and receiving. Whereas the idea of character type blamelessly accounts for people's biases and blindnesses in and around giving and receiving—giving us a way to bypass our moral judgments by seeing both "giving to others" and "getting others to give to us" as blameless acts which, at times, can be overdone or underdone.

In addition, the idea of character type shows us that regardless of who we are, at the heart of everything we do lie inherent biases as to who can have needs—and who should meet these needs. These biases then explain why we can sometimes seem to ignore—or even be completely blind to—our own needs or to the needs of others. As well as that the forces underlying these biases are neither ignorance—nor malice—nor injury.

Another natural force which the idea of character type explains is the attractions which occur between people—both romantic attractions and friendly attractions. Here common sense tells us that—in romance, opposites attract—and that in friendships, like-minded folks attract. And for the most part, these beliefs are true. But why? It turns out that your character type is the principle filter though which everyone you come in contact with is sorted into one of these two groups. For obvious reasons, I call the relationships which fall into the romance category, your family-making relationships—and the relationships which fall into the friend category, your friendship-making relationships.

What's the difference?

Start with this. All people have a character type—and all people have relationships—even when these relationships are extremely dysfunctional or entirely imaginary. Yet despite the many ways two people may or may not fit together, the driving principle behind this fit is rather simple. And seemingly cliché. In family-making relationships, opposite character types attract—and in friend-making relationships, like character types attract.

Know that when I say opposite and like, I am not merely referring to having common likes and dislikes. Rather I'm referring to the primary character state in each of the two people's character types. Either their character types both begin in the same character state—or they do not. Here only people whose character types start in the opposite character state can have true family-making relationships (one person's character type starts in a Me state—and one in a You state). And only people whose character types start in the same state can have true friendship-making relationships (two Me-first character types—or two You-firsts).

What does this mean out in the real world?

Ones are more romantically attracted to Twos than to any other character type. And vice versa. And Three's are more romantically attracted to Fours—and Fours to Threes. Whereas people with the same character type feel more drawn to have friendships with each other, and to a lesser degree, with those whose character type starts in the same state as theirs.

Are there ever exceptions to this family-making, friendship-making relationship rule? Yes. But even here people's character type is what underlies these attractions. For instance, you can sometimes be romantically attracted to someone—then have this attraction disappear. This sometimes happens when you meet someone at a time wherein either their character type—or yours—is "inverted." Meaning what exactly? Let's see.

Temporary Changes to Your Character Type: Inversions

In the case of Ones and Twos, inversion means simply that their typical urges intensify. This looks similar to what half-baked Ones and half-baked Twos look like. Only in this case, the condition is temporary—not permanent—as in the temporary state of being tyrannical Ones and self-centered Twos. In the case of the two bistate character types, however, inversion reverses the order of their primary and secondary character states. Here Threes temporarily become intense caricatures of Fours, as in "forced-to-give-to You, then mousy Me" Threes—and Fours become intense caricatures of Threes, as in "urgently Me, then tentative You" Fours.

The thing to notice this time is how these changes to people's primary character state affect the kinds of relationships they can have. For instance, when Twos become inverted, they can often become friends with Ones—as for all intents and purposes, their primary character states appear identical to all others except to the Two's currently designated needy person.

Likewise inverted Threes can—and often do—fall in love with half-baked Ones. Here a good example would the relationship my friend, Ed, was in when I first met him. As I mentioned previously, back then, Ed was an inverted Three—a forced-to-give-to You, then mousy Me Three. At the time, he was madly in love with a big Me One. Truly a match filled with falls from heaven into hell.

At the same time, the character type of Ed's future wife, Inetta, was also inverted. In her case, she was a self-centered Two whose designated needy person—her husband, Carl—was also a big Me One. Yet another example of how inversions can affect romantic attraction.

All this changed however when Ed and Inetta met and fell in love two years later. How? Both Ed's and Inetta's character types righted themselves. This redefined their sense of romantic attraction—Ed became a normal Me then You Three—and Inetta a normal Two. And not long afterwards, they both left their partners and married each other.

Know these kinds of changes also explain the times wherein people who were intensely attracted to each other at the beginning of a romantic relationship fall out of lust—the "I still love you, but only like a brother or sister" syndrome.

Finally, as complicated as all this may sound, in truth, there are only four inverted character types. As I said, there are tyrannical Ones—self-centered Twos—forced-to-give Threes—and urgently Me Fours. Here the demanding nature of Ones becomes intensely punitive whenever people don't give them what they want—the giving nature of Twos becomes entirely focused on giving to one person to the exclusion of all others—the insistent nature of Threes begins to resemble self-centered Twos who demand that you take what they're offering—and the gentle nature of Fours starts to resemble tyrannical Ones who have somehow learned to feel remorse.

As for how you can tell inverted character types from half-baked character types, know we'll be discussing this in depth in Book III: chapter eleven, when we explore Understanding Relationships.

For now, the thing to keep in mind is that half-baked character types have never been fully baked—while inversions happen only to fully baked types. Moreover, the main thing to take away here is that your character type is the foundation for the whole rest of your personality. Thus becoming familiar with all the possible incarnations of character types is essential to having healthy relationships—especially when it comes to discerning the personal truth about these relationships. And lest you think this is just too much to learn, realize, the whole enchilada fits in this one section of the book. Learn what's in these few pages and you'll feel like you've wearing the first pair of eye glasses to ever enable you to see people clearly.

Progressed Character Types: Being Needy With a Choice

In Book III, we'll talk a lot about how all personal truths form geometric patterns—and how knowing this can help you to recognize when a truth is complete. One of these patterns is a pair of crossed continuums, wherein the second continuum derives from the first (e.g. black to white, black white to white black).

Applying this pattern to what I've told you about the various forms of character types, right away, you should see that something is missing. To wit, I've only described three forms so far. A whole truth must include four. There are four wise men, remember?

So what is the fourth form of character types?

Essentially, it's the state wherein you consciously alternate between your fully-formed character type—and being connected to others. Here by "consciously," I mean you are fully aware of your character type and can tell when you're inverted *and* can also choose more times than not to make connecting more important than getting your needs met.

This is not to say you don't care about getting your needs met. You do. But one of the greatest ironies revealed by the idea of character types is that the more you focus on connecting—the more your needs get met.

Admittedly, learning to think this way can feel quite counter-intuitive. Logically, the less you focus on your needs, the less they should be met. Here again, we'll talk a lot about this idea in Book III: chapter eleven when we talk about relationships.

For now, just try to keep in mind that the fourth form which character types can take holds the path to the spiritual realm. Meaning what? Again, you'll find out in Book III: chapter eleven.

A Brief Review of the Four Character Types

Does this seem like way too much to learn? In reality, it's not. People's character type merely describes their default assumptions as to who has needs—and who should meet these needs. Moreover, these two assumptions always derive from people's experience of their primary and secondary character states. Here being in a Me state causes people to assume that the needs they feel exist only in themselves, not in others—and that in order to feel better, they must get others to meet their needs. And being in a You state causes people to assume that the needs they feel exist only in others, not in themselves—and that in order to feel better, they must meet these people's needs.

As for how this looks out in the real world, Ones experience the sequence of Me then Me. This means they assume they are the only ones with needs. They also assume that other people, not themselves, should meet these needs. Thus like infants, Ones are blind to the needs of others and assume that others should—and will—met their needs. And if this doesn't happen, then they protest loudly and feel ignored, wronged, and unloved.

Twos experience the opposite sequence—You then You. Thus Twos can see other people's needs fine. But they're blind to their own needs—even when they're pointed out to them. This means Twos live as if only other people have needs—and that if they don't meet these needs for them, then their needs will go unmet.

At the same time, Twos, more times than not, feel uncomfortable when people offer them help or try to return the favor. Indeed, most Twos prefer to have their needs remain unmet rather than burden others. God forbid they inconvenience anyone else.

Then we have Threes. Threes experience a combination of what Ones and Twos feel. First, Threes see only their own needs. Then they see only the needs of others. This means Threes have both sets of assumptions—but never at the same time. First they assume that the neediness they feel exists only in them—that only they have needs and that someone else should meet these needs. Then they assume that the neediness they feel is someone else's—and that they are responsible for meeting this other person's needs.

Lastly, Fours experience this same sequence, only in reverse—the sequence of You then Me. Thus at first, Fours see only other people's needs, then they only see their own. This means Fours assume that other people will need their help. They then assume these others will reciprocate and automatically return the favor. Unfortunately, this assumption doesn't always come to pass. Thus it often results in hard feelings. For instance, despite being grateful, most Me-first people don't reciprocate.

In addition to these four fully-baked character types, there are three alternate forms character types can take—half-baked, inverted, and progressed. Half-baked character types are the immature form which comes from being taken out of the oven abruptly. Inverted character types are the fully-baked form under stress. And progressed character types are the fully-baked form with options.

Finally, we have the idea of how long character types last. Here the fully-baked and progressed forms are permanent—while the inverted and half-baked forms are temporary.

Overall then, the main points to remember are that layer 7—first and foremost—describes what happens to people when they feel needy. And Layer 7's first sublayer—character type—describes people's urges to give and or get when in the presence of neediness.

Know these urges are always unidirectional. Either they seem to be coming from inside the person or from outside the person—but never from both places at once. Moreover, these assumptions as to who the needy person is—and who should meet this person's needs—always derive from how people's character states fit together. As do all interpersonal relationships. Two Me-firsts or two You-firsts? A possible friendship. A Me-first with a You-first? A possible romance.

The Idea of Good and Bad Character Types

Back in chapter five, I promised I'd tell you about a seven year old who taught parts of the wise men's personality theory to his class. Obviously, this is far from the norm. What seven year old is even interested in such a thing? At the same time, it points to one of the more important ideas to know about character types—the idea that there are no good or bad ones. They all have their good and bad side.

The story involves my friend Lauren's son Jacob again, now quite bit older than he was at the time the dirt-eating story took place. Indeed, what had triggered this event was that Lauren had had a talk with Jacob about his character type, hoping to get him to see his "three-ness." Unfortunately, not long after this, Jacob began to equate being a One with being selfish and bad. So one day when Lauren picked him up from Hebrew school, she wasn't surprised when Jacob's teacher told her that he had been teaching his class about Ones, Twos, Threes, and Fours—and that the Pharaoh was a One!

Okay. On the one hand, this is amazing. A seven year old teaching character types. At the same time, it's not surprising. Most people—when they first hear about character types—make value judgments as to which character type is the best and which is the worst. Despite these first impressions however, in truth no character type is better than any other. They're just different. And yes, I realize it may take time to accept this as true. Even so, all four character types have their up side and down. It's simply a matter of how well a particular character type fits a particular situation.

For instance, take Twos. From what I've told you so far, they can sound self-sacrificing and altruistic. And they are. However, they also tend to do these things at their own—and others—expense. Conversely, Ones can sound like the least self-sacrificing and least altruistic. And this too is true. However, if you were a soldier in a war and your commanding officer was a Two—the likelihood you'd get killed because of indecision would be far greater than if your commanding officer was a One.

At the same time, if your commanding officer was a One and the mission was a suicide mission, the likelihood the mission would be a go would be far greater than if your commanding officer was a Two.

So which is better? You tell me.

The point of course is that there are life situations wherein each character type excels and each is a fish out of water—yet another benefit of knowing people's character type. Moreover, nowhere does knowing this benefit you more than in classroom settings wherein matching teachers to their students can optimize the whole learning process.

Equally valuable is using your character type to make career choices. Even from the little I've told you, it should be obvious that there are good matches and bad. Know we'll be looking at this in detail in Book III: chapter twelve, when we talk about finding personal truth in learning and career settings.

This said, the thing to see is that no character type—in and of itself—is bad or good. Each character type simply adapts better to certain life situations—and worse to others.

Character Types Exist in Only Seven of the Ten Layers

Before moving on to the second sublayer, social priorities, I need to mention one last thing—the idea that there are only seven Layers wherein your character type has an effect. After all, needs do not come into existence until Layer 7. Thus your character type does not begin to exist until you reach Layer 7.

This means, whenever you're in one of the three Layers which nest within Layer 7, for all intents and purposes, you have no character type.

For instance, in Layer 8—universal non-existence—you experience the total absence of personal experience. Thus you can't very well experience your character type, as you cannot feel needy. And in Layers 9 and 10, you are connected. Thus you cannot experience suffering of any kind—including the suffering known as "pure needs."

Know that when we come to the part where I tell you about the personality tests, it will be very important to keep this in mind. All but one of these tests look to define an aspect of people's Layer 7. Thus, in order to get valid test results, the person being tested cannot be connecting to nor disconnecting from anyone while the questions are being asked, as this will make the person unable to experience a need.

Fortunately, meeting this criteria is not too difficult. All the test questions center on making decisions about needs. Moreover, we humans have a seemingly inexhaustible amount of needs. Indeed, the Buddhists teach that desire—which is just another word for need—is the underlying source of human suffering, and this is not far from the truth. Besides the pain of disconnections, pure needs are the most potent form of human suffering. And the most visible.

Now let's look at how we define these needs. What kinds of needs can we feel? Curiously enough, what we're about to look at offers some powerful insights into what underlies our main interests in life—including which subjects we'll likely excel at in school and which career we'll be happiest in. Sound intriguing? Useful? You have no idea.

Section Two

Social Priorities: Your Core Personality—Part Two

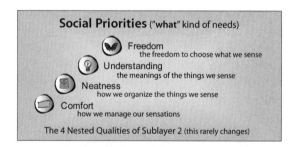

The Four Social Priorities: What Kind of Needs?

In the first sublayer of layer 7, we figure out whose needs we should focus on—our own or someone else's. Thus character type is essentially about two things—"who" has needs and "who" should meet those needs. Once we know these things, we then move on to the second sublayer of layer 7 wherein we determine "what kind of needs" we're dealing with. Here we use our social priorities to divide all needs into four categories.

In one sense then, the four social priorities are our four basic categories of needs. But they're also the four "holy grails" of human nature in that they are the four things we believe will eliminate our needs.

Why call these categories, "social priorities," and how do they come into being? To see, we'll need to take another look at what I've been calling, "needs." Only this time, we're going to discuss needs in the everyday sense. And yes, as a theorist, my formal way of describing needs is to say they are what people feel when they experience disconnects. But how do normal folks define their needs? Let's see.

The Four Kinds of Needs

To begin with, all needs are rooted in sensation itself. We can't experience a need—or even imagine a need—if we can't sense it. Moreover, all unmet needs in some way resemble having an itch. Some sort of unpleasant sensation creates the "need" in us to change something.

What kinds of unpleasant sensations do we look to change? There are four, exactly. Voiced as theoretical categories, they are Sickness (internal physical need)—Chaos (external physical need)—Nescience (internal mental need)—and Weakness (external mental need). And voiced as real world categories, they are Discomfort (internal physical need)—Disorganization (external physical need)—Ignorance (internal mental need)—and Dependence (external mental need).

Not surprisingly, each of these four classes of unmet needs has a corresponding class of met needs. Here "met needs" is just another way to refer to the goals of the four social priorities—the four holy grails I mentioned. Voiced theoretically, the goals of four social priorities are to master Sensation, Organization, Meaning, and Free Will. And voiced as real world goals, the four holy grails are Comfort, Neatness, Understanding, and Freedom.

As for how all this fits together, in theory, when we experience Sickness, mastering Sensation becomes our goal. When we experience Chaos, mastering Organization becomes our goal. When we experience Nescience, mastering Meaning becomes our goal. And when we experience Weakness, mastering Free Will becomes our goal. Or voiced as real world goals, when we experience Discomfort, Comfort becomes our goal. When we experience Disorganization, Neatness becomes our goal. When we experience Ignorance, Understanding becomes our goal. And when we experience Dependence, Freedom becomes our goal.

Overall, the thing to pay attention to here is what we do with these four social priorities. Whenever we experience unpleasant sensations—either physically or mentally—we turn to our social priorities to define the problem. Moreover, we each employ all four strategies. We differ only in the way we prioritize them. Hence my calling them "priorities."

The Four Categories of Needs
(both in theory and in the real world)
(© 2007 Steven Paglierani The Center for Emergence)

The Theoretical Categories of Needs

(unmet need)   (met need)

(internal physical need)
Sickness   the Mastery of Sensation

(external physical need)
Chaos   the Mastery of Organization

(internal mental need)
Nescience   the Mastery of Meaning

(external mental need)
Weakness   the Mastery of Free Will

The Real World Categories of Needs

(unmet need)   (met need)

(internal physical need)
Discomfort   Comfort

(external physical need)
Disorganization   Neatness

(internal mental need)
Ignorance   Understanding

(external mental need)
Dependence   Freedom

So what are needs?

As I've said, theoretically, they are the unpleasant urges we feel each time we disconnect from someone or something. Thus in the real world, *needs* are simply the pressure to resolve the unpleasant experience of disconnecting. Moreover, since all disconnections result in this same kind of pressure, in effect, each time we experience a disconnect, we feel the "need" to change something—either inside ourselves or outside ourselves.

Remember too that I've previously defined stress as *the experience of adapting to change.* Thus since needs are the pressure to change something unpleasant, in a real sense, needs equate to stress. Here as unmet needs, the four social priorities become the four ways to define stress—and as met needs, they become the four goals we hope will help us to adapt to change.

Finally, it should come as no surprise that each wise man has his preferred method of responding to needs. The materialist wise man prefers Comfort—the mastery of Sensation. The empirical wise man prefers Neatness—the mastery of Organization. The rationalist wise man prefers Understanding—the mastery of Meaning. And the spiritual wise mans prefers Freedom—the mastery of Free Will.

Why Needs are a "Social" Experience

At this point, it should be easy to see why I'm calling these goals, "priorities." But why am I calling them, "social?" Do we experience needs only while in the presence of other people? Or can we experience a need alone?

The answer to this question may surprise you. It turns out that you cannot experience a need without being in the presence of another person. And yes, it's obvious you can be physically alone and still feel needy. But as it turns out, you cannot experience neediness and be both physically and mentally alone.

So who else is there when you're physically alone? Why it's you, of course. And to see how this works, take a look at the diagram on following page, the one titled, "Why Needs are Social." In it, you'll find three circles, each representing a perspective wherein you feel needy.

Let's start with the circle on the left. What does this circle represent?

In this, the "observer" circle, you become aware that you are observing two people—one feeling scarcity, and the other feeling abundance. Moreover, when I say "two people," I mean that you're either literally observing two people—or you're observing yourself at two different times. Either way, whenever you're needy, you're observing two people.

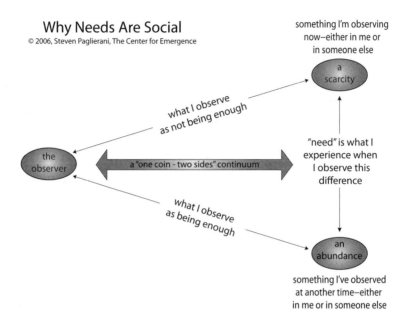

Why Needs Are Social
© 2006, Steven Paglierani, The Center for Emergence

something I'm observing
now—either in me or
in someone else

a scarcity

what I observe
as not being enough

the observer

a "one coin - two sides" continuum

"need" is what I
experience when
I observe this
difference

what I observe
as being enough

an abundance

something I've observed
at another time—either
in me or in someone else

Why must you be observing two people in order to experience a need?

Because all needs derive from the experience of losing a connection, even if this disconnection is merely imaginary. Moreover, you must have been connected to someone in order to disconnect. So in order to feel needy, you must experience a disconnect through the eyes of two people—the one who formerly felt connected, and the one who now feels needy.

How do we pull this off when we're physically alone?

All normal humans are capable of imagining themselves and someone else simultaneously. In addition, those who can sense things in after-age-seven time can imagine themselves in two different times as well. Either way, to feel a need, you must be doing one of these things. Either you must be sensing two different people, or sensing yourself in two different times.

What is it you are observing in these two people? To see, notice what's happening in the upper right circle. Here you're observing someone experiencing scarcity. Either this person feels that he lacks something or he feels that he's running out of something.

Now notice what's happening in the lower right circle. Here you're observing someone feeling what most people would call an abundance of the thing person number one is lacking or losing.

Know the whole trick to understanding this lies in having a personally true meaning for the words "scarcity" and "abundance." The trick here is to place these words on a continuum of complementary opposites. Moreover, it turns out these two words are not complementary opposites. What would make this continuum whole then? Let's see.

The Continuum of Personal Needs
© 2002, Steven Paglierani, The Center for Emergence

the experience of having
enough of something
(abundance is what I see whenever I'm connected)

excess — abundance — scarcity

the experience of
having too much
of something

"need" is what I
experience when
I observe this difference

the experience of
having too little
of something

Using Scarcity and Excess to Define Abundance

Let's start by looking at scarcity and abundance again, only this time we'll use one of the wise men's favorite tools for finding personal truth—a continuum. I've titled this one, "The Continuum of Personal Needs." What does it represent?

To begin with, this continuum references three words—not two—as it extends from scarcity through abundance to excess.

To what do these three words refer?

Scarcity refers to the unpleasant experience of having too little of something—not having enough Comfort, not having enough Neatness, not having enough Understanding, or not having enough Freedom. Excess then refers to the unpleasant experience of having too much of something—too much Comfort, too much Neatness, too much Understanding, or too much Freedom.

The thing to see here is how scarcity and excess are actually two sides of the same coin. This makes them complementary opposites. Moreover just as we cannot have one-sided coins, we cannot feel scarcity without also feeling an excess somewhere in the picture.

Why don't we see this excess? Because more times than not, we focus on the scarcity and don't notice this excess at the time.

Where does abundance come in then?

I define "abundance" as *the pleasant experience of having enough of all four needs*—having enough Comfort, having enough Neatness, having enough Understanding, and having enough Freedom. Clearly, this is not how most people would define abundance. Most people see abundance as having an excess. However, abundance can't refer to having an excess as having an excess means there is a scarcity somewhere else—and how could something be both scarce and abundant.

This makes excess the complementary opposite of scarcity, and abundance the mysterious experience which lies between these two states—the illusive experience of being satisfied; the experience of having enough.

Why call abundance, illusive and mysterious? Because like being "on time," it exists only in theory. In other words, with being on time, you can either be early and the on time state passes through you later, or you can be late and miss this mythical moment. Either way, in the real world, you cannot actually be on time. You can only be early or late.

Does what I'm saying seem counterintuitive? Admittedly, it is. We are asked to be on time all the time, no pun intended. In truth though, even if you synchronize your watches, in the real world, it's nearly impossible to be on time. Either you can be early and in position when the on-time moment comes. Or you can miss this moment and be late. Thus to be on time in the real world, you must be early.

Having abundance is similar. It's more a description of something you feel in spiritual moments than any literal reality, albeit, I may need a moment to explain why.

Scarcity and Excess as the Two Ways We Perceive Needs

What makes us feel like things are scarce or excessive? Only one thing. Our perception of how needy we are in the present moment. Moreover, being as we're talking about perception rather than reality, these ideas hold true even if it turns out that we had exactly what we needed.

Said in other words, the scarcity, excess, and abundance I'm referring to here do not necessarily refer to anything literally true. Rather, they refer only to our perceptions of these three states.

And if these perceptions turn out to be inaccurate? Then, oh well. Since the needs I'm referring to here are our "personal" needs, these needs may or may not exist literally. Indeed, more times than not, our perceptions of these three states do not relate to any literal reality.

Abundance as How We Perceive Connection

The point of course is that scarcity and excess are just two more ways to refer to unmet needs. The things you "need" are the things you feel are scarce and so, need more of—or excessive and so, need less of. This makes abundance just another way to refer to the experience of having no needs. Thus it's just another way to refer to the experience of being in Layers 10 or 9—the feeling of being connected.

Can you see this yet—that abundance is just another way to refer to how you feel when you have no needs? If not, then think back to the last time you felt abundance. Can you recall how it felt? In truth, you cannot feel abundance without feeling connected. Indeed, the moment you connect to someone or something, your needs seem to vanish. And in this moment, you feel as if you have—and have always had—everything you need.

No coincidence people who seek spiritual experiences frequently describe their successes this way. They feel as if they finally have enough of what they need—that they are enough, that life is good enough, or something similar. In a way then, the continuum of personal needs explains clichès like, "you always want what you can't have" and "the grass is always greener." Both these expressions refer to what it feels like to simultaneously be observing both scarcity and abundance.

The reason I'm telling you all this, of course, is to point out that all neediness is a social experience. In other words, to experience need, we must be observing two people who are disconnected from each other. Otherwise, we cannot experience need.

Seeing Unmet Needs as "Social Distractions"

So far, I've referred to the unpleasant experiences which follow disconnections in several ways. The four wise men call these experiences, "unmet needs." Psychotherapists and medical folks call them "stress." And Hindus and Buddhists call them "desires" or "the hungry ghosts." Yet another way to refer to these experiences, though, is the way educators refer to them—as "distractions."

Why call unmet needs, "distractions?" It's simple. Can you have an itch and not feel distracted? No one I know can. Thus a basic quality of all unmet needs is that they impair your ability to mentally and physically focus. They distract you.

Realize, this impaired ability to focus is just another way to refer to the inability to connect, yet another reference to needs being "social." In effect, we seek the met-needs versions of the four social priorities (comfort, neatness, understanding, freedom) as a means to restore our ability to connect to each other. Moreover, nowhere does this matter more than in classroom situations wherein we must connect to a teacher in order to learn. This in fact is the idea which led me to discover the four social priorities, albeit, at the time, I had no idea Layer 7 held anything other than the four character types. Indeed, my goal at the time seemed entirely unrelated to character types and needs. I was looking for the underlying nature of learning disabilities. Did I find it? You tell me.

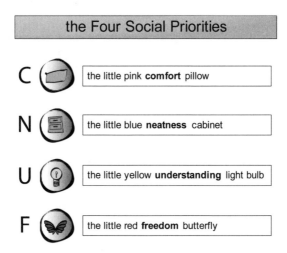

the Four Social Priorities

C the little pink **comfort** pillow

N the little blue **neatness** cabinet

U the little yellow **understanding** light bulb

F the little red **freedom** butterfly

Seeking the Root Cause of Learning Disabilities

Some years back I was attending a three-day workshop on using visualization to heal and by the second morning, it was clear to me that the workshop was going to be a great disappointment. Talk about feeling needy. And angry. Rather than wallow in self pity though, I decided to try to gain from my suffering. So I set a goal for myself. I decided that before the workshop was done, I would try to discover the underlying nature of learning disabilities. What is it that interferes with our ability to learn? Do you know? I wanted to find out.

Can you imagine making such an extravagant promise to yourself? In hindsight, this decision sounds insane, even to me. Never underestimate the power of well-directed anger however. Pointed in the right direction, anger can be a powerful agent for change.

So there I was, sitting a few rows back from the speaker, frantically taking dictation from the four wise men and scribbling on a white pad. Those who know me know I'm constantly drawing on one of these pads, or writing in a notebook, or sketching diagrams on napkins. No surprise then that two days later, I'd filled an entire pad with what I now believe is the nature of what prevents people from learning.

At the heart of this lies the idea that there are only four things which can prevent learning, at least in normal people. These four things are what I have been calling the four social priorities. Voiced as theoretical distractions, they are Sickness (uncontrolled sensations)—Chaos (uncontrolled things), Nescience (uncontrolled meanings)—and Weakness (uncontrolled free will). And voiced as real world distractions, they are Discomfort (being distracted by not having enough Comfort)—Disorganization (being distracted by not having enough Neatness)—Ignorance (being distracted by not having enough Understanding)—and Dependence (being distracted by not having enough Freedom).

The Four Wise Men's Symptom Tool as a Route to Discovery

How did I arrive at this conclusion? It's pretty simple, actually. I thought about the four worst case scenarios with regard to conditions which impair learning—Kanner's Autism, OCD, Asperger's Syndrome, and ADHD. Then rather than treat these four conditions as brokenness or diseases, I used another one of the four wise men's favorite truth finding tools to explore them—the idea that *all symptoms are a compulsive replaying of what was once a normal, healthy, natural response to life.*

Can you see what makes this approach different? Rather than limit the search to what is broken, you focus on finding a similar—but normal—process which occurs in all personalities. This assumes that what you're looking for is some otherwise normal process which has gotten stuck in an endless loop, making it compulsively replay—in predictable ways, but at unpredictable times—in the personality of the afflicted person. This endless loop is then assumed to be the mechanism underlying the condition. Thus as soon as you find a normal condition which resembles the painful condition, you understand the nature of the painful condition. It's either an excess or a scarcity of the normal condition.

Realize this focus on what something looks like violates an aspect of the primary drive in human nature, specifically, the drive to avoid future suffering by determining the cause of this suffering. We'll spend all of Book III: chapter eight exploring this drive. Even without having read this chapter though, it should be obvious why I'm saying this. Indeed, we've already spoken at length about how impossible it is to track the data necessary to determine cause. Rain clouds and super computers, remember? Thus to understand symptoms, we must limit our focus to what we can track and measure—the natural fractal patterns.

Ironically, the more we can picture a painful condition, the more we can zero in on the causes. And yes, I said causes, not cause. Why? Because all people exhibit the fractal patterns underlying Kanner's Autism, OCD, Asperger's Syndrome, and ADHD. Normal people just exhibit these patterns to a lesser degree. Moreover since the fractal patterns underlying these conditions always repeat differently, the so-called causes of these four conditions will always repeat differently even within the same person.

This means the actual causes of these conditions will forever remain outside of the scope of what we can measure—even when these conditions are clearly recognizable. Thus no single set of conditions will ever prove to be the cause of these four conditions—nor of any painful condition really. Indeed, this holds true even in cases wherein severe biological symptoms are present. No two cases will ever be the same. Thus regardless of how well we can generalize the symptoms of a painful condition, the exact causes of each specific instance of this condition will always remain unknowable. And this includes the causes of the four conditions I've just named—Kanner's Autism, OCD, Asperger's Syndrome, and ADHD.

What the Four Wise Men's Symptom Tool Reveals

So what can the wise men's symptom tool teach us about these four conditions? For one thing that each of them is indeed a compulsive replaying of what was once a normal, healthy response to life.

For instance, take Kanner's Autism. What compulsively replays in people with Kanner's Autism? The need to master sensation. People with Kanner's Autism feel compelled to master their five senses.

When is this focus normal? From birth to about six months old. We all look to master sensation during this time.

How does one end up with Kanner's Autism?

The precise causes are and will remain unknown, certainly for each individual case—the data in the rain cloud problem again. Fortunately, we need not know these causes in order to offer help, as the four wise men's symptom tool reveals the mechanism underlying this condition—an interrupted mastery of sensation. This is what we must address.

In effect, Kanner's Autism is simply a significant impairment of this particular learning process. Thus our interventions must focus primarily on helping these folks to master their five senses—and only afterwards on helping them to master doing things in life (neatness), knowing what things mean (understanding), and acquiring free will (freedom).

What about OCD? What learning process underlies this condition?

Here we're talking about learning to arrange the things we sense. Babies normally spend from about age six months to about one year old trying to master this ability. However, if something significantly impairs this learning process, then they end up with OCD. Thus OCD is the compulsion to master arranging the things you sense.

What about Asperger's Syndrome? What learning process underlies this condition? Here we're talking about learning the meanings of the things you sense. Children normally spend most of their second year of life focused on mastering this ability. However, if a child gets stuck in an endless loop during this learning process, then he or she ends up with Asperger's Syndrome. Thus Asperger's Syndrome is the compulsive need to learn the meaning of everything you sense.

What about ADHD? What learning process do these children get stuck in? This time we're talking about the ability two to four year olds normally focus on—free will. Here by "free will," I'm referring to the need to be free of having to master the first three abilities—sensation, organization, and meaning. And if something significantly impairs this learning process, then you end up with ADHD.

The Four Distractions as the Four Learning Disabilities

The thing to see of course is how each of these compulsions resembles a skipping phonograph record "compulsively" replaying a small section of what may, in fact, be beautiful music. Even the most beautiful music endlessly replayed will eventually drive you to distraction. Thus while preventing these four conditions does matter and so, finding their "causes" has it's benefits, our ability to help individuals with these conditions more relies on determining the nature of what's wrong with these folks than on determining what caused these conditions—more on putting out the fire than on worrying how the fire began.

The main thing to come away with then is what these four conditions have in common. They each involve the compulsion to master a specific kind of learning. This compulsion then impairs the person's ability to connect with teachers and socially normal peers—especially in learning situations which provoke these needs. Hence my associating these conditions with learning disabilities and my calling them, "distractions."

Finally, since none of us ever completely masters these four abilities, we all have some degree of impairment with regard to these four distractions. Complete mastery would mean we'd never feel needy, and no normal person ever achieves this, not even the Dalai Lama. This means we all have things in common with folks with Kanner's Autism, OCD, Asperger's, and ADHD. We differ only in the degree to which these classes of needs distract us. Which is why, when people off-handedly remark that they must in part be autistic, have OCD, have Asperger's, or have ADHD, they're right.

The Twenty-Four Social Priority Groupings
(the twenty-four ways we can prioritize our needs)
(© 2007 Steven Paglierani The Center for Emergence)

Group 01	Group 02	Group 03	Group 04	Group 05	Group 06
Comfort	Comfort	Comfort	Comfort	Comfort	Comfort
Neatness	Neatness	Understanding	Understanding	Freedom	Freedom
Understanding	Freedom	Freedom	Neatness	Neatness	Understanding
Freedom	Understanding	Neatness	Freedom	Understanding	Neatness

Group 07	Group 08	Group 09	Group 10	Group 11	Group 12
Neatness	Neatness	Neatness	Neatness	Neatness	Neatness
Understanding	Understanding	Freedom	Freedom	Comfort	Comfort
Freedom	Comfort	Comfort	Understanding	Understanding	Freedom
Comfort	Freedom	Understanding	Comfort	Freedom	Understanding

Group 13	Group 14	Group 15	Group 16	Group 17	Group 18
Understanding	Understanding	Understanding	Understanding	Understanding	Understanding
Comfort	Comfort	Neatness	Neatness	Freedom	Freedom
Neatness	Freedom	Freedom	Comfort	Comfort	Neatness
Freedom	Neatness	Comfort	Freedom	Neatness	Comfort

Group 19	Group 20	Group 21	Group 22	Group 23	Group 24
Freedom	Freedom	Freedom	Freedom	Freedom	Freedom
Comfort	Comfort	Neatness	Neatness	Understanding	Understanding
Neatness	Understanding	Understanding	Comfort	Comfort	Neatness
Understanding	Neatness	Comfort	Understanding	Neatness	Comfort

In other words, beneath all neediness lie the four social priorities we all use to define our needs—the need for comfort, the need for neatness, the need for understanding, and the need for freedom. Here we all focus on meeting these four classes of needs, and differ only in when and how much. Indeed, should these urges become so pervasive that they impair your ability to connect, you then end up with one of the four learning disabilities—Kanner's Autism, OCD, Asperger's Syndrome, or ADHD. Hence each of these conditions is merely a distorted and exaggerated version of one of the four normal social priorities.

How Connection Bypasses the Four Distractions

What if you have one of these conditions and you enter layer 9 or 10? Amazingly, these conditions cease to exist. Thus if you have ADHD or Asperger's—and if you connect to a teacher—in effect, you no longer have ADHD or Asperger's. At least, not while this connection exists.

How does this happen? It's simple really. Picture the onion. Needs exist only from Layer 7 out. Thus if you're in a layer which nests inside of Layer 7, for all intents and purposes, you have no needs. Nor wounds for that matter. Wounds exist only from Layer 6 out.

The Twenty-Four Normal Social Priority Groupings

So far, what I've told you is that we each have the same four basic needs—the need for Comfort, the need for Neatness, the need for Understanding, and the need for Freedom. We differ only in how we prioritize these four needs. Moreover if you were to list the possible arrangements of these four needs in a hierarchal order, you'd find there are twenty-four core social priority groupings.

Mathematicians will immediately see this as the permutation of 4 things taken four at a time—4 factorial. Or, 4 x 3 x 2 x 1 = 24. But even non-mathematicians can easily count these twenty-four core possibilities. Know that each of us falls into one of these twenty-four groups. Hence, after your mind body preference and your character type, your social priority grouping is the most significant part of your core personality—the part of you that makes you, you.

How do we end up with our particular social priority grouping? Do we choose this using reason? Is it the luck of the draw? Is it something that changes situation by situation?

Actually, it is none of these things. Like character type, stress bakes our social priorities into us during the first four years of life. However, unlike character type wherein the period of highest stress finishes the baking process—with social priorities, we prioritize these categories based on which strategy led to the least stress.

For instance, say the period wherein you were under the least stress was age birth to six months. It's likely Comfort would be your highest priority. And if the period wherein you were under the least stress was age one to two, then your highest social priority would likely be Understanding.

Know this idea is borne out in real life in that when we are under the greatest stress, our lowest social priority rises to the top. And as we're about to see, these temporary changes to the ordering of our social priorities can happen in three ways—one-quarter (stressed), one-half (fully inverted), and three-quarter (righting).

The Seventy-Two Abnormal Social Priority Groupings

Like your character type, then, which can get inverted by stress, so your social priority grouping can invert as well. Here there are three possible inversions—*stressed* (tipping over), *fully inverted* (upside down), and *righting* (tipping back up). In all three cases, what these states refer to is that you feel an increased pressure to meet a particular need. This then changes your focus. Indeed, in two of the cases this pressure is so great that it causes the order of your social priorities to reverse.

For example, say we're talking about your *fully inverted* social priority grouping. If your normal grouping is Understanding, Freedom, Neatness, Comfort (UFNC), then your fully inverted grouping will be Comfort, Neatness, Freedom, Understanding (CNFU). Here your main focus becomes giving or getting Comfort (C). But say we're talking about your *stressed* social priority grouping. If your normal grouping is Neatness, Understanding, Comfort, Freedom (NUCF), then the order of your priorities won't change. But you'll feel an abnormally high pressure to get or give Understanding (U).

Overall, there are two things to notice here—how the order of your four priorities can change, and how your focus can change. As far as changes in the order, there are two possibilities. Either it stays the same as the normal order or it completely inverts. With the *stressed* variation, the order stays the same as the *normal* order. Whereas with the *inverted* and *righting* variations, the order completely inverts.

As for changes in your focus, here there are three possibilities. With the *stressed* variation, your focus shifts to what is normally your second highest priority. With the *inverted* variation, your focus shifts to what is normally your lowest priority. And with the *righting* variation, your focus shifts to what is normally your next-to-lowest priority.

The Four States of Social Priority Groupings
(normal, stresed, fully inverted, righting)
(© 2007 Steven Paglierani The Center for Emergence)

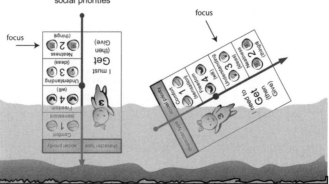

Normal
character type
and
social priorities

Stressed (with normal order)
(losing one's sense of Social Priorities)

I need to get
(then give)
Comfort

I really need to get
(then give)
Freedom

Fully Inverted
character type
and
social priorities

Righting (with inverted order)
(regaining one's sense of Social Priorities)

I must give
(then get)
Neatness

I really need to get
(then give)
Understanding

How Knowing about Social Priorities Can Benefit You

Admittedly, social priorities can appear complicated at first. So why would you want to know about them? For one thing, if you know your normal social priority grouping, then you have a way to gauge how much stress you're under—the lower your priorities shift, the more stressed you are. You also gain a clear sense of how you'll act when you're at your worst—when you're at your worst, your priority will shift to what is normally your lowest priority. Finally, you'll know how to pull yourself up out of this state—you simply focus on what is normally your next-to-lowest priority.

For example, my normal social priorities are UFNC—Understanding, Freedom, Neatness, Comfort. Thus when I'm at my worst, I become a CNFU—with the focus on C. Here I tend to do comfort-based things like overeating, pacing the floor, and taking naps. But because Neatness is normally my second-to-lowest priority, I can bring myself out of this fully inverted state by doing Neatness oriented activities—mail a letter, organize a drawer, sweep the kitchen floor, and so on.

Know that what I'm suggesting here will not work for everyone. It works for me because Neatness is my normal, next-to-lowest social priority. This means, whenever I need to get myself back on track, I purposely engage in activities which center on organizing my life—and accomplishing menial tasks. In effect, crossing things off my list literally helps me to regain control of my life. Moreover, because these activities hook directly into my core personality, doing this doesn't just work for me some of the time. It works every time.

Now contrast me with the woman in the drawing on the previous page—the one titled, *The Four States of Social Priority Groupings*. She is a character type Three—and her normal social priority grouping is CFUN (Comfort, Freedom, Understanding, Neatness).

Now look at the stressed variation of her social priority grouping. Notice how the overall order of her social priority grouping remains the same—while her focus shifts from getting Comfort (her normal first priority) to getting Freedom (her normal second priority). If she continues to feel this way for long enough though—or if she inadvertently relives a wound—then the order of her social priorities may fully invert, at which point her focus would shift from Freedom (her normal second priority) to Neatness (her normal lowest priority).

In addition, the order of her social priorities changes from CFUN to NUFC, at which point she starts to demand that someone help her organize her life. Unless, of course, she shifts her focus from Neatness (her normal lowest priority) to Understanding (her normal, next-to-lowest priority). At which point her focus would shift back to Freedom, and from there it's only a matter of time before she'd be back to her normal, Comfort-first self.

Now consider how knowing people's social priorities could improve your life. For instance, do you ever deal with difficult people? Knowing their social priority groupings would give you good insights into how they may behave—as well as how to best deal with them. It could also improve your chances to be heard by showing you the best ways to phrase things. And each time you did this, you'd increase your ability to connect to people by a magnitude or more—certainly, no small thing.

One final note. From the drawing, some may assume that character type and social priorities always invert together. Frequently, they do. But not always. My point? Be aware this doesn't always happen.

How Professionals Could Benefit

Obviously, one of the things professionals must face is how best to help people. In the cases of Kanner's Autism, OCD, Asperger's Syndrome, and ADHD, knowing the mechanisms underlying these four conditions would go a long ways toward doing this. For one thing, it would give psychotherapists the ability to more accurately diagnose these conditions. For another, educators would get a better sense of what it is they are trying to address when they offer these folks help.

Another thing professionals often try to do is to get people to connect. Here I'm referring to things like matching solutions to business clients and teaching methods to students. To wit, teachers familiar with their student's social priorities could tailor their lessons to the individual students within each social priority grouping. And talk therapists could find better ways to voice their interventions, directly tuning what they say to each person so that they say it in words which focus on the need this person wants met.

More important still is the way a knowledge of people's social priorities gives us a sane way to make sense of their distractions. For years, I've watched anyone who has trouble focusing get labeled as ADHD. This has become so commonplace that even folks who normally focus well will at times say they must have ADHD. No surprise here. We all have trouble focusing at times. But do we all have ADHD? I think not.

Sadly I've seen far too many unqualified people make these assertions, often in educational settings. Never mind that they don't take the time to find out what's actually distracting these folks. They're treated as people with broken brains and pressured to take medications.

Aren't the brains of folks with ADHD different though?

Brains scans reveal the brains of folks with all four of these conditions are. But so what. Treating people like their bodies are all that's real is one of the more serious examples of what happens when you honor one wise man while ignoring the rest. These folks don't heal. They only behave better.

More to the point, don't these folks deserve more of an explanation than that their brains are broken? Indeed, don't they deserve the kind of help which could permanently improve their ability to focus?

So am I saying no one should take medication for ADHD?

I am absolutely not saying this. However, to treat medication—or anything physical—as the whole answer is a travesty. Moreover, taking the easy way out while not addressing the real mechanism underlying distractions means we don't, as a society, get healthier. We get more medicated and use medicine to fake normal. And while I doubt this represents your personal truth, in the end, it's up to all of us as to how much longer this travesty will go on.

Do Social Priority Groupings Ever Change Permanently?

Before moving on to the third sublayer, Decision Trees, I first need to address one final thing—the question as to whether your social priorities can ever change permanently. The quick and dirty answer? Yes—but almost never. Thus like your character type, once your social priority grouping forms, it pretty much stays the same for life. However, on rare occasions—such as during serious life events—the order of your social priority grouping can permanently shift. This is similar to what can happen to tides after hurricanes, wherein the levels of high and low tides can change permanently.

In this way, your social priority grouping differs markedly from your character type in that once your character type is baked, it's baked for life. And while we can experience temporary shifts, inversions, and the like—as well as a delayed baking process as in the half-baked character types—even then, the pattern I'm referring to as character type doesn't change. Rather, it either continues to move forward towards a more idealized version of our assigned character type—or it temporarily varies, but based only on this same assigned character type.

The point is, unlike character type, social priority groupings can, on rare occasions, permanently change.

Section Three

Decision Trees: Your Core Personality—Part Three

Decision Trees ("how" will we meet these needs?)

	Digression	External Locus of Control (person feels forced)
Internal Locus of Control (person feels empowered)	Precision	
	Correction	External Locus of Control (person feels forced)
Internal Locus of Control (person feels empowered)	Bluntness	

The 4 Nested Qualities of Sublayer 3 (this rarely changes)

The Four Decision Tree Processes: Deciding on Needs

Okay. So you've identified who has needs—and you've determined what kind of needs you're dealing with. Now it's time to decide on an action plan. What are you going to do about meeting these needs? It turns out that human beings use only four styles of decision making to resolve their needs. Here by "styles," I'm referring to the four decision-making processes with which all decisions are made—the Bluntness process, the Correction process, the Precision process, and the Digression process. Indeed, every decision you make employs one or more of these four processes. Moreover, while we each employ all four processes at times, we favor only one. Yet another indication that the four wise men are at work.

What makes you favor one process over the other three? Do you choose which you use, for instance?

To put it bluntly, you don't choose. Life decides for you, in part, based on your mind body orientation and in part, based on your preference for trusting theoretical versus real world observations. To wit, if you're biased toward the mind's way of making decisions, then you'll favor either Precision or Digression. But if you're biased toward the body's way of making decisions, then you'll favor either Bluntness or Correction. And if you're biased towards trusting theories, then you'll favor either Precision or Bluntness. But if you tend to trust real world observations, then you'll favor either Digression of Correction.

How does this preference affect you?

For one thing, it determines whether you feel in control of your decisions. When you use Bluntness or Precision to make a decision, you feel in charge of this decision. Whereas when you use Correction or Digression to make a decision, you feel as if something's forcing you to make this decision.

As for how I refer to this quality, here I defer to Julian B. Rotter and his social learning theory of personality. Rotter saw our sense of being in control as a primary feature of personality. He saw the origin point of this control—which he called, our "locus of control"—as existing either inside us or outside us.

Applied to the four decision-making styles—with Bluntness and Precision, you feel the locus of control exists somewhere inside of you. Thus when you use these two styles of decision making, you feel empowered and in control. Whereas with Correction and Digression, you feel the locus of control exists somewhere outside of you. Thus when you use these two styles of decision making, you feel powerless and out of control—as if some external force is pressuring you to make decisions based on what they need rather than on what you need.

How does this play out in real life?

People with an internal locus of control feel like they are in charge of their decisions. So they tend to want to face them. Whereas people with an external locus of control feel controlled by their decisions. Thus they tend to want to avoid them. Hence people whose decision trees begin with Bluntness or Precision tend to face or even leap at decisions. Whereas people whose decision trees begin with Digression or Correction tend to avoid or to grasp at decisions.

Have I made it sound like this would be an easy choice to make, given it was up to you? In control, all the way?

If the choice were based on logic, it would be easy. Most people would choose a decision tree which empowered them. Unfortunately, we're talking about a part of personality which forms long before we understand decision making. Moreover once formed, decision trees rarely change. Thus, if your decision tree is one of the two wherein people feel the world is dictating to them, realizing this about yourself can feel pretty bad.

On the other hand, like all things in our world, all four styles of decision making have an up side and a down. For example, people with an internal locus of control can be overconfident at times. And impulsive. Whereas people with an external locus of control tend to be more careful when it comes to making choices—and this can lead to decisions which have been more thought out and ultimately, to better choices.

So which would you choose? Careful? Cautious? Confident? Clear? In truth, we don't get to choose. It simply happens to us. Ultimately then, like all things in personality, what's important is to know is who you are. After all, while you can always choose to take a leap of faith, you can't consciously choose to change what you can't see. Or more to the point, you can't consciously decide to do something which you can't imagine doing.

The Four Decision Tree Quadrants

As I've mentioned, we all use these four processes to make our decisions. However, similar to how we each favor a wise man, we each favor a decision-making style. This means we each have our own way of prioritizing these four processes. Moreover while the mathematical possibilities for prioritizing these four styles should in theory resemble the twenty-four social priorities, in actuality, there are only four primary decision trees—the BPCD tree, the CDBP tree, the PCDB tree, and the DBPC tree.

What are these trees like? Take the PCDB decision tree. People who have this tree tend to seek precise solutions—and correct them as they go. However, if they expand their correction search-criteria too far, they can get lost in digressions—then bluntly quit.

Obviously, this means that many people share the same decision tree. However the strength of these four processes can vary a great deal between people. Moreover if the variations in intensity between your four decision tree processes are great enough, this can indicate a social learning disability. For instance, take the PCDB tree. If you're like me, then your P is quite intense and your B dull. This could indicate Asperger's Syndrome. Similarly, the DBPC decision tree. If your D is quite intense and your C is quite minimal, then this could indicate the opposite social learning disability—ADHD.

The Quadrant of Decision Tree Strength
(How the Four Decision Tree States Become Decision Trees)
(© 2007 Steven Paglierani   The Center for Emergence)

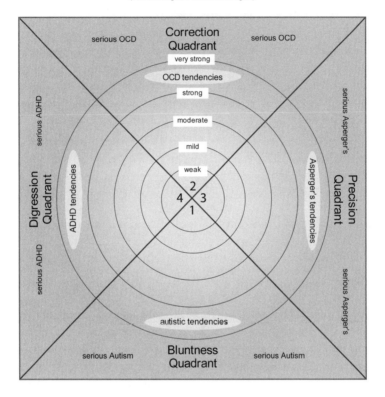

How do the four decision trees come into being? To see, you'll need to explore *The Quadrant of Decision Tree Strength* drawing. In it, you'll find the four decision tree processes, numbered one through four. These numbers represent the order in which these four processes first appear—with the Bluntness process appearing at birth—the Correction process appearing at about age six to eight months—the Precision process appearing at about age one or so—and the Digression process appearing at or just before age two. You'll also find five concentric circles which represent how intensely each process manifests in your life—from weak to very strong.

Know too that each wise man has a preference. Here the material wise man prefers Bluntness, the empirical wise man prefers Correction, the rationalist wise man prefers Precision, and the spiritual wise man prefers Digression.

What does this have to do with the four decision trees? Let's see.

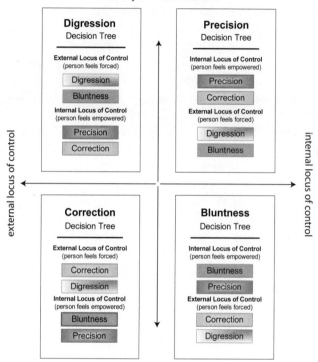

The Four Primary Decision Trees
(Layer 7's 3rd Level)
(© 2007 Steven Paglierani   The Center for Emergence)

The Four Primary Decision Trees

Start with the first decision tree—the Bluntness tree. To see the origin of this tree, start in the Bluntness quadrant. Now move counterclockwise around the four quadrants. Thus the Bluntness Decision Tree is Bluntness, Precision, Correction, and Digression. Likewise, if you start in the Correction quadrant, then move counterclockwise around the four quadrants, you get the Correction Decision Tree—Correction, Digression, Bluntness, and Precision.

If you then start in the Precision quadrant and move counterclockwise, you get the Precision Decision Tree—Precision, Correction, Digression, and Bluntness. And if you start in the Digression quadrant and move counterclockwise, you get the Digression Decision Tree—Digression, Bluntness, Precision, and Correction.

Finally, if you look at the drawing on the previous page titled *The Four Primary Decision Trees*—and if you notice where these four trees are placed—you'll notice something quite interesting. It turns out that like all things in personality, if you plug these four decision trees into the wise men's map, you can learn things about them. For instance, you find that the Bluntness and Correction trees are the body's opposites, whereas the Precision and Digression trees are the mind's opposites. So having ADHD is like having OCD of the mind and vice versa. And having Kanner's Autism is like having Asperger's Syndrome of the body and vice versa.

Know we'll have a lot more to say about the implications of this placement in Book III when we talk about learning disabilities in depth. For now though, something to consider is that, if these four trees are truly complementary opposites, then no one can have more than one of these conditions. At least, not simultaneously. For example, if Asperger's and ADHD are a pair of complementary opposites, then no one can have both conditions. Complementary opposites contain none of each other. Likewise Asperger's and OCD. And Kanner's Autism and ADHD.

This brings us to the next thing to know about these four decision trees—that one of the main things which makes these trees complementary opposites is the differences in how information flows through them. Which means what exactly? Let's see.

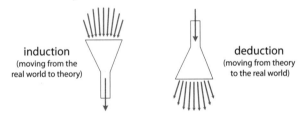

induction
(moving from the
real world to theory)

deduction
(moving from theory
to the real world)

Decisions as Information Flowing Through Funnels

One way to understand how we make decisions is to look at how information changes as it flows through funnels. It turns out that there are only two ways information can move—it can either condense or it can expand. Here by "condense," we're talking about the truth-seeking process called *induction*—going from the many details to the one big picture (from the specific to the general). And by "expand," we're talking about the truth-seeking process called *deduction*—moving from the one big picture to the many details (from the general to the specific).

Why funnels? Because they give you a way to visualize the four decision tree processes. Each of these processes is either inductive or deductive. Thus the more you understand induction and deduction, the more you understand how to make decisions. And the better you become at finding personal truth.

Let's start with induction. Induction is the truth-seeking method said to have been favored by Francis Bacon. It is symbolized by the upright funnel—decisions made by going from the many to the one. With induction, the way to find truth is to infuse the coldness of theory with the warmth of the real world. Thus there are two parts—a theoretical part and a real world part. The theoretical part is called *Bluntness*—and the real world part is called *Correction*.

Realize that with induction, decisions start with real world observations and end in a theoretical truth. Here the focus is on the process—on the real world, on observing how things change—rather than on the outcome. Thus with induction, you move from the real world to a theoretical truth.

So what is deduction?

Deduction is the truth-seeking method Descartes is said to have favored. It's symbolized by the inverted funnel—decisions made by going from the one to the many. With deduction, you find truth by imposing the clarity of a theory onto the vagueness of the real world. Thus like induction, there are two parts—a theoretical part and a real world part. The theoretical part is called *Precision*—and the real world part is called *Digression*.

Realize that with deduction, decisions begin with a theory and end in real world observations. Thus the focus is on proving an outcome—on finding things that don't change—rather than on engaging in the process. Thus with deduction, you move from a theory to a real world truth.

Overall the thing to see here is that, once again, finding truth involves four perspectives. But we tend to favor one. Moreover, rather than consciously choosing which processes we'll use, more times than not we simply do what we're programmed to do.

At the same time, like all things which involve personal truth, good decisions require you to use all four processes. So how do you do this?

You begin with the decision tree process which feels most comfortable. From there you keep going until you've used all four processes. If at this point you've made a decision, then you're done. If not, then you keep trying to satisfy all four wise men until you make this decision.

Problems arise only if you get stuck in one of the four decision tree processes. Or leave one or more out. This is what us makes believe Bacon favored induction and Descartes, deduction. In truth, this assertion is absurd. Both men employed all four perspectives. They differed only in how they moved through the four decision tree processes. And the process where each of them began is how we've chosen to remember them.

Induction and Deduction as Funnel Movements
(the nature of the four decision tree processes revealed)
(© 2007 Steven Paglierani   The Center for Emergence)

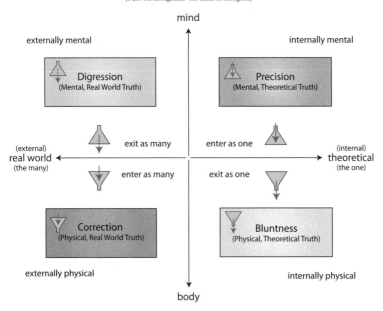

Finally, like all things in personality, with decision trees, each wise man has a favorite. Here the materialist wise man favors the Bluntness tree (truth seeking begins with gathering facts), the empirical wise man prefers the Corrections tree (truth seeking begins with arranging these facts into a story), the rationalist wise man endorses the Precision tree (truth seeking begins with getting ideas about these stories), and the spiritual wise man trusts only the Digression tree (truth seeking begins with feelings).

The Wise Men's Map as a Test of Internal Integrity

Speaking of the four wise men, some of you may be wondering why they've been so quiet in Book II. To be honest, they've been bugging the heck out of me for the past hundred pages or so. After all, their map holds the key to understanding everything I've been telling you—including the nature of these four decision trees. You should also realize though that their map also gives us a way to test for the internal integrity of all these concepts—a way to prove that they're true. How?

The Map of the Four Wise Men
(Four Wise Men's Realms)
(© 2007 Steven Paglierani The Center for Emergence)

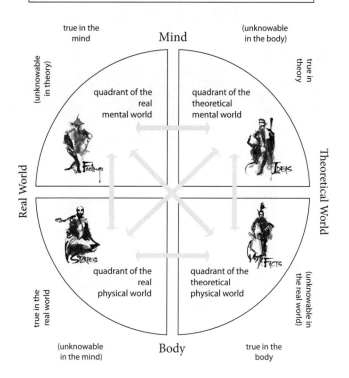

To see, take a look at this version of the wise men's map. Notice the six continuums in the center of this map. These continuums exist to make sure that whatever gets plugged into this map meets the strict standards of the four wise men. Here, everything at the ends of these continuums must be the complementary opposite of everything else.

Now turn the page and look at the wise men's map I've placed there. In particular, notice how I've plugged the four decision tree processes into this map. For instance, for Precision to fit into this map correctly, it must be the complementary opposite to all three of the other processes.

In addition, together, these four processes must account for all possible decision-making efforts. And they do. Precision is defined as "to enter as one." Bluntness is defined as "to exit as one." Correction is defined as "to enter as many." And Digression is defined as "to exit as many."

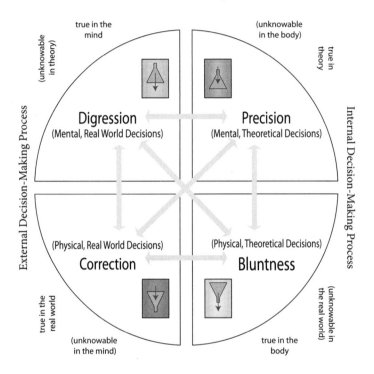

For instance, if you look at the drawing on the next page, you'll find the four decision trees pass this test. And if you turn the page to the four character types drawing, you'll find they also pass this test.

Know that every part of the wise men's personality theory must pass this test for internal integrity. Either six continuums exist between what is placed into the four quadrants—or the internal integrity of this part of the theory fails.

For instance, if you look at the drawing on the next page, you'll find the four decision trees pass this test. And if you turn the page to the four character types drawing, you'll find they also pass this test.

Likewise the drawing I've placed on the page after that, wherein the four social priorities pass this test. And in the next section, you'll find the four gender orientation-settings pass this test as well.

Can you imagine holding any other personality theory to such a standard? Indeed, this level of internal integrity is the one of the more amazing things about this book. Everything in this book passes this test.

How Induction and Deduction Lead to the Four Primary Decision Trees
(the four paths your decisions can take)
(© 2007 Steven Paglierani   The Center for Emergence)

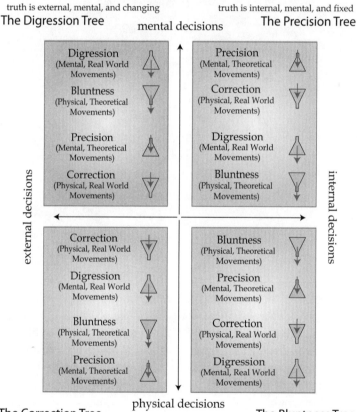

More amazing still is how this simple map can unearth such elegant discoveries. Incredible, isn't it? Who would have thought that redefining four words—facts, feelings, stories, and ideas—could reveal so much about human nature.

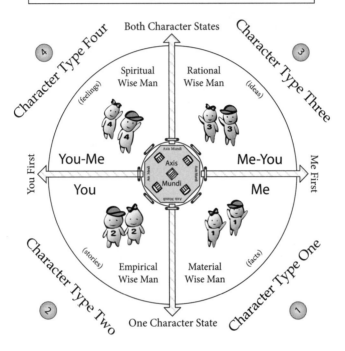

The Four Character Types
(per the Four Wise Men's Map)
(© 2007 Steven Paglierani The Center for Emergence)

Then again, without the map, these definitions would hardly warrant this fuss. To wit, it's the way these words have been placed into the map that matters most. It is after all a map. Still, isn't it surprising how plugging a few words into a little geometry can explain so much about personality.

This, in part, exemplifies the degree to which the wise men's personality theory is capable of revealing the beauty hidden in each of us. As well as how their map could possibly hold the key to finding your personal truth. Moreover, the odds that every aspect of an untrue theory could pass these tests are near impossible. This many coincidences? I think not.

A Brief Review of the Wise Men's Map

Finally, just in case you're having a hard time seeing how all these drawings are based on the same map, let's briefly review the elements which define the map. After all, I've drawn these maps in several styles.

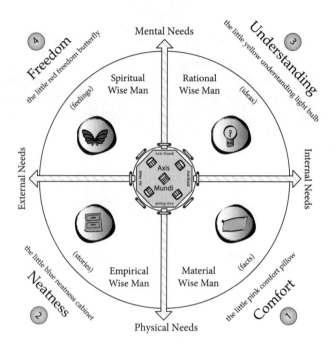

The Four Social Priorities
(per the Four Wise Men's Map)
(© 2007 Steven Paglierani The Center for Emergence)

However if you recall the basic elements I outlined in Book I: chapter three, you'll find they all contain the same basic elements.

First, every map has a horizontal axis which extends from the real world to the theoretical world. Here the tipping-point-based test is, does this truth change? Real world things do. Theoretical things do not.

Second, every map has a vertical axis which extends from the mind to the body. Here the tipping-point-based test is, is this truth visible? Physical truths, including the body, are. Mental truths are not.

Third, these two axes then create four quadrants, each of which contains a truth which is the complementary opposite of the truths in the other three quadrants. These four truths then create the six continuums which define the axis mundi—the truth seeker's seat. Together they represent all possible versions of this particular truth.

In the original wise men's map, these topographical divisions mark the four realms of the wise men—the four aspects of the mind. And in the Layer 7 maps, they mark divisions between different aspects of the sublayers I've just presented—the four character types, the four social priorities, and the four primary decision trees. In every case, the perfect way in which these ideas fit into the map offers strong support for that they cannot be just coincidence or pseudoscience.

The Wise Men's Map as a Guide to Personal Truth

Now take a moment to consider this aspect of the wise men's map. Why should you care that this theory has this sort of internal integrity?

As I mentioned in the reader's guide, we each favor one wise man and leave one out. Because we do, we struggle to find our personal truth. In other words, because we ignore—or dismiss as unimportant—parts of ourselves, we find it hard to know what to believe.

This is like to trying to balance a checkbook without accounting for all the checks. Leave out even one check and you get the wrong answer. The same thing happens when you leave out even one wise man. Do this enough and you end up depending on others for your truth.

Here then is where the map comes in. The map allows you to know when you've accounted for all aspects something, including all aspects of you. Moreover while it's obvious we all have biases, the goal here is simple. Account for all four wise men and you'll find your truth.

Know you need not treat these wise men as equals. You need only account for them all. And if you can find it in you to do this, then it's likely you'll find your truth.

Why Aren't There Twenty-Four Primary Decision Trees?

At the beginning of this section, I told you there were twenty-four possible decision trees but that we need learn only four. Why only four? Why not the whole twenty-four?

To be honest, if you can identify your first decision tree process, then you know more than enough to guide your decisions. So while in theory, each primary decision tree does have six possible forms (e.g. six trees that start with Precision, six with Digression, and so on), you need not trouble yourself with trying to pin down your exact variation.

At the same time, were you to do this, you might come to some interesting conclusions. For instance, for years I wondered if Descartes had Asperger's. If he did, he would have had the Precision tree—PCDB. During the course of writing this chapter however, I realized he had the Digression tree—DBPC. Thus Descartes had ADHD.

What makes me so sure? Because his four step method for finding truth plugs directly into the Digression decision tree—digression (intuition), bluntness (pick a starting truth), precision (arrange the pieces in a sensible order), correction (refine this order so it has a cohesive meaning).

At the same time, when I tried to plug Bacon's method into the wise men's map, I found that his decision tree matches none of the four primary decision trees. Bacon's tree in fact is the sequential opposite to Descartes'—correction, precision, bluntness, digression.

What does this mean?

It means that Bacon's decision tree is a variation of the Correction first tree—where the second, third, and fourth processes are the same as the primary tree but in reverse. Here we can easily see why Bacon's truth finding method is considered the opposite to Descartes'. They are exactly the same tree, only reversed. This means both men used the same four processes, just in reverse. This makes them far more alike than most people have previously believed.

The point? Knowing which primary decision tree best matches your tree is all you need to know. But knowing the rest can at times tell you some interesting things.

Do Core Decision Trees Ever Change Permanently?

Before addressing the fourth and final sublayer, we've one more question to answer. Can your core decision tree change?

The quick answer? Yes. But for most people, it won't. You'll likely have the same tree for life. However, I have seen a few exceptions. This happens similarly to how going through a life changing experience can change the ordering of your social priority group. Life changing experiences can, on rare occasions, change the order of your decision tree processes as well.

This said, in truth, the possibility this will happen is quite low. Moreover, as I've said, knowing your primary decision tree process is all you need. And while my letting you in on these secrets seems to be aggravating the four wise men to no end, I've convinced them that they owe you some degree of disclosure. After all, they've been screwing with your head since the day you were born.

Wise asses, one and all.

What did they expect, that you'd just keep blindly following their instructions for the rest of your life?

I, for one, certainly hope not.

Section Four

Gender Orientation: Your Core Personality—Part Four

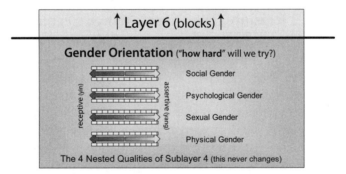

Your Gender Identity: Meeting Needs

Okay. So you've used your character type to determine who has needs and who should meet these needs. You've used your social priorities to determine the kind of needs you're dealing with. And you've used your decision tree to decide on a method by which to try to meet these needs. Now you arrive at the fourth and final sublayer of layer 7—the gender orientation sublayer. What do you try to do here?

To see, you're going to have to start with what may be one of the more controversial and counterintuitive ideas in this book—the idea that your gender identity has two sides—one somewhat fixed and the other rather fluid. By this, I mean that while your gender *orientation* is indeed largely determined by your biology, influenced by societal pressures, and more or less fixed by age four—your gender *presentation* is far from the polarized and unchanging schema most people assume gender to be—as in men versus women, masculine versus feminine, straights versus gays, and so on.

So what do I mean by *gender presentation,* and how does this differ from *gender orientation*? Start with this.

Gender presentation is external—while gender orientation is internal. So gender presentation is essentially how you look to others—physically, sexually, psychologically, and socially. Whereas gender orientation is *the direction—and degree of force—with which you execute need-meeting decisions within these four gender realms.*

Are you getting this? With gender, you have an inside gender and an outside gender—and only your inside gender is considered part of your core personality. And of course, your outside gender will in many ways reflect your inside gender. However, these two genders don't always match, and when they don't, you'll experience all sorts of conflicts.

Obviously, I've got a lot of explaining to do including why the drawing on the opposite page refers to our having four "genders." Then again, some of you will not be surprised by this, as by now it should be apparent that the number four holds a special place in the wise men's personality theory. Why these four though? We're about to find out.

The Four Gender Realms: Where Decisions Get Executed

As I've just defined it, gender orientation is the direction and degree of force with which you execute your need-meeting decisions. The four gender realms are the four places in life wherein you execute these need-meeting decisions—in your physical life, in your sexual life, in your psychological life, and in your social life.

This means there are four realms in which gender exists, one for each wise man. There's the realm of your Physical gender (the materialist wise man's gender)—the realm of your Sexual gender (the empirical wise man's gender)—the realm of your Psychological gender (the rationalist wise man's gender)—and the realm of your Social gender (the spiritual wise man's gender).

How do these four gender realms come into being?

Like the previous three layer 7 sublayer-qualities, they originate during the first four years of life. Know the order I've listed them in is the order in which they appear. Here your Physical gender appears first and develops from birth to about age 6 months. Your Sexual gender comes next and develops from about six months to about age one. Your Psychological gender appears third and develops from about age one to about age two. And Your Social gender comes last and develops from about age two to about age four.

The Four Gender Realms

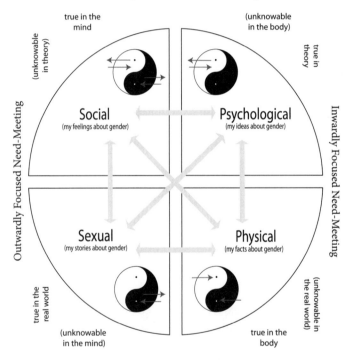

Mentally Oriented Need-Meeting

Physically Oriented Need-Meeting

Plugging Gender into the Wise Men's Map

If we now plug these four gender realms into the wise men's map—and if we then refer to the characteristics which define each wise man's realm—we gain insights into what defines each of these gender realms.

For instance, since the *Physical* gender realm exists in the lower right quadrant, we know that it refers to whatever physical, theoretical forces you're exerting—your facts about gender. Thus your urges/efforts in this gender realm focus inward, feel private, and create your desire to exist as a separate being. Whereas the *Sexual* gender realm exists in the lower left quadrant. So we know it refers to whatever physical, real world forces you're exerting—your stories about gender. Your urges/efforts in this gender realm involve the physical forces coming both at you and from you. Thus they feel mentally private—but physically vulnerable—and look to satisfy your physical needs.

The *Psychological* gender realm exists in the upper right quadrant. So we know it refers to whatever mental, theoretical forces you're exerting—your ideas about gender. Your urges/efforts in this gender realm involve the mental forces coming both at you and from you. Thus they feel physically private—but mentally vulnerable—and look to satisfy your mental needs.

Finally, the *Social* gender realm exists in the upper left quadrant. So we know it refers to whatever mental, real world forces you're exerting—your feelings about gender. Your urges/efforts in this gender realm simultaneously focus inward and outward—are both mental and physical—feel both vulnerable and private—and seek to connect your mind and body to the outside world.

As for how these four realms reflect the primary motive—to avoid suffering—here again, we can learn a lot about gender by seeing how these genders interconnect. Here your physical gender pertains to your need to exist as a separate being—your sexual gender to your need to override the physical aloneness created by your physical gender—your psychological gender to your need to override the mental aloneness created by your physical gender—and your social gender to your need to eliminate your aloneness entirely, in other words, your need to coexist with all other beings as one conscious self.

Have I just turned your head into a mixing bowl once more? If so, please don't fret. The four gender realms are just the four containers which hold your need-meeting efforts. Moreover, once you learn how to chart these efforts on paper, they become the easiest sublayer of all.

Measuring Your Gender: Direction & Degree of Force

As I've said, there are two kinds of measurements when it comes to gender—the direction and degree of force with which you execute your need-meeting decisions. With regard to *direction*, you can either make inward moving or outward moving efforts. And with regard to *degree of force*, you can make very meek, meek, bold, and very bold efforts.

That there are four degrees of force is no surprise, yet another nod the four wise men. But why only two directions?

Here the answer is simple. These two directions refer to one person. Hence, there can be only two directions, those which focus inward (the person's receptive/yin efforts)—and those which focus outward (the person's assertive/yang efforts).

The Gender Identity Charts

All this comes together in the Gender Identity Charts. You'll find an example of one on the following page. Start by noticing that there are actually two groups of four arrow-headed continuums. The upper group represents your Core Gender Orientation—the part of you that does not change; your inside gender—your need-meeting efforts. And the lower group represents your Gender Presentation—the part of you that does change; your outside gender—how these efforts appear to others.

Now notice the arrow-headed continuums themselves. These continuums describe the style of need-meeting efforts you make in each gender realm. Fully receptive efforts get charted on the left. Fully assertive efforts get charted on the right.

Next notice the segmented bars which appear above and below each of these arrow-headed continuums. The bars which appear above each continuum represent how your efforts play out in *friend-type relationships*. Here we're talking about the relationships you have with folks whose character type starts in the same character state as yours—another You-first person if you're a You-first person, for instance. The bars which appear below each continuum then represent how your efforts play out in *family-type relationships*. Here we're talking about the relationships you have with people whose character type starts in the opposite character state from yours—a Me-first person if you're a You-first person, for example.

Finally, notice that every segmented line has a gray bar on it. The position of these gray bars represents how assertive or receptive these need-meeting efforts are, whereas the length of these gray bars represents the size of these efforts—from very meek to very bold.

Adding all this up, we find that there are four marks for each gender realm, two friend-type marks and two family-type marks. And being that each mark represents two measures, this totals thirty-two measures in all. Here each mark has a position—ranging from being fully receptive to fully assertive, and a strength—ranging from very meek to very bold.

What can you learn from these charts? One, you can see how closely your orientation and presentation match—how well your insides match your outsides. And two, you can see how closely your friend-type relationships match your family-type relationships.

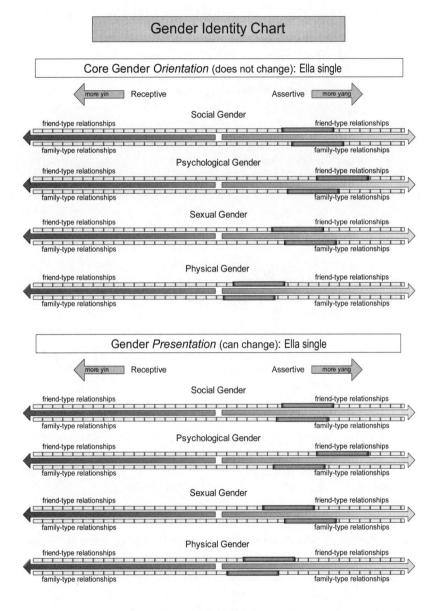

For instance, in healthy people, it's normal for your friend-type and family-type measures to differ a bit. Under stress however—and in unhealthy people—these two measures sometimes differ so greatly as to contradict each other. This then leads to internal conflicts which cause gender confusion. We'll talk more about this in a moment.

An Interesting Example: Ella's Gender Chart

Admittedly, all this theory means nothing if it can't improve people's lives. Thus at this point, I'll need to tell you a story. This story involves a former client of mine, a woman whom I'll call Ella, who, after spending four years in a heterosexual relationship, came out as lesbian. She then had a year long relationship with a woman, only to fall in love with—and get engaged to—a man.

Okay. So in our times, coming out as lesbian isn't as big a deal as it once was. Most folks even see these admissions as acts of courage. However, at the point at which Ella became engaged to a man, even she and I were confused to say the least. Who was she really, gender-wise?

Coincidentally, as a personality theorist, I'd been trying to make theoretical sense of gender for years. For example, in a case wherein I'd helped someone transition from male to female, I'd been struck by how many gender-related things stayed the same in this person—her literal sense of sexual orientation, for one. In fact, at one point, this second person hypothesized that when she transitioned, that her sexual orientation might change—that she might feel attracted to men.

She and I even argued at times as to whether this kind of change is possible. In the end though, she remained sexually attracted to women, this despite having gone through reassignment surgery and even after living for years as a woman.

Thus with regard to her sexual gender, her transition entailed little more than changing the words she used to refer to her sexual preference. In other words, the only thing that changed was that she went from calling herself a heterosexual male to that she was a lesbian. Either way, she was still attracted to women, not men.

Believe it or not, helping Ella sort out her sexual orientation was far more complex. Was she bisexual? Heterosexual experimenting with women? For a while, it was hard to say. Just as we were ready to defer to calling her bisexual though, I identified the four gender realms. At which point, we did her gender identity chart and realized what had been happening.

What did we find? It turned out that when Ella was single, her insides would match her outsides. Her presentation and orientation would match. As would her friend-type versus family-type continuums.

However, whenever she got into a romantic relationship, within several months her family-type versus friend-type measures would gradually drift apart. This would then cause her to question her sexual gender orientation. And to see why, we'll need to contrast and compare her single versus in-a-relationship presentation charts.

Being Single vs in a Relationship: Charting the Changes

Admittedly, Ella was not a typical person, gender-wise. So her ambivalence is understandable. Even so, per the wise men's sense of gender, we all experience some degree of gender ambivalence and differ mainly in the degree to which we suffer from this.

What does this gender ambivalence look like?

Start by reviewing the Gender Identity chart a few pages back. This chart shows what Ella was like when she was single.

Now notice the left to right *placement* of the gray bars above and below the arrow-headed continuums. This placement indicates the direction of each of Ella's gender orientation measures—whether she tends more toward being assertive or toward receptive in each gender realm.

Now notice the *length* of these gray bars. This length represents the degree of need-meeting force of each of these efforts. Here some bars are longer and some are shorter. And the longer ones represent more force, while the shorter ones represent less force.

What can we tell about Ella from this chart? For one thing, that when she's single, she can be herself. We can tell this because according to her chart, her gender presentation more or less matches her gender orientation. Thus when she is single, she is more or less she same person—gender wise—in both friend-type and family-type relationships.

What else can we tell?

From the placement of the gray bars on her sexual, psychological, and social gender continuums, we can see she's normally a rather assertive person in these three of the gender realms. Whereas in the fourth realm, the physical realm, she's less assertive. Here her physical appearance is only slightly yang, meaning, she's bit more "masculine" than "feminine."

How strong are these tendencies? All the bars on Ella's chart represent the bold degree of force. Here bars 1 click long would represent very meek, bars 3 clicks long would represent the meek degree of force, bard 5 clicks long would represent the bold degree-of-force, and bars 7 clicks long would represent very bold. All of Ella's bars are roughly 5 clicks long.

Why is there no "medium" degree of force—no even number of clicks? Because the only way to measure real world qualities is to use tipping-point based tests—tests which employ pairs of complementary opposites and measure tendencies rather than quantities. In a sense then, because all natural things tip, all natural things have a gender. And in truth, this is where the idea of gender derives from—from nature's tipping points.

Thus gender is nature's way of expressing the duality present in all things. Moreover, because the idea of "medium" in personality refers to a statistical mean—and since statistical means are theoretical measures which do not translate to recognizable measures in the real world—no real world measure of gender can be medium. What would we call it? Non tendencied? Bi-gendered? Genderless?

Of course, in theory, there can be medium bar strengths—just as there can be perfectly bisexual people. However because these charts measure real world values, they contain no theoretical "medium" measures. Thus in a way, every measure on these charts is like a coin toss. So while in theory a coin can land on end and a gender measure can be medium, in the real world, the coin must land on a side to be a valid coin toss. Likewise, all measures of gender.

How Gender Charts Reveal Gender Confusion

What about when Ella got romantically involved? Did she change much? To put it mildly, she changed a lot. So for instance, when Ella was single, her outside gender—her gender presentation—would more or less match her inside gender—her gender orientation. And her friend-type relationships would more or less match her family-type relationships. But whenever she got into a romantic relationship, aspects of her outside gender would gradually weaken. She would become unnaturally receptive. And because her inside gender would remain the same, gradually, she'd become unhappy the more her outsides ceased to match her insides.

Now to see what this looked like, compare the two *Presentation* charts which follow. Pay particular attention to way Ella's need-meeting efforts tended to shift left. Also, notice the decreases in the degree of need-meeting force of these efforts—they weakened in all but three of her measures. This means she took up less personal space in many of her relationships. Hence her increasing unhappiness.

As for specifics, sexually and socially, Ella took up less space overall. Psychologically, she took up roughly the same space with her friends, but less with her partner. And she also became less assertive among friends, but next to invisible with her partner. Finally, physically, Ella changed little if at all. Thus Ella's physical gender presentation was the only setting in which she remained true to herself.

That these patterns were the same regardless of whether her partner was a man or a woman explained her tendency to see herself as being "bisexual"—a term more indicative of the sexual gender of the partners she had been sexually attracted to than anything else. More significant though was the degree to which Ella grew less and less true to herself. Hence her tendency to become confused in romantic relationships.

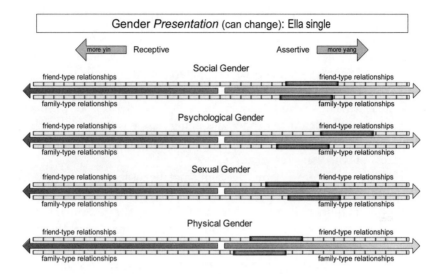

Gender *Presentation* (can change): Ella single

What is most surprising about all this is how Ella changed after we did her gender orientation chart. She literally stopped doing this. How could this one event so have altered her life? My explanation. It seems that becoming able to visualize her gender orientation gave Ella the ability to stay true to herself in romantic relationships. The proof? Not long after this, she got married and is still happily married. Yet one more example of how things can change when you find your personal truth.

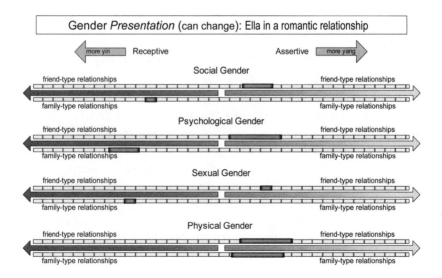

Gender *Presentation* (can change): Ella in a romantic relationship

Orientation vs Presentation: the Value in Seeing Differences

Obviously, most of us change when we get into romantic relationships. And in general, most of us find it a bit more difficult to be ourselves when we're around people whose character type starts in the opposite place. That this happens regardless of people's sexual preference is yet another nod to that sexual attraction is not the main indicator of gender. Rather, the main thing to see with regard to gender and being happy is how mismatches within and between your orientation and presentation create suffering regardless of who you're attracted to.

Equally important is how these mismatches affect your ability to find personal truth. In Ella's case, her chart clearly shows the nature of her former inability to be true to herself. Whenever she got romantically involved, her presentation and orientation would drifted apart. That this improved from doing her gender identity chart a single time still amazes me, not so much because she got married not long afterwards but more, because of the degree to which she and I had—in a single session—defined her personal truth about gender.

At the same time, Ella had been working on herself for years, some of this time in therapy with me. Thus while her gender chart did indeed open the door on her self realization, it was more like she had many realizations all queued up and waiting to get in, and doing her gender chart opened the door.

The point?

Healing does not instantly give you life skills. It opens the door on your ability to learn these life skills.

Do Core Gender Orientations Ever Change Permanently?

The upshot of all this of course is that only your outer gender can change. Thus while your inner gender—your gender orientation—remains more or less fixed after age four, your outer gender—your gender presentation—does vary. Sometimes briefly. Sometimes widely. And sometimes indefinitely.

Know these changes include not only the occasional manly-man dressed in a dress for Halloween. They also include the more than occasional wardrobe makeovers which completely shift a person away from—or towards—their actual gender orientation, such as with cross-dressers. As well as the folks who identify themselves as transgendered— both trans men and trans women.

With regard to occasionally cross-dressed men wearing Halloween costumes, we regard this as simply funny and oddly uncomfortable. But with regard to the folks who identify themselves as transgendered, for most people, oddly uncomfortable is putting it mildly.

The thing is, if you consider what I've been saying about gender presentation versus gender orientation, you realize that the changes these folks make are more external than internal—more presentation than orientation. In fact, based on this idea alone, we could define transgendered folks as people whose gender presentation is seriously out of sync with their gender orientation. Here the "transition" they effect simply brings their gender presentation more in line with their gender orientation.

The point? Even folks who identify as transgendered do not change their inside gender—their gender orientation. They alter only their outside gender—their gender presentation—so as to feel more comfortable in their own skin. That this can include physically altering their bodies is explained by the fact that there are four gender orientations—one of which is physical. Thus even bringing your body more in line with your gender orientation does not change this part of your core personality—the part I'm calling, your core gender orientation.

Finally, the main thing to come away with here is simply this. Your gender happiness depends largely on how well your orientation and presentation match. If they differ mildly, then you'll be more or less happy. Fluidity is a sign of health. But if they differ greatly—or if they rigidly never differ—then you'll likely be unhappy with your gender.

Section Five

Instructions for Administering the Core Personality Tests

The Test Criteria

Where are the tests? You'll find them in the appendix. Before you can administer them though, you'll first need to know the conditions under which these tests should be given. Moreover while these conditions are easy to describe, they can take a bit of effort. So remember, it's personal truth you're seeking. Just do your best.

- Condition One. *The explorer shouldn't self-administer these tests.*

Even if you think you can do it, don't administer your own tests. Have someone else do it. Best is someone you've known for a while. Ideally, she'll also have determined her own core personality, giving her experiences with which to guide you through the process.

- Condition Two. *The test administrator and the explorer cannot be connected while this explorer searches for answers.*

Except for the mind body tests, all these tests measure aspects of people's pure needs—who they are in Layer 7. Thus the accuracy of the test results largely depends on that the test administrator and the explorer do not connect *while the questions are being answered.* People have no needs while they're in Layers 9 and 10, remember? Thus if, while the answer is being sought, the administrator and the explorer connect, there won't be any needs to test for.

How can you prevent this? The best way is to ask people to picture themselves in the test question situations, then have them answer without thinking. Admittedly, this can take effort. However, if you use the wise men's method, you'll find it's easier than it sounds.

What is the wise men's method again?

- One: a truth must feel emotionally true—you must let go of all you know and trust your intuition to guide you to a starting point.
- Two: a truth must be factually true—measurements must be taken.
- Three: a truth must be empirically true—the measurements must tell a story.
- Four: a truth must be rationally true—the pieces of this story must fit together logically.

Why does starting with the spiritual wise man's truth improve the chances you'll get personally accurate results? Because when people do this, it prevents them from rationalizing an answer. That this mirrors Descartes' idea that we must rid ourselves of all preconceptions only points to how wrong people are for seeing him as the "rationalist." Intuitively, Descartes knew to honor the wisdom of all four wise men, *beginning with the spiritual wise man*. Why? Because by its very nature the spiritual wise man's truth takes us beyond words, and this rids us of any preconceptions.

The point? If people picture themselves in the test-question situations—then answer without thinking—they'll do fine.

And if they can't picture themselves in a situation?

Then ask them to trust their intuition and answer without thinking. More times than not, this answer will be their personal truth even if the rationalist wise man—and their logical mind—later tell them it's not.

- Condition Three. *If the explorer uses logic to find answers, this will invalidate the test results.*

Why does rationalizing answers cause problems? Because it prevents people from picturing the test question situations. Rational truths are non-visual truths, remember? The thing is, spiritual truths are also non-visual truths. Thus logically, they should be a problem as well. It turns they aren't a problem however as the easiest path to a spiritual truth is to begin picturing something then let it happen. Whereas the opposite is true for rational truths. If you begin by picturing, you'll find it's harder to find a rational truth.

What if the explorer can't picture a test question situation?

Then ask them to try answering—as quickly as they can—with their first impulse. More times than not, people's quickly-answered first impulse will be their true answer even if they feel like taking it back the minute the words leave their mouth.

Here again, the thing to keep in mind is where Descartes and the wise men tell us we must begin. They tell us *we must let go of all we think we know and trust our intuition*. Admittedly this can be hard, especially for those who favor the two theoretical wise men—the rationalist wise man and the materialist wise man. Here reminding them that beginning with the spiritual wise man is the best path to personal truths may help them to let go.

- Condition Four. *All answers should be validated with secondary questions voiced in the opposite state. All questions should be posed both positively and negatively.*

One way to improve the reliability of the test results is ask a second round of questions, checking to see if they agree with people's first answers. Even better would be to voice these questions in the opposite state from the one used for the original questions, as posing questions in both directions raises the likelihood people's results will be valid. Know the test questions have purposely been designed so they can be posed both positively ("which would you prefer...") and negatively ("which would feel worse...").

- Condition Five. *If either person is reliving a wound while a question is being asked, this too will invalidate the answer.*

Whenever people relive a wound, their core personality distorts in some way. Their character type may invert, their current social priority may change, their decision tree processing may get stuck, and so on. When this happens, at the very least, they become blind in some area of life. And if they answer a question while they're in this state, then the validity of this answer will be questionable at best.

How can you know if this has happened? Watch the explorer for overreactions and underreactions. For example, say you're asking a person which she prefers—a day off or a day at a spa? Say too that right after you ask her this question, she blurts out that she hates spas. As we'll discuss in Book III, hating an ordinary person, place, or thing is an overreaction. Moreover since spas are ordinary places, this would mean it's likely this question triggered a wound. Thus any answer she offered at this point would likely be wrong—and certainly suspect.

What about underreacting?

Here we're talking about things like when people abruptly go blank or lose their words. For instance, say the explorer goes blank after being asked which is harder, losing a day's pay or losing a day off? Since most folks experience both these things at some point in their life, they're ordinary events. So if this person goes blank when asked this question, it's likely this question triggered a wound.

What should you do if this happens? Ask the explorer to take a breath, then wait a minute before trying an alternate question.

And if the person still over or underreacts? Then do the test another time. Valid test results can change a person's whole life for the better. Thus it's well worth the trouble it takes to repeat the tests another time.

- Condition Six. *All questions must be phrased as tipping-point based measurements. Only "coins tosses" lead to certain results.*

One thing to keep in mind is the logic underlying the test questions. Understanding this logic can help you to state the test questions clearly and with more confidence. It can also inspire trust in the person being asked the questions, as doing this will help you both to access the spiritual wise man's truth.

What kind of logic underlies the test questions? The idea that real world measurements require tipping-point based tests. As opposed to using scale-based measurements which can only measure theoretical constructs accurately.

What I'm saying is, in theory, you can base personality test questions on scale-based measurements. In theory, scales are the norm. But since nothing in the real world occurs in scalable, evenly dissectible measures, self-report scales are at best vague measures and at worst useless.

For instance, take other-centeredness (neuroticism), one of the more commonly referred to measures in personality tests based on the Five Factor Model of personality. Here people are asked questions related to this trait, then asked to rate on a five point scale from very accurate to very inaccurate how accurately this trait describes them.

Unfortunately, this test question treats other-centeredness as a condition which people can have measurable amounts of. Indeed, the entire Five Factor Model treats personality this way—as a set of linear personal values, each of which can be statistically averaged then summed to arrive at a meaningful description of personality. Through self reporting no less.

The Coin of Truth
(How Tipping Points Resolve to 100% Certainty)
© 2008, Steven Paglierani, The Center for Emergence

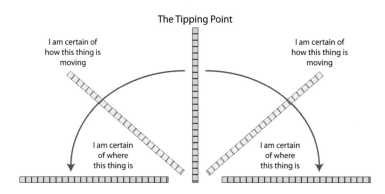

Contrast this with the wise men's personality theory wherein other-centeredness is treated as one pole on a continuum which extends from other-centeredness (the You state) to self-centeredness (the Me state). Here people's character type is assumed to begin either in a Me state or in a You state. The explorer is then asked questions designed to tip an answer one way or the other. Thus no scales are needed here as these questions treat personality traits as continuums of complementary opposites—each a set of stochastically self-similar patterns which become measurable *only after they tip*.

Are you having trouble seeing how scale-based questions and tipping-point based questions differ? Then consider this. How scientifically accurate would it be to rate snow flakes on a five-point scale from more of a snow flake to less? In truth, all snow flakes are equally snow flakes or they're not snow flakes at all.

Likewise personality tests which ask you to quantify personality traits. At what point does someone become other-centered, let alone have a meaningful way to interpret this vague request. A neurotic person and a narcissistic person could be equally focused on other people—yet rank themselves as complete opposites.

The point is, personality is fractal. Thus the only way to measure it is to base the questions on pairs of complementary-opposite fractals, then ask people which fractal they normally tip towards. Doing this treats personality traits like coin tosses, in that valid results require only that people's answers clearly tip in one direction. As such, these results suffer from none of the shortcomings of scale-based measures.

In other words, unlike scale-based measurements which require contrived test situations and statistical validation, tipping-point based measurements can be 100% accurate—even in messy, real world situations using very few cases. This makes getting valid answers on these tests a lot easier than you might think. Because the questions are phrased like coin tosses, each question has only two possible outcomes. And because these answers exist only after they tip, the answers you arrive at will be 100% certain.

Know this kind of certainty would not be possible if the personality theory underlying these tests was not based on pairs of complementary opposites as well. Because it is, correctly phrasing the test questions comes naturally. No effort required. Hopefully knowing this will make you feel less anxious, both about taking/administering these tests and about the validity of the test results.

The Mind Body Orientation Tests

Now let's discuss the Mind Body orientation tests. What do these test look for?

Mind body orientation is primarily a measure of how quickly or slowly people take in and process life. Moreover, since the accuracy of this test depends on using tipping-points, this test is simply a measure of which experience people favor—faster experiences or slower experiences.

Know you're not looking to find mere preference here. Rather you're looking to see which speed feels more natural (positively biased questions) and which causes more discomfort (negatively biased questions). Does having to rush through something feel exhilarating—or debilitating? Mind first folks love speed. Body first folks love suave.

With the mind body orientation tests then, there are only two possible test results. Either a person is mind first or body first. Mind first people process life first mentally and only afterwards consider the physical effects. Body first people do the opposite.

Know these tests are wonderful bridge-building tools for couples wherein one person thinks the other is ignoring them or just doesn't want to talk. You can also use them to help body-first people understand why classroom settings make them uncomfortable. In addition, you can use them to teach people the basic skill underlying all good communication—that both people must communicate at the same speed. And you can also use them to open people's minds to the idea that thinking quickly doesn't make someone smart. Only quick.

You'll find the tests in the appendix—section 1.

The Character Type Tests

Character type is primarily a measure of people's automatic assumptions as to who has needs. Here there are only four possible test outcomes, the four character types—Ones, Twos, Threes, and Fours.

- Ones normally experience only their own needs. That's it. *From their perspective*, only they have needs. Seen through the eyes of a One then, who has needs? First Me, then Me again. And who should meet these needs? First You, then You again.

- Twos normally experience only the needs of others. *From their perspective*, only others have needs. So according to Twos, who has needs? First You, then You again. And who should meet these needs? First Me, then Me again.

- Threes normally experience only their own needs, then only the needs of others. Thus *from their perspective*, at first, only they have needs. Then only others have needs. According to Threes then, who has needs? First Me, then You. And who should meet these needs? First You, then Me.

- Fours normally experience only the needs of others. Then they experience only their own needs. Thus *from their perspective*, at first, only other people have needs. Then only they have needs. So according to Fours, who has needs? First You, then Me. And who should meet these needs? First Me, then You.

Know that determining a person's character type is usually not that hard, given this person can be self honest and see past the obvious logic and social discrimination against self love. At the same time, because there are four possible outcomes, not just two, making these tests tipping-point based requires a bit of finesse.

How do you tip something with four possible outcomes? The answer is, you use questions to divide these four answers into two tests. First you ask questions meant to tip the four possible test results into one of two groups. Either a person's character type begins in a Me state (Ones and Threes)—or in a You state (Twos and Fours). Then you ask questions to determine whether the two character states which make up this person's character type are the same state or opposite states. Either both states are the same and the person is a character type One or Two. Or the two states are opposite states and the person is a character type Three or Four.

Can you see how this sequence of two tipping-point based tests divides the four test outcomes? Know this kind of divide and conquer approach occurs in many of the tests. Moreover because all the questions are tipping-point based, as long as you can determine which tendency is more obvious, your results will be valid.

Are you beginning to see why I've been boasting about the accuracy of these tests? The concept of tipping-point based measurement is both elegant in theory and doable in the real world. Indeed, the more comfortable you become with how tipping-point based measurements work, the easier the tests become.

My point? Don't get hung up on getting perfect answers. Perfect answers, like all things theoretical, don't exist in the real world. This includes perfect personal truth.

What are these tests good for? For one thing, they discern between family vs friend type relationships. So they're great for clarifying the nature of all kinds of personal relationships—parent/child, employer/employee, teacher/student, and so on. They also explain why a person can get intimidated when some folks raise their voice and yet, when others do this, it's no big deal. And they also describe the best ways for people to approach others—their boss, their wife, their closest friend.

You'll find these tests in the appendix—section 2.

The Social Priority Tests

What kinds of needs are most important to you? The social priority tests identify this part of personality. Here again, there are four categories to choose from—comfort, neatness, understanding, and freedom. This time however you won't be looking to arrive at one of these four answers. Rather, you'll be using all four.

So what are you looking to see then? The order in which people prioritize these needs. Moreover since there are twenty-four ways in which people can prioritized their needs, there are twenty-four possible test outcomes.

How do you determine which of these twenty-four social priority groupings people have? By far, the easiest method is to again divide and conquer. You do this by asking a series of questions wherein people must choose between juxtaposed pairs of social priorities. You then look for the underlying pattern.

How many questions do you need to ask to arrive at the final outcome?

At minimum, you must ask six tipping-point based questions to determine the ordering of these four priorities.

Why six questions? Because three tipping points exist between each of the four priorities and the other three. Not an easy thing to picture.

But if you picture the four categories of need as the corners of a square, it's a bit easier. Now consider how many pairs of opposites exist between each of these four points. In truth, each corner is opposite three other corners. Which makes it sounds like there should be twelve tipping points. However if you eliminate the duplications, you find there are only six unique tipping-points between these four corners, the six continuums I mentioned earlier.

This explains why it takes six questions to pare down the twenty-four possibilities to one. You ask one question for each of the six tipping points.

As for meeting test condition four wherein you must voice these questions both positively and negatively, know I've included eight positively-voiced tests and eight negatively-voiced tests. The positively-voiced tests ask people things like which "met need" they prefer. The negatively-voiced tests ask people things like "which unmet need distracts you more," or "which need unmet feels worse" questions. Moreover as long as you ask at least one set of test questions from each category, it doesn't matter which style of test you begin with.

For instance, say begin with a positively-voiced test wherein the questions ask people to choose between two positive things. Things like, "which would you prefer, a massage—or a day off?" This order works well with people who are in a good mood. Whereas, with folks who are having an off day, beginning with a negatively-voiced test can help. Here the questions ask people things like, "which distracts you more, being uncomfortable—or being disorganized."

Either way, when you're done with the first question set, go on to the alternately-voiced set.

What if the two tests result in conflicting or incomplete outcomes?

The first thing to know is that this can happen to the best of folks. So don't take it too seriously. Worst case, you'll need to do the test on another day. At the very least, you'll need to review the test criteria.

Then again, the problem may be that the explorer is converting the tipping-point based questions into scale-based questions. In effect, when you split the two tipping points of a single question into two separate questions, you remove the tipping-point between them.

How can you tell if this has happened? The answer will refer to *how well* one of these points describes the person—a quantity. Here this amount is the key. Tipping-points never measure amounts.

If you see this happening, try reviewing test criteria three and five. Three says the person should answer without thinking. Five says you can't get a valid answer if the person is reliving a wound. Also, you might state a few examples of how scale-based conversions happen. Hopefully, this will enable the person to stop doing this. At which point, you can either try another question set—or try doing the test another time.

What about ambivalent results which stem from other than logic, wounds, and converting to scale-based measurements? What might you try then?

For one thing, more times than not, it's easier to identify people's first and second priorities than their third and fourth priorities. A good thing to keep in mind then is that people's fourth priority is the category of need which comes to the top of their priority list *when they're at their worst*.

For example, when people tend to overeat—or sleep all day—when they're at your worst, then Comfort is likely their fourth social priority. Whereas, if they tend to clean like a demon when they're at their worst, then neatness is likely their fourth social priority. And if they tend to demand explanations when they're at their worst, then it's likely understanding is their fourth priority. Whereas if they just look to escape from bad things—or to get away from it all—when they're at their worst, then it's likely freedom is their fourth priority, and so on.

Of course, as I've said, to know for sure, you'll need to see if the reverse is true as well. For example, if people tend to demand explanations when they're at their worst, then their fourth priority is likely understanding. If this is true, then the reverse will be true as well. Do they normally not care why things happen? If so, then you've verified your answer. Clearly, if understanding is their fourth priority, then it can't be their first priority.

Likewise, if people tend to clean like a demon when they're at their worst, then neatness is likely their fourth priority. This means the reverse must be true as well. They'll normally do everything they can to avoid cleaning and straightening. Again, the same priority can't be both their fourth priority and their first priority.

As for what you can do with these tests, I personally find them the most interesting of the bunch. And the most useful for teaching people to connect. Here I'm referring to things like matching teachers to students and matching people to careers. In addition, these tests are great for identifying people's academic and personal interests and skills. So they're great for guidance counselors and job coaches. They can also be used to match people up based on having common interests, as well as determining the best methods to teach people things.

You'll find these tests in the appendix—section 3.

The Decision Tree Tests

What do people do to decide how to best meet their needs? The decision tree tests look to determine this. Here there are four processes people can use to make these decisions. They can use the Bluntness process (they can make decisions decisively). They can use the Correction process (they can make decisions carefully). They can use the Precision process (they can make decisions incisively). And they can use the Digression process (they can make decisions comprehensively).

Know that all people use these four processes. They just prioritize them differently. In addition, while in theory there should be the same number of possible test outcomes as there are for the four social priorities (twenty-four), with decision trees, the order doesn't count. So there are only possible four outcomes—the four *primary* decision trees. The Bluntness tree—BPCD. The Correction tree—CDBP. The Precision tree—PCDB. And the Digression tree—DBPC.

How do the tests determine which one it is? They simply determine where people begin their decisions—which of the four decision tree processes they normally turn to first. Once this is determined, you know which primary decision tree this person has. It's the one which begins with this process.

How do the test questions tip the four possibilities into one? They do the same thing the character type tests do. They divide and conquer. This time though you need ask only two questions. The first question divides the four into two; the second decides between the two in the chosen pair.

Question One. When you make decisions, where do these decisions come from? *From inside you*—as in you feel in charge of making your decisions. Or *from outside you*—as in you feel someone else is in charge of making these decisions?

If people feel like their answers come from inside them, then their decision tree is either the Bluntness tree or the Precision tree. Whereas if they feel like their answers come from some place other than inside them, then their decision tree is either the Correction tree or the Digression tree.

Question Two. Do your decisions tend to feel more like *beginnings* or *endings*?

If people feel like they start at the beginning when they make decisions, then their decision tree starts with either Precision or Correction. Both of these processes are beginning processes. Whereas, if they feel like they start by reviewing an already made decision, then their decision tree starts with either Bluntness or Digression. Both of these processes are ending processes.

Do these two questions seem vague and unscientific? If so, remember, you're asking people which process feels more normal; in effect, which feels more comfortable. That's it. Moreover if after answering these two questions people still feel unsure of their answer, then you can validate the results by asking which answers feel more uncomfortable.

The point is, you're just looking to identify two tendencies. One, whether or not people tend to feel in charge of their decisions—in other words, whether they normally feel like they are making their own decisions. Two, where in the process they begin these decisions.

If it feels to them like they are making their decisions, then these decisions are coming from *inside them*. Whereas if it feels like someone else is making these decisions, then they're coming from *outside them*. And if they feel like their decisions have already been made as they begin, then they have an *endings* decision tree. But if they feel like their decisions are just beginning, then they have a *beginnings* decision tree.

Know these tests are great as a way to assess for learning disabilities and social interaction problems. They can also be used to identify how and where people get stuck in learning situations. They can also help folks who tend to either be overconfident or lack confidence, by showing them where the problem is. As well as helping people who find it hard to finish things to know where they get stuck.

You'll find these tests in the appendix—section 4.

The Gender Orientation Tests

Finally we come to the gender orientation tests. Here you're looking to identify the strength and direction of people's need-meeting efforts. This time you'll need a lot more tipping-points to arrive at your result. However these tests involve only the two qualities I previously mentioned—direction and degree of force. So they're not that hard to do. With regard to *direction*, you're looking for whether people tend to make outward-moving efforts (assertive, or yang efforts)—or inward-moving efforts (receptive, or yin efforts). And with regard to *degree of force*, you're looking to see how strong these efforts tend to be—very meek, meek, bold, or very bold.

Does the second measure appear to be scale-based? Indeed, it does. However here again, you'll use the divide and conquer method. To wit, you'll start by dividing the strength of people's efforts. Do they tend to be meek or bold? Then you'll subdivide these results. Either they tend to be meek and very meek—or bold and very bold.

What are you looking to measure here? There are three categories of things.

• First, you're looking to see if the direction and degree-of-force of people's efforts differ physically, sexually, psychologically, and socially.
• Next, you're looking to see if the direction and degree-of-force of people's efforts differ in family-type vs friend-type relationships.
• Finally, you're looking to see if people's gender orientation (their internal gender—*their urges*) differs from their gender presentation (their external gender—*their efforts*).

Putting all this together, what you're looking for is sixteen direction results and sixteen strength results, thirty-two results in all. Moreover, because thirty-two results is a lot to picture, allow me to list them for you. With regard to family-type relationships, what you're looking for is:

• The direction and degree of force of people's *physical* need-meeting *urges* in family-type relationships (internal, physical gender).
• The direction and degree of force of people's *physical* need-meeting *efforts* in family-type relationships (external, physical gender).

ooooo

• The direction and degree of force of people's *sexual* need-meeting *urges* in family-type relationships (internal, sexual gender).
• The direction and degree of force of people's *sexual* need-meeting *efforts* in family-type relationships (external, sexual gender).

ooooo

• The direction and degree of force of people's *psychological* need-meeting *urges* in family-type relationships (internal, psychological gender).
• The direction and degree of force of people's *psychological* need-meeting *efforts* in family-type relationships (external, psychological gender).

ooooo

• The direction and degree of force of people's *social* need-meeting *urges* in family-type relationships (internal, social gender).
• The direction and degree of force of people's *social* need-meeting *efforts* in family-type relationships (external, social gender).

Now apply these same eight pairs of measures to people's friend-type relationships and you have it all, the thirty-two gender identity measures.

How Hard Are These Tests to Do?

Obviously, this is a lot to consider. Yet in truth, I think you'll find these tests easy to administer. Moreover, since these tests reveal a great deal about who people are, doing them is well worth it.

One final note.

I mentioned that there are two levels of testing for strength—dividing the four possibilities into meek and bold, then subdividing these results into very meek or meek, or into bold or very bold. Know that the second, subdividing step is optional. Thus while many people will prefer the comfort of using both tests and thus, getting a finer result, I find that dividing strength into meek or bold urges offers more than enough detail to determine a person's core personality.

At the same time, if you're dealing with someone who has gender issues, then by all means consider doing the second level testing as well. Here the possibility for emergences is just too great to ignore. Thus in cases where a person is struggling, it's well worth the extra effort. And you never know. Doing these tests may just be the ticket to give this person a clearer sense of self.

You'll find these tests in the appendix—section 5.

Interpreting the Tests Results: Synthetic Interpretations Revisited

Okay. So you've completed the tests. What do you do with the results?

Simply put, you *natively* interpret them. As opposed to *synthetically* interpreting them. Do you remember the difference?

Native interpretations stem from your natural reactions to visually observing fractal patterns. When you see a snow flake, you know it's snowing. There's nothing more to say. Whereas synthetic interpretations arise from the efforts you make to understand things when you don't see fractal patterns. Is it cold enough to snow? Will it hold off until you get home? Until it's snowing, it's anyone's guess.

Keep this in mind then when you're done administering the tests. Synthetically interpreting your results will render these results useless. Why? Because the main purpose of personality tests is to make personality more visible. However, synthetic interpretations derive from logic and reason alone. So logic and reason function fine even in the absence of visual input. This means synthetically interpreting your results could actually make your personality less visible, as it's possible to make these interpretations *even without making observations*.

Still not clear as to what I'm saying? Then consider this. Can you imagine what it would be like to have the weatherman interpret your tests? Synthetic interpretations all the way.

"There's a 50% *chance* you're a Two."

"You *may* have a PCDB decision tree."

"You're *partly* mind first, *partly* body first."

To me, this is what makes weather reports so unreliable. Supposedly, we're talking science. And data wise, this is true. Yet were you to remove every instance of the words "chance of," "may," and "partly" from these forecasts, I'm sure their accuracy would drop to below ten percent. Maybe twenty on a good day, no pun intended.

All this would change if the weatherman only had a window. Imagine that. Observations would rule the day. Moreover whether it rained, hailed, snowed, or sunned, his accuracy would rise to one hundred percent. Cloudy would mean cloudy. Windy would mean windy. And "chance of," "partly," and "may" would all go the way of the Dodo. At least, with regard to their role in passing off weather reports as science.

Likewise most personality tests. The questions they ask—and the data they collect—are often quite good. Where they fall down is in how they then interpret this data. For instance, it's one thing for a personality test to proclaim that people are neurotic (as per the Five Factor Model). It's another to use this "data" to predict how they'll react when the picnic gets rained out.

The point is, don't ruin your hard work by synthetically interpreting your test results. It's one thing to derive your sense of what it means to be a Two from logical guesswork and lexical rationale. It's quite another to be able to recognize this pattern *natively*—based on what you see. Go slow then, at least until you've learned to recognize these five measures of personality out in the real world. Until then, it's better to simply admit that you've yet to find a personally true meaning for your test results than to settle for logically possible—but likely questionable—and certainly misleading meanings.

How Having Wounds Leads to Synthetic Interpretations

If only it was this easy. Advise you to steer clear and that's that. The problem is, we all have wounds, each of which function like a personal black hole. Not only do they keep us from visualizing certain parts of ourselves. They also draw us toward them with incredible strength.

In addition, they make us behave at times like we're mentally ill. For example, say you have that same old fight with your spouse again—the one about putting out the recycling. Repetitive patterns of painful behaviors always point to wounds.

So what makes us vulnerable to engaging in the same stupid crap, again and again? We synthetically interpret what we can't see—the source of the suffering—by proposing causes and motives which offer reasonable explanations for why we do these things.

"You just don't give a fuck about how this makes me feel."

"You're such a nag, who would want to give you what you ask for anyway."

"You've always been a shirker. Your father was the same way."

"Your mother was a toad of a woman who just lived to find ways to control your dad."

If only we could reserve judgment until we could natively interpret these painful events. Spousal wars would dramatically decline. Unfortunately, as long as we continue to define wounds as the painful things we *can* see, we'll have all the proof we need to believe that our synthetic interpretations are true.

Why then do we synthetically interpret painful events?

In part, because these interpretations require no visual input. Thus we can make them even when we go blank—such as during arguments or personal tirades. In effect, what we're doing is using logic and reason to guess what's inside of our personal black holes. And if what we come up with sounds good enough, then we feel justified in treating it as facts.

Imagine if scientists did this with astronomical black holes? How scientific would that be? And yes, doing this as a way to come up with theories is fine. We theorists are a strange lot anyway. But when it comes to evaluating people's personal lives, it's never okay.

Now add to this the idea that painful events draw our attention far more than normal events and you begin to see why I've been saying that our wounds drive our need to synthetically interpret life.

Are you thinking you could learn to resist these urges? Perhaps you could treat them like we treat driver's mirror blind spots—know they're there and just be careful? If so, then ask yourself this. What's it like to not understand something about yourself, especially something painful? Most people feel really uncomfortable. Some folks feel stupid. And some folks feel downright unsafe. No surprise then that we so often turn to synthetic interpretations, when they so easily explain away this discomfort.

Applied to these personality tests, can you see how this tendency could impair your ability to interpret your results? The amount of new ideas in this chapter alone is enough to make even the smartest person's brain fart. In essence, I am claiming that five simple tests can completely define who you are. Thus the idea that anyone recently introduced to these concepts could expect themselves to grasp these results boggles my mind.

Additionally, there is the idea that because we all have wounds, we all feel this bias toward making synthetic interpretations—*even when we do understand things.* This happens because it takes less effort to logically describe something than to consciously picture it. In truth, you don't even need evidence to synthetically interpret things. Words, statistics, logic, and a good dictionary are all most people need. This and internet access.

Please keep these things in mind then as you process your test results. We all have wounds which hide from view parts of who we are. Because we do, we feel urges to fill in our blank spots with the easily accessed comfort of synthetic interpretations. Unfortunately, if you give in to these urges, you'll likely know even less about yourself than when you started.

How Synthetic Interpretations Lead to Groundless Science

Now consider how this tendency to make synthetic interpretations explains the many seemingly logical—but nevertheless wrong-headed— conclusions professions like psychiatry, medicine, psychology, politics, and the people-sciences in general arrive at. These are the folks we turn to when we cannot understand ourselves.

Unfortunately more times than not these professionals base their advice primarily on synthetic interpretations. Thus this advice often has more in common with superstring theory than with common sense.

For instance, take the talk therapies which developed during the second half of the twentieth century. With a few notable exceptions, these therapies base their conclusions almost entirely on synthetic interpretations. For example, take the idea that poor relationships come from poor choices, in effect, that we pick the wrong people. This is obviously an entirely synthetic interpretation. How can we be choosing something we have yet to see, in effect, picking from a menu we haven't been handed?

But don't we all at times make bad choices when it comes to relationships? From a logical standpoint, in hindsight, yes, we do. But if you grasp the significance—and necessity—of being provoked into healing crises, then you see that what these therapists have been calling dysfunction functions perfectly. It shows us where our wounds exist.

Contrast this with how the late nineteenth century, early twentieth century, personality theorists/therapists sought truth. Their standard operating procedure was to first gather case studies, then interpret what they saw. They were literally taught to first psychophysically observe, then to record both what they saw and their natural reactions to what they saw. Only then did they posit conclusions as to what things meant.

More important still, these conclusions were not the end of the process. There was no end to the process. Personality was seen as fluid and dynamic. Thus they simply carried their conclusions forward with them as they continued to make more observations, and so on and so forth.

Not coincidentally, this same cycle—psychophysical observation, personal reaction, record keeping, and native interpretation—is what guided the physicists of the same era. Not a one of them would have thought to call something true based on logic alone. Moreover, despite Descartes' reputation for being a man who believed reason was the only path to truth, as I've mentioned, his method derives out of what he calls, his "meditations." Here Descartes is referring to his lifelong habit of spending mornings looking out at his garden while exploring his inner life. Translation. Descartes began his searches for truth, first, by observing, and only then by making what I have been calling native interpretations.

My point? Truth begins with making observations—visual, not logical. Base a truth on anything less, e.g. on synthetic interpretations, and your truths will be groundless science. Literally.

Likewise personality test results. Base your interpretations on anything less than personal reactions to what can be visually observed and the accuracy of your test results will forever be questionable. And groundless to boot.

How Synthetic Interpretations Hide Wounds

Of all the truths you could possibly learn, certainly one of the more important is how to find your wounds. Without this knowledge, all conclusions become suspect, whether personal or not. Fortunately, knowing your core personality gives you a baseline from which to test for these wounds. However since synthetic interpretations can be used to explain away wounds, if this baseline includes synthetic interpretations, it won't be of much help.

How do synthetic interpretations explain away wounds?

All synthetic interpretations derive from logic and reason. And to be honest, there aren't many wounds a clever person can't find reasons for. For example, say it's morning and you walk by your spouse without saying hello. Were you ignoring her? Still mad from last night's fight? Resentful that you didn't have sex? Or perhaps you were just deep in thought?

Amazingly when faced with situations like this, most folks are more likely to believe the worst case and less likely to consider things like that this person might have a wound about making noise in the morning.

The thing is, for personality test results to make sense, you must have a personality theory to guide you. After all, it's this personality theory which gives these test results their meaning. But if you interpret what you find synthetically, even results based on the best personality theory become questionable at best. At which point, you can't even know for sure if the problem lies in the theory or in you.

What about the criteria I defined in the previous chapter, those necessary for a theory to be called a legitimate personality theory? Couldn't we use these criteria to verify the theory? For instance, one of these criteria is that a legitimate personality theory must form a theoretical to real world feedback loop with a therapy. The thing is, if we synthetically interpret what we see, in effect, we break this loop. At which point we end up with no baseline at all from which to ascertain who we are. Including what is normal and where we have wounds.

Am I being difficult again? Okay. I admit it. Like my mentors—the four wise asses—I can be a pain in the ass. However, if you keep in mind that it's your personal truth I'm trying to help you to find, then my reasons for trying to dissuade you from making synthetic interpretations become clear. I want you to know yourself. I want you to succeed.

At the very least then, synthetically interpreting your test results will confuse you. At worst it will permanently throw you off track by accounting for the very blindnesses which would otherwise lead you to identify and perhaps, heal your wounds. Left unhealed, these blindnesses guarantee you'll have flaws in your personal truth. Certainly this alone should be enough to convince you to do your best to steer clear of synthetic interpretations.

How Synthetic Interpretations Affect Other Theories

So, synthetically interpreting personality test results will confuse you and cover up your wounds. Isn't it ironic then that most current personality theories base their conclusions on this kind of nonsense. For instance, take the system of personality measurement I referred to a few pages back—the Five Factor Model (FFM). This theory posits that all of human personality can be represented by the five factors of Openness, Conscientiousness, Extraversion, Agreeableness, and Neuroticism. Here we're talking about a theoretically sound endeavor which derives most of its observations directly from people's self observations—from questionnaires. Moreover, while the questions on these tests are actually quite good from a psychological perspective, the accuracy of these tests rests largely on the test taker's ability to synthetically interpret—on a five-point scale—how well the questions agree with their psychologically-observed life experiences.

So for example, say I wanted to see how high on this scale you score for the trait of Openness. I might ask you a series of questions like—do you spend time reflecting on things, do you have a vivid imagination, do you use difficult words, or do you have excellent ideas. In each case, you'd be asked how accurately the question describes you on a scale from very inaccurate to very accurate.

Questions posed like this do several things wrong. For one thing, they force people to psychologically interpret the questions. What is a "difficult" word?

What is an "excellent" idea? Without placing these words on continuums of real world opposites, you cannot be sure what you're being asked.

Then there's the problem inherent in all scale-based measurements. In order to rank yourself, you have to interpret the very scale that's being used to make these measurements. This is like buying shoes without trying them on. By what criteria are you judging the difference between something which is inaccurate and something which is very inaccurate? Without tipping-point based measures, you simply can't.

Finally, there's the idea that these questions ask you to consider making potentially pejorative judgments about yourself. This ignores the fact that we all have wounds which in part blind us to both our good qualities and our faults. This alone is enough to skew the test results of even the most honest person. You cannot report what you cannot see, no matter how hard you try.

The Limits of Synthetically Interpreted Scales

Do all the questions in this model ask you to evaluate yourself based on synthetically interpreted scales? Yes. Not a one poses a question as a tipping-point based choice. For instance, if they were testing you for the trait of Neuroticism, you might be asked things like—are you easily disturbed, do you get irritated easily, do you get stressed out easily, or do you get upset easily?

For Conscientiousness, you might be asked things like—do you get chores done right away, do you like following schedules, do you like order, or do you pay attention to details?

For Extraversion, you might be asked things like—do you feel comfortable around people, do you start conversations, do you talk to a lot of different people at parties, or are you quiet around strangers?

And for Agreeableness, the questions might be things like—do you have a soft heart, do you make people feel at ease, do you sympathize with other people's feelings, or do you take time out for others?

The thing is, on the surface, all these questions would seem to be psychologically probing. As I read them back, I like them myself. Unfortunately, in order to answer these questions, you have to first synthetically interpret each question, then synthetically scale your response.

Do you have excellent ideas? An egoist and a neurotic might have opposite opinions as to what an excellent idea is. Do you get stressed out easily? In what situations? We all get stressed out easily when we relive a wound. Do you start conversations? About what? The weather? Your suicidal thoughts? Your excess methane problem? Do you pay attention to details? Obviously, it would depend on how important something is to you. Even people with severe ADHD pay great attention to the details in video games.

How Emotional Logic Adds to the Confusion

Now as if this were not already confusing enough, there's also the effect our wounds have on our ability to make sense of things. What I mean is, when you make synthetic interpretations, how do you know whether your interpretations come from intellectually sound judgments, from the discomfort that being unable to visualize examples provokes in you (from a wound), or from sheer laziness wherein you don't bother to look for any real life examples.

For instance, were I referring to the wise men's personality theory, I might rate myself as very accurate on the "do I have excellent ideas" question. However, the people who believe in the Five Factor personality model might tend to disagree. Even vehemently, perhaps.

Who is to say which theory is true? Me? Them? To be honest, both systems have their merits even without real life examples.

The thing is, while in theory, scale-based measurements look wonderful on paper, in the real world, they at best resolve to questionable validity. Conversely, while on paper, tipping-point based measurements seem terribly vague, in the real world, they resolve to one hundred percent validity.

In the end, of course, the problem is deeper than questions about the validity of these data-gathering methods. It is more that the real world value of any theory based on synthetic interpretations is questionable at best. Add to this that every decision you make as to whether a theory is true gets filtered through your personality, and you begin to see how important having a legitimate personality theory really is.

How then can you know whether a theory is true?

If you limit your allegiances to theories based on tipping-point based measurements which get natively interpreted, you'll do fine.

What Good Does Knowing All This Do?

So here we are at the end of Book II, another long and thoroughly complex tome of truly epic proportions. And after being put through all this, I wouldn't be surprised if you'd lost sight of the point of this chapter.

We've been trying to define a method which can give you a true picture of your personality. Why? In a word—choices. With a true picture of yourself, many previously unseen choices appear, each of which may improve your life. And yes, I realize this claim flies in the face of the common sense wisdom that says the tiger can't change his stripes. You are who you are, right? But in truth, we're not talking about changing the tiger. We're talking about the tiger learning to see the parts of herself which prevent her from choosing a better life.

To me, this idea sounds a lot like what I imagine German biochemist Otto Rössler had in mind when he wrote that "to recognize limitations is even more important than to be free of them." I so agree with Rössler. To know your limitations is to know where to focus your efforts. And this is where personality tests come in.

Personality tests, if they're psychophysical, create a theoretical baseline from which to discover your limitations—including your wounds. How do they accomplish this? By giving you a sense of who you'd be *if you had no wounds*. After all, this unwounded self—the forever-innocent child in you—is what gets stored in layer 7. And this innocent child is the only true baseline from which to measure your health. And improve your life.

Of course, with every change you make come worries as to how it will all turn out. This brings us to the focus of Book III.

Specifically, we're going to be looking at how a simple sequence of six geometric shapes can unlock the secrets of the universe, teach you to have your own original ideas, and possibly even raise your IQ. Seriously.

We'll also be looking at how the everyday suffering we call "uncertainty" drives much of who we are. And how we can use what we've learned so far to help us to feel less uncertain. In other words, while in theory, avoiding layer 8, returning to layers 9 and 10, and resolving the conflict these two things create in us are our three main drives, in everyday life, it's the uncertainty we feel in everyday life that colors everything we think, feel, say, and do—astrophysics to astrology, zoology to xenophobia. And lest you worry we're headed for yet another voluminous morass of complex theoretical stuff, relax. The most theoretically difficult book in this series is behind you. What lies ahead are the chapters which describe all the wonderful things we can do with what we've been discussing, things like how to improve your relationships—how to heal wounds—how to get children to love learning, and so on.

Still feeling skeptical? Think it's all been pseudoscience? In the next book, I'll offer concrete proof for that most of what we've been taught about how to find truth is less than pseudoscience. It's straight-up nonsense. Scientists, therapists, and educators, load your guns. The wise men and I are coming for you and I promise, it won't be pretty.

Notes Written in the Margins of Chapter Six

On the Difference Between Feeling Needy and Pure Needs

Something I failed to address in this chapter is the idea that people can appear to be needy and yet, have no sense of their pure needs—another example of people's outsides not matching their insides. For instance, young children often display extremely needy behaviors. Yet if asked—even repeatedly—what it is they need, many times, they have no idea.

My point for telling you this?

If you're feeling especially needy when you take the tests, you'll skew the results. Likewise, if you're feeling abundance when you take the tests (the total absence of neediness), the tests will likely fail as well, as you'll be unable to access your needs.

Keep this in mind then when you take the tests. Since what you're looking to measure is your core personality, the more normal your state when you take the tests, the more accurate your results will be.

On the Importance of Tipping Points

Nowhere is the idea of tipping points more important than when it comes to personality tests. In a very real sense, tipping points are what turn otherwise useless subjective reporting into genuinely scientific results. Of course, whether this will happen or not depends entirely on how you design the test questions. They must be phrased as choices between the two sides of a single tipping point. And while learning to do this can take some effort, once you learn this, you'll have quite a powerful tool.

For instance, take the idea of losing and gaining weight. Nowhere have scaled-based measurements been more abused. The thing is, in Book III, in the chapter on science, I'm going to introduce you to the real secret to losing weight, something so obvious and simple, it's amazing no one's noticed it before. And no, it's not to cut off an ugly limb so as to lose 10 pounds. It's simply that you're either losing weight or gaining weight—and this change is a tipping point.

In truth, no one can lose weight and keep it off simply through bonsai calorie counting and kamikaze exercise. However, if you know the four qualities which describe the nature of how weight changes, you can use this knowledge to rebalance your weight each day, tipping where you need to when you need to. And yes, there are six tipping points which derive from those four qualities and you'll need to manage them all. But if you can see them, you can manage them. Yet another variation on the theme I've been proclaiming throughout the book—that you can't change what you can't see. And vice versa.

Know this same principle applies to recovery from addictions. You're either in recovery or you're not—and this change in state is a tipping point. Thus rather than recovery being a scale-based measurement like those psychologists tend to use, it's more accurate to describe it in the language AA-ers have been using for decades—that you're either moving toward a drink or away from a drink. Here you've either tipped toward sobriety—or toward relapse.

Seen in this light, tipping points are truly amazing, certainly with regard to knowing what is true in the real world. Indeed, without them, nothing in this book would be comprehensible—let alone defensible. Not a single idea. In truth, your ability to understand this book, and more, your ability to find personal truth, rests entirely on your ability to grasp tipping points. Please do your best to learn them well then, grasshopper. Your entire real world truth depends on knowing how to use them.

How Calculus and the Wise Men's Personality Tests are Similar

Although I've never read this idea before, it may well be out there. If so, I offer the credit to whomever said it first. This said, it is obvious to me that what made Newton's (and Leibnitz's) idea of infinitesimal calculus so astounding was that, for the first time, it made mathematical use of tipping points. And for those who are unfamiliar with the idea of infinitesimal calculus, it's simple.

Whenever you calculate enormous amounts, you can never know the exact number. What's infinity times 2? However, sometimes you need to know an approximate number in order to calculate things like the distance to the sun and so on. To do this, Newton simply started with two things—what he could be certain was a greater number, and what he could be certain was a smaller number. By doing this, he book-ended the actual number. He then continued to reduce the distance between these two bookends until he arrived at a usable number.

Many people know this idea. It's not hard to grasp. However, what most people don't realize is that the mechanism underlying this mathematics is tipping points. You see, there is no way to arrive at a real world mid-point. This point is always changing. However, if you use tipping points to arrive at this number, you've translated your theoretical calculations into a real world result—a truth which will always be correct and certain. At least in theory.

Geometric Bisections and the Wise Men's Personality Tests

Similarly, I've not previously seen the ancient Greek method of bisecting geometric distances with pendulums referred to as tipping-point based measurements either. Here in order to find the mid-point between two end-points, you make two overlapping, pendulum-based measurements, one from each end point. Each of these pendulum-based measurements marks an arc from a distance shorter than the mid point to a distance longer than the mid point. A line is then drawn between the two points at which these arcs intersect.

How are these measurements based on tipping points? It's the part wherein the arc swings from less than the mid-point distance to more and back. And while in theory, this will give you a theoretical measure that does translate to the real world, it's still never going to give you a linear, real world result. In the real world, arc swings are fractal. Thus they never repeat the same way twice.

On Calculating the Number of Layer 7 Sublayer Personality Factors

Some of the calculations used to determine the total possible core personalities are simple. Take character types. There are two possible character states—and all character types are comprised of a sequence of these two states. Thus each of the two states can be in two positions.

This means, there are 2 possible positions times 2 possible character states—4 possible character types in all.

The calculations used to determine primary decision trees are similarly simple. Because there are four decision tree processes, and because each tree begins with one of these decision tree processes, there are 4 times 1 trees—4 primary decision trees in all.

Some calculations are harder though. Take social priorities. To figure out the possible social priorities, we need to use something called *permutations*, meaning, the possible non-repeating orderings of a set. To figure out permutations, the formula is n!/(n-k)!, where n = the total number of data, and k = the number of data used in each ordering. Here any number followed by a "!" means the number multiplied by itself-minus-one down to one. For instance, 5 factorial (5!) means 5x4x3x2x1. Thus 5! = 120.

This means, when it comes to determining the number of possible social priorities, we need to know two things—how many categories we have and in how many positions these categories can be. This means, because there are four categories of need—and because each person's social priorities include some ordering of all four categories—there are 4 possible positions of 4 categories, (4_P_4). Thus there are 4 factorial (4!) possibilities—4x3x2x1—meaning 24 possible social priorities in all.

As hard as this sounds, figuring out the total gender orientations is the hardest calculation of all. Here each continuum has 4 possible positions and four possible gender strengths. Thus each continuum has 16 possibilities.

If we now consider that there are 8 continuums on which one of these 16 possibilities exist, we get 16x16x16x16x16x16x16x16 = 4,294,967,296—an overwhelming number of possibilities. Obviously this number would be untenable, making it useless as a real world measure. Thus like my choice to limit the possible decision trees to the four primary trees, I have chosen to limit the number of basic positions to the two directions—assertive and receptive—and the basic strengths to 2—meek and bold.

This gives us 4 possible results which can occur on each of the 8 continuums. Thus the actual calculation for the possible core gender orientations is 4x4x4x4x4x4x4x4. Result. 65,536 possibilities.

On Why There Are Not Sixteen Character Types

As I told you during the chapter, each character types has four forms—normal, half-baked, inverted, and progressed. So why have I chosen—in my calculations for the measurably unique core personalities—to say that there are only eight forms of character types and not sixteen?

The sixteen forms character types can take can be divided into two groups—those which are temporary, and those which are permanent. The half-baked and inverted forms are considered temporary—while the normal and progressed forms are seen as permanent. This means there are only eight, not sixteen, permanent forms. Hence my using the number 8 in my character type calculations as to the total possibilities for core personalities.

On the Sixteen Jung/Myers-Briggs Personality Types

As far as I know, there is only one other kind of personality tests based on tipping-points—the sixteen Carl Jung/Myers-Briggs types. For those who may be interested, here's a thumbnail sketch of the tests which lead to these sixteen types.

In the Myers-Briggs version of Carl Jung's personality theory, there are four pairs of complementary opposites, each of which is referred to as a "dichotomy." They are, [1] the energy pair (the extroverted-introverted dichotomy), [2] the perceiving pair (the sensing-intuiting dichotomy), [3] the judging pair (the feeling-thinking dichotomy), and [4] the judging-perceiving pair.

Here the extroverted-introverted pair refer to your preference for *where you observe* (outside yourself or inside yourself)—the sensing-intuiting pair refers to your preference for *how you observe* (with your body or your mind)—the feeling-thinking pair refer to your preference for *how you interpret what you observe* (natively or synthetically)—and the judging-perceiving pair refer to your preference for either interpreting or observing.

It is from these four pairs that the sixteen possible types emerge. However, each pair derives from what are called *facets*—five categories of tipping point-based questions per each of the four pairs. If recorded, this would result in 32 possibilities per dichotomy—or over one million possible personalities, with the only downside being that these facets are not nested.

What makes the wise men's personality theory so elegant then is that every single facet is nested somewhere within other facets. In other words, the entire wise men's personality theory is based on a single, nested fractal. Thus as good as the Myers-Briggs tests are—and they are good—unfortunately, they lack the elegance of the wise men's theory.

Resources for Chapter Six—The Personality Tests

On the Locus of Control
Rotter, J.B. (1966). Generalized expectancies of internal versus external control of reinforcements. *Psychological Monographs*, 80 (whole no. 609). Storrs, CT: University of Connecticut.

Lefcourt, H.M. (1976). *Locus of Control: Current Trends in Theory and Research*. Hillsdale, New Jersey: Lawrence Erlbaum Associates.

On Tipping Points
Gleick, James. (2004). *Issac Newton*. New York: Vintage Books. (I find Gleick's books amazingly clear, and sufficiently detailed. For instance, my sense of infinitesimal calculus as a tipping point emerged from reading this book.)

Gladwell, Malcolm. (2002). *Tipping Point: How Little Things Can Make a Big Difference*. New York: Back Bay Books.

Allman, George Johnston. (1976). *Greek Geometry from Thales to Euclid (History of Ideas in Ancient Greece)* Manchester, NH: Ayer Co Pub.

Heath, Thomas Little. (1921, 2006). *A History of Greek Mathematics: Volume 1. From Thales to Euclid*. Boston: Adamant Media Corporation. (My idea that the Greeks used tipping points to find midpoints emerged right after the one about calculus. Indeed, were I to spend time looking, I'm sure I'd find that tipping-point based measurements have been used in many sciences. That no one's pointed out this simple yet profound concept for making real world measurements never ceases to amaze me.)

On the Five Factor Model of Personality
John, Oliver P., Robins, Richard W. & Pervin, Lawrence A. (2008). *Handbook of Personality: Theory and Research*. 3rd Edition. New York: The Guilford Press. (Chapters four and five give an excellent overview of the state of FFM. And while I certainly consider this approach to be of limited value in the real world, I admit I remain fascinated by it from a theoretical perspective.)

On Astrology as a Personality Theory
Fuzeau-Braesch, D.Sc., Suzel. (2009) *Astrology off the Beaten Track*. San Antonio, Texas: Anomalist Books. (I found this book to be remarkably balanced and thoroughly scientific. To wit, many astrologers would cringe reading Fuzeau-Braesch's list of astrology's scientific errors. As would many so-called scientist debunkers cringe reading her list of their errors. Whatever your bias, her impeccable scientific studies with animals show numerous positive scientific correlations which cannot be

denied. And her courage to voice her personal truth while adhering to strict scientific methods is truly admirable. A fascinating read from a truly brave woman.)

Bobgan, Deidre & Bobgan, Martin. (1992). *Four Temperaments, Astrology & Personality Testing*. Pasig City, Philippines: EastGate. (A good example of the pseudoscientific nonsense Fuzeau-Braesch debunks. Worth reading just to see the lengths to which so-called debunkers need to be debunked as well. Maybe even more.)

On the Myers-Briggs Personality Tests

Quenk, Naomi L. (2009) *Essentials of Myers-Briggs Type Indicator Assessment*. 2nd ED. New York: Wiley, John & Sons, Incorporated.

(Prior to reading this book, I had tried—and failed on numerous occasions—to make sense of the Myers-Briggs tests. However, Quenk's book is so clear and concise that I found myself repeatedly having aha's as to the many things Jung's theory and my theory have in common. Including that every question on the Myers-Briggs tests is based on tipping-point based preferences, not on quantitative measurements. Wow.)

On Personality Tests in General

Craig, Robert J. (1999). *Interpreting Personality Tests: A Clinical Manual For The MMPI-2, MCMI-III, CPI-R, And 16pf*. New York: Wiley, John & Sons, Incorporated.

Birnbaum, Debra & Freed, Jennifer. (2001). *The Ultimate Personality Guide*. New York: Penguin Books USA.

Appendix

Administering the Personality Tests

The Test Criteria

- Condition one. *The explorer shouldn't self-administer these tests.*
- Condition two. *The test administrator and the explorer cannot be connected while the explorer searches for answers.*
- Condition three. *If the explorer uses logic to find answers, this will invalidate the test results.*
- Condition four. *All answers should be checked with secondary questions voiced in the opposite state. All questions should be posed both positively and negatively.*
- Condition five. *If either person is reliving a wound while a question is being asked, this too will invalidate the answer.*
- Condition six. *All questions must be phrased as tipping-point based measurements. Only "coins tosses" lead to certain results.*

Overall, the thing to keep in mind is the first step of the wise men's method—*a personal truth must feel emotionally true.* Thus to arrive at valid answers, *you must let go of all you know and trust your intuition.* Applied to these tests this means just let go and let it happen.

Section One—the Mind Body Orientation Tests

The following tests are reprinted from Book I. I've included them as they are part of core personality. At the same time, I realize I've not discussed mind body orientation in this book. So for those who have not yet read Book I, I offer this brief explanation.

All people broadcast and receive information both with their body and their mind. However normally, we do not broadcast and receive with both simultaneously. And yes, like all aspects of personality, there are exceptions. But these exceptions are few. So in essence, we all have a bias towards either the body or the mind. In other words, we all tip in one direction.

Why does this matter?

Because your mind body orientation is the filter through which everything else in personality passes. In effect, this filter determines the manner in which you process life. Either you tend to process life first through your mind and only then through your body—the faster path. Or you tend to process life first through your body and only afterwards through your mind—the slower path.

What causes this difference?

As I told you in Book I, we have two physiological brains. By this, I mean we literally have two distinctly separate areas in our bodies where there is a significant amount of brain tissue. One is in our cranium—the brain in our head. The other is in the lining of the esophagus, diaphragm, and small intestine—the brain in our gut. Moreover, like being right-handed, we each develop a personal preference—more an unconscious tendency really—for one of these brains. Here, mind first people are like right handed folks and vice versa.

What does this tendency tell us about a person's personality?

Mind first people tend to process the mental aspects of life more quickly than their body first counterparts, especially experiences involving words. Having conversations, thinking with words, deciding what to write, reading to oneself—all come easier to mind first people. Whereas body first people tend to need more time to process these things. But this predisposes them to having an easier time learning to draw, play sports, dance, learn a musical instrument, do yoga, and read aloud.

What's behind these differences? It's simple. Minds are not subject to the physical restrictions inherent in physical movement. Thus minds can process life more quickly. At the same time, because bodies process life more slowly, they process life more thoroughly. So while body first people usually need more time to decide what to say, when they take this time, the things they say often feel more grounded. And more personal.

Why does knowing this matter? There are many reasons. For one thing, the world mistakes quick thinking for intelligence, and this biases educators towards mind first students. Sadly, this often leads body first students to be classified as learning disabled, when in fact they're not.

For another, mind first people often mistake the slower responses of body first people for a reluctance to talk or worse, that these folks are shutting them out. I can't count the number of marriages I've seen wherein this misunderstanding has poisoned the relationship.

Also, we tend to see people who have careers in sports, technical trades, cooking, and the arts as being less important than people with careers in science, medicine, law, business, and finance. So we're surprised for instance when an athlete has a great mind, or when a computer genius is good at sports.

In addition, we assume from a person's mind body orientation what this person can and cannot learn well. We then perceive limits to this person's choices in life which do not exist. That these limits undermine this person's greatest resource—self worth—only makes things worse, as ultimately this will limit this person's ability to find personal truth.

Overall then the thing to keep in mind is that mind body orientation is like having a favorite radio station. Here the analogy would be that mind first people tend to like stations which broadcast on higher frequencies and body first people on lower frequencies—something like 106.7 vs 93.7 FM. Obviously, having a higher broadcast frequency does not indicate more intelligent programming. It simply indicates the speed at which this station broadcasts.

A Few Things to Keep in Mind as You Administer the Tests

Something to keep in mind as you administer these tests is, if people mentally prepare before doing a test this will screw up the test results. This makes learning to see people doing this—and having ways to get them to stop doing this—an absolute necessity.

What's the best way to accomplish this? Simply ask people to respond to your requests as quickly as possible and without thinking. In general then, the less people think before responding, the more valid the test results.

Also keep in mind that mind body orientation is like handedness. Even right handed people do some things left handed. Thus to get a clear outcome, you'll need to do several tests, including a few voiced negatively.

Also when it comes to interpreting the results, know you'll have a much easier time if, prior to giving the tests, you've taken them yourself.

Finally, be careful not to logically assume how a test will turn out as these expectations may skew what you see. Now the tests.

Mind-Body Orientation Test #1—Throwing Fives

Like all mind-body orientation tests, this test is relatively simple. You simply ask the person to do the following.

Without thinking—and as quickly as possible—fully extend an arm, palm face forward and with all five fingers spread apart, while simultaneously saying the word *five*.

Can you picture someone doing this?

Try it. Stand up. Now as fast as you can and without thinking, extend an arm—palm face forward—as if you are signaling someone to stop. At the same time, say the word *five* as quick as you can.

What will happen?

Either your arm, hand, and fingers will begin to extend before you start saying the word *five*—or you'll start saying *five* before your arm, hand, and fingers begin to extend.

Did your hand start first? Then your normal mind-body orientation is body first. Did you say the word *five* first? Then your normal orientation is mind first.

Know I've seen people so mentally control themselves that the outcome is repeatedly invalid. Here you'll likely see people mentally preparing rather than following the part of the instructions which ask them to respond as quickly as possible and without thinking.

If this happens, you can compensate for it by asking people to deliberately cause one action to begin before the other. Either they must have their arm begin to extend before they start saying the word *five*—or they must say the word *five* before their arm begins to extend. Moreover, there must be no observable prep time spent inbetween doing these two things. If there is, again, the results will be invalid.

What are you looking for this time? Essentially, for which outcome is easier to reach. In other words, did this person find it easier to begin to extend an arm before starting to say the word *five*? Or did this person find it easier to say the word *five* before beginning to extend an arm?

If the former, then this person is body first.

If the latter, then this person is mind first.

Lastly, know you can significantly improve your ability to administer this test if you practice deliberately causing both outcomes. First cause your hand to extend first. Then say the word *five* before your arm begins to extend.

You'll be surprised at how this simple exercise can improve your ability to discern people's mind-body orientation.

Mind-Body Orientation Test #2—the Draw and Speak Test

Have you ever had to give someone driving directions? This test looks at which comes easier, drawing the map or speaking the words. Here all you need do is ask the person to draw the roads while describing the drive. If the drawing is occurring ahead of the words, then the person is body first. And if the words are being spoken ahead of the drawing, then the person is mind first.

Here again, a good way to validate this test is to ask people to reverse their normal order, then watch for discomfort and disorientation. If they normally draw then speak, ask them to speak first then draw. And if they normally speak then draw, then ask them to draw then speak.

What if the results of this test contradict the previous test?

If this happens, don't be alarmed. One of these tests represents the person's norm—the other, a counter preference. Indeed, finding people's counter preferences is a good long term goal, as it gets them to see options they usually don't consider. Thus if this happens, just make a note of it and go on to the next test.

Mind-Body Orientation Test #3—the Sing and Tap Test

For the less inhibited, another good test is to have people sing or hum while tapping a hand on their leg. Or while snapping their fingers. Know it usually doesn't matter whether people sit or stand. All that matters is that you witness a clear preference for which comes first, the singing/humming or the tapping/snapping.

Here again, asking people to deliberately get the opposite outcome gives you a way to arrive at a false outcome, and by doing this you can validate the results. Moreover once you've done these tests a few times, you'll realize how easy it is to get clear and distinct results. Mind-body orientations are literally this obvious.

Mind-Body Orientation Test #4—the Ultimate Test: Slow Talking

This test is my favorite as it's nearly impossible to fake the results. It's also one of the easier tests to administer and gives accurate results. I usually use it in a couple's first therapy session, as well as with anyone whom identifies as having ADHD. It's also a good test for determining the severity of Asperger's, as well as for one's general vulnerability to overeating.

Here's all you do.

With both of you sitting—or with both of you standing—say something to this person at an exaggeratedly slow pace. What should you say? It doesn't matter really, albeit simple is better.

For instance, you might say to this person, "How ... do ... you ... feel ... when ... people ... talk ... this ... slowly?" Or, "Do... you ... ever ... get ... annoyed ... when ... people ... talk ... too ... quickly?"

When mind first people get spoken to like this, they go out of their minds. Literally. Slow talk makes them so aware of their body that it ruins their ability to think. Conversely, body first people love it when you talk this slow. Indeed, doing this will often make them smile as hearing words at this pace brings what you're saying into focus.

How accurate is this test?

I once attended an all day seminar wherein one of my favorite neuro researchers was presenting on the brain. I respect this man a lot and see him as having done some particularly good original work on the relationship between neurotransmitters and hormones with regard to brain functioning. He literally discovered a fractal for this relationship. However when I, at the end of his seminar, asked him to comment on the brain in the body (the enteric brain), his faced deadened and he became noticeably angry. At which point, he told everyone, "this question is easy to answer—there is no enteric brain."

Right after this, people began exiting the seminar and as they did, I approached him and asked him to comment more. Moreover, as my work relies heavily on the existence of the enteric brain, I was feeling quite deflated. I then tried to dialogue with him about what made him so mad, and the more I tried to get him to comment, the more annoyed he got. At which point, I slow talked, rather loudly, to all the people still in room, that "this ... is ... what ... the ... non ... existent ... enteric ... brain ... feels ... like." Whereupon every person listening to our exchange—and everyone in the process of exiting, some hundred plus people actually—froze in surprise, including the neuro researcher. We then proceeded to have an entirely different conversation, the tone of which was now respectful and curious.

In another seminar—this one an Asperger's/Autism seminar being given by my one of my favorite speakers, psychologist John Ortiz—I was asked to briefly describe to the conference attendees my work on mind-body orientation. At which point, I slow talked a single sentence to a room of several hundred people, mainly professionals, with the same result. They all froze in surprise at how obvious the effect of this test was.

What makes me begin couples therapies with slow talk?

Mainly, it's that most couples include one person of each orientation. One spouse will be mind first, and the other, body first. Here, the mind first spouse will usually see the body first spouse as being distant and unwilling to communicate, when in truth, body first people merely hear and speak words differently than mind first people.

Remember too that we're talking about a relative difference here, not an absolute one. In other words, all I'm saying here is that, by comparison, one person is noticeably more mind orientated than the other. Indeed, there is a point at which slow talking to body first people makes them uncomfortable too. Thus what's more relevant here is the relative difference between these two people and not some absolute measure.

What does this difference do to relationships?

Misread, it causes people to feel unloved. Indeed, often the body first spouse will have endured years of being accused of being unwilling to communicate, while the mind first spouse will look to the world like a critical control freak.

What happens when a couple realizes the truth about what's been happening?

Usually, the body first person grins with delight, as he or she knows right away that someone hears them and speaks their language. Whereas the mind first person usually looks dazed and confused as, for the first time, they see evidence for there being a lot more to their spouse's lack of communication than that he or she just won't try. Or doesn't love them.

Know we'll be looking in depth at these problems in Book III, in the chapter on relationships and the chapter on learning. For now, all you need be concerned with is learning how to determine this difference.

A Few Tie-Breakers

Generally, determining people's mind body orientation is not that hard. However occasionally, people's counter preferences can cast doubt on the test results. With this in mind, I offer the following potential tie-breakers. Know that these observations are valid mind body tests only if you treat them as tipping points, as in, "which do you *tend* to do more."

- **Deciding What to Eat:** Mind first people tend to make choices based what they think is "healthy." Body first people tend to make choices based on taste.
- **How Fast You Eat:** Mind first people tend to hurry through meals. Body first people tend to eat more slowly.
- **The Type of Clumsiness:** All people are clumsy at times. Mind first people tend to be *physically* clumsy, whereas body first people tend to be *mentally* clumsy.
- **The Timing of When You Swing (baseball, tennis, golf):** Mind first people tend to think too much before they swing. Body first people swing when it feels right.

Section Two—the Character Type Tests

The first thing to know about determining people's character type is that it takes two steps. In the first step, you determine the primary state of people's character type—whether it begins in a Me state or in a You state. In the second, you use the results of the first step to arrive at people's actual character type.

Know it may be helpful—and sometimes necessary—to begin the testing by briefly describing the stages babies go through when developing a character type. Here the point would be to make sure that being seen as Me first will not be interpreted as being selfish. Indeed, in order to properly administer these tests, you yourself must be free from this bias. And to do this, you'll need to know your own character type and the character types of the major players in your life.

Lastly—and perhaps most important—you must be able to tell the difference between the needs of the person you're testing and the needs of everyone else in this person's life.

For example, say you're testing a man named Tom. Say also that Tom is a Two. In all likelihood, if asked, Tom would probably say that he "needs" to do things for other people. And in truth, he probably does feel this way. The thing is, character type is not just about how a person feels. That would make it the purview of just one wise man. Rather, character type is about whose needs your urges reference. Literally.

Needing to meet *other people's needs* does not make these needs your own. And even if you do feel the need to do things for others, the needs you'd be meeting would still be other people's needs.

Now let's start with the questions which determine people's primary character state—the step one questions.

Me State or You State? Where Does Your Character Type Begin?

This step divides all people into two groups—those whose character type begins in a Me state (Ones and Threes) and those whose character type begins in a You state (Twos and Fours). Again, remember, you're not testing for selfishness. Or for selflessness. Rather, you're looking only to see where this person focuses first—on his own needs or on the needs of others.

Also, you need not ask every question. Ask only as many as you need to reveal a clear tendency. In truth, if you're testing a person who has a good sense of what character types are, he or she should be able to decide between being Me first or You first with just one question.

We'll start with the positively voiced questions.

- When you feel needy, which feels more comfortable, having someone else meet your needs or meeting these needs yourself? Someone else = Me first. Yourself = You first.
- Which do you prefer, getting or giving? Getting = Me first. Giving = You first.
- How do you react to compliments when they're said more than once in a row? Comfortable with successive compliments = Me first. Uncomfortable the more times the compliment is said = You first.
- When you make a mistake, where do you look first for the problem, in yourself or somewhere else? Somewhere else = Me first. In yourself = You first.
- When you and someone else want to move through or occupy the same physical space (e.g. go through a door, drive through a toll booth, sit in the only empty seat), which feels more normal, for you to go first or for the other person to go first? You go first = Me first. The other person goes first = You first.
- In romantic relationships, whose needs usually get met first, yours or the other person's? Yours = Me first. The other person's = You first.
- Do you hate imposing on people—or can you ask for your needs without guilt? Ask without guilt = Me first. Hate imposing = You first.
- One of your parents was a Me first person; the other, a You first person. Which parent do you feel more at ease with—the Me first parent or the You first parent? Your character type starts in the same place as the parent you feel more at ease with.
- What were the character types of the people you've been romantically attracted to? Girlfriend or boyfriend? Husband or wife? Your character type starts in the opposite place.

Now ask the negatively voiced questions.

- Which feels less comfortable, getting or giving? Giving = Me first. Getting = You first.
- When you feel needy, which feels less comfortable, having someone else meet your needs or meeting these needs yourself? Someone else = You first. Yourself = Me first.
- How do you react to compliments when they're said to someone else and not to you? Comfortable with other people getting compliments = You first. Uncomfortable with other people getting compliments = Me first.

- When someone else makes a mistake, do you usually feel like you too might have done something wrong? Yes = You first. No = Me first.
- When you and someone else want to move through or occupy the same physical space *and* the other person goes first, how do you feel? Resentful = Me first. Fine = You first.
- In romantic relationships, if your everyday needs don't get met, how bad do you feel? In a foul mood = Me first. Like it's no biggie = You first.

Hints on Administering the First-Step Questions

Something which may help here is to remember that character type is essentially about just one thing—the direction in which a person's "river" flows. Here it either flows in the direction of giving or in the direction of receiving. Me first people's rivers flow in the direction of receiving. You first people's rivers flow in the direction of giving.

What do I mean by this? Consider these examples.

When Me first folks get compliments, they usually bask in them. And when people give them gifts, they generally beam and express gratitude. But when You first people get compliments—or when they get gifts—they often respond with anything from mild discomfort to an overwhelming need to get this giving to stop. For them, compliments go against the grain and gifts feel unnecessary.

Hence for Me first folks, getting gifts goes with the grain. But for You first folks, getting a gift is like trying to push water back up river. They'd rather give.

Conversely when you ask You first people for help, they usually beam with delight. They may even say, "thanks for asking." Whereas when you ask Me first people for help, even if they say yes, you can often feel their reluctance. Or annoyance. Again, because their river flows in the direction of getting, for them, giving is like pushing water up river.

What is Your Character Type (asking the second-step questions)?

At this point, you know which group the person you're testing belongs to, the Me first group or the You first group. Now you're ready to determine this person's actual character type. To do this, you'll ask the second-step questions and by doing so, divide the group you've arrived at into an actual character type.

Realize that because there are four character types, that there must be two sets of questions—those designed to split the Me first folks into Ones and Threes, and those designed to split the You first folks into Twos and Fours.

We'll start with some questions designed to separate people in the Me first group into *Ones* (Me then Mes) and *Threes* (Me then Yous).

- After someone meets your needs, do you then want them to get their needs met? Yes = Threes. No = Ones.
- When something bad happens, do you eventually blame yourself? Yes = Threes. No = Ones.
- When you've had an argument with someone—after you get over being mad—do you then feel bad for what happened to the other person? Yes = Threes. No = Ones.
- When people tell you you've hurt them and after you're done being mad, do you sometimes then feel responsible for their suffering (can you feel remorse)? Yes = Threes. No = Ones.
- How entitled do you feel to have other people meet your needs *without reciprocating*? Entirely = Ones. Somewhat = Threes. Here *somewhat* means less than *entirely*.

Now let's look at some questions designed to separate You first folks into *Twos* (You then Yous) and *Fours* (You then Mes).

- After you've had an argument with someone—and after you feel bad for how this has affected the other person—do you then feel bad for how this has affected you? Yes = Fours. Not usually = Twos.
- After you've given someone what they want, do you then expect them to reciprocate? Yes = Fours. Not usually = Twos.
- When something bad occurs between you and another person *and* when you've finished feeling bad for this person, do you eventually feel bad for yourself? Yes = Fours. Not usually = Twos.
- When something bad occurs between you and another person *and* when you've finished blaming yourself, do you then blame the other person? Yes = Fours. Not usually = Twos.
- To what degree are other people entitled to have you meet their needs? Entirely = Twos. Somewhat = Fours. Here *somewhat* means less than *entirely*.

Using Your Own Character Type to Validate Your Answers

At this point, you should have a good idea as to this person's character type. However, it's a good idea to use yourself to validate your results. Here again, you'll be looking to first divide all people into two groups—the Me first group and the You first group—and then to divide this result into an actual character type.

The thing is, this time, rather than ask the person questions, you're going to use what you know about your own character type to see if your conclusions hold up. For instance, consider how it would be to ask yourself the following first-step question.

- As I sit with this person, do I feel any sense of age? No sense of age means this person has the same primary state as you. A sense of age difference—either older or younger—means this person has the opposite primary state as you.

When people with the same first character state meet, they usually feel no sense of age difference. That this happens even when there is a great age difference is one of the more interesting things character types explain. Indeed, I recall a time when I, a died-in-the-wool Two, and my friend Ed, a card-carrying Three, were sitting at a table in an outdoor cafe. Next to us, there was a young mother and a baby in a stroller. I remember realizing that I felt an age difference between me and this baby, this despite the fact that he was obviously in the middle of his second year. And when I asked Ed if he felt any age difference, he said no.

What did this mean? That the baby's character type had already been decided. The baby was a one. If not, then the baby would have been at least trying on the Two character type. If this had been true, then I would have felt no sense of age. And yes, obviously Ed could rationally see this age difference. But even so, he felt no sense of age.

My point? Even when the chronological age difference between two people is several decades, you should still feel either a sense of age difference or the lack thereof. Unless of course, you and the other person are connected meaning you're both in Layer 9 or 10. In which case the test is invalid, as the experience of character type won't exist.

Still not clear as to what I mean here by a "sense of age." Then change this question to, "When I first interacted with this person, how comfortable did I feel?" Here you're looking to gauge whether you immediately felt at ease or whether you felt a bit guarded.

What do these feelings indicate?

When you're in the presence of people whose character type starts in the same place as yours *and* when you're in a normal state of mind (not in Layer 9 or 10), you'll feel at ease almost immediately. Whereas when you're in the presence of someone whose character type begins in the opposite place from yours, you'll feel anything from a bit on edge to downright guarded. Something like what most folks feel like around their parents.

Even here though, there are considerations.

For instance, because all romantic relationships—including our parent's—occur between people with opposite character types, we all have a "friend" parent and a "parent" parent. The *friend* parent is the parent whose character type starts in the same place as ours. The *parent* parent is the parent whose character type starts in the opposite place.

The point is, we all have a parent we find easier to talk to—and one we go to when the shit hits the fan. The easier to talk to parent is your friend parent. Your character type begins in the same place as this parent's does. The "shit hits the fan" parent is the parent parent.

Your character type starts in the opposite place from this parent's.

Now consider how you can use this knowledge to determine whether a person is Me first or You first. You simply compare how you feel around this person to how you feel in the presence of each of your parents. For example, you might ask yourself the following question.

- Does this person feel more like my friend parent or my parent parent? Friend parent? Then his character type starts in the same place as yours. Parent parent? Then his character type starts in the opposite place as yours.

Taking this a step further, if you've met this person's spouse or romantic partner, then ask yourself the same question. If you've correctly found this person's character type, then how you feel—age-difference wise—with this person should be the opposite of how you feel with the person being tested.

Addressing the Second Step

Now you'll need to address the second step Admittedly, this can be a bit harder. Twos and Fours—and Ones and Threes—can at times appear quite alike. However if you use your sense of your own character type, you should be able to sense this difference. Indeed, eventually you'll just develop a sense for people's character type. Ones will feel like they take up all the space in a room. Threes will feel like they take up much less space. Fours will feel like they take up little to no space in the room. And Twos. Well, they often feel like they're apologizing for taking up any space at all.

Ones will also feel like they see themselves like a king or queen. Threes will see themselves as the boss or manager. Fours will feel like they want to offer help but get something in return. And Twos will feel like they want to help you even when you say no.

Finally, the most important thing of all to remember is to get input from all four wise men. This means trust your intuition—then collect personal facts—then solicit life stories—and then use your logic.

Section Three—the Social Priority Tests

The first thing to keep in mind as you administer these tests is that these test questions are designed for adults not children. Indeed, even some adolescents may struggle to come up with answers. This said, many adolescents can take these tests and arrive at meaningful outcomes. Moreover, if you know a younger child well enough, you may be able to answer the questions for them and in doing so, get at least a working sense of their social priorities.

In truth, people's social priorities are often visible by age four and certainly discernable by age seven. Moreover, if you've read chapter six with enough care, you should be able to devise test questions for just about anyone you know. I, for one, would love to hear about this if you do decide to try. So if you do, please consider forwarding me your tests.

As for how to administer these tests, there are only two things to keep in mind. First, advise people that they must answer these questions without thinking with the first thing that comes to mind. In other words, don't allow people ruminate on the question. Second, do not allow people to change their first response or allow them time to reconsider their answer.

Now you're ready to begin.

Start by asking the first tipping-point-based question. Then circle the person's preference. Now continue until all six questions have been answered. Again, if you see people hesitating for more than a few seconds, gently urge them to respond with the first answer that comes to mind. Then when you have all six answers, it's time to convert these answers into a set of social priorities. To do this, just follow the directions on the process part of the form.

For example, in the example of the opposite page, there were three circled answers where *freedom* was on top. Notice how I've transferred these three answers to the three topmost boxes in the social priority ladder. There were also two answers which had *neatness* as the upper priority. I transferred these two answers to the second line of the process boxes. Finally I located the remaining answer and copied it into the bottom process box.

Next I copied the social priorities which had arrows next to them into the appropriate social priority answer boxes.

Finally if, during the testing, the person struggles to get an answer, note this in the Notes section. Ambivalence often leads to doubtful answers. And if no priority gets three results? Then you'll need to try another test.

Positively Biased
Social Priority Question Set 8

Social Priority Questions	**Choices**

Which sounds better,
massages or seminars?

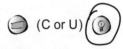 (C or U)

Which sounds better,
to do it your way or to do it well?

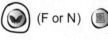 (F or N)

Which would you rather get, an
expensive vacuum or a good professor?

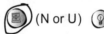 (N or U)

Which would you rather be,
outspoken or well cared for?

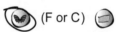 (F or C)

Which would you rather be,
rested or organized?

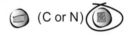 (C or N)

Which would you rather be,
bright or blunt?

 (U or F)

Process

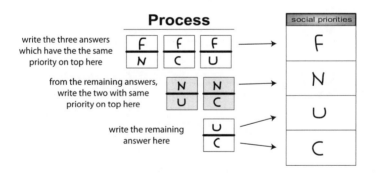

write the three answers
which have the the same
priority on top here

from the remaining answers,
write the two with same
priority on top here

write the remaining
answer here

Notes

Ambivalent on question 2. Try a few
f/n negatively phrased questions

Sample

Positively Biased
Social Priority Question Set 1
©2005 Steven Paglierani The Emergence Alliance Inc

Social Priority Questions	**Choices**

Which is more important,
being comfortable or being neat?
 (C or N)

Which would you prefer,
being smart or being free?
 (U or F)

Which is better,
being pampered or being tutored?
 (C or U)

Which is better, being
independent or being organized?
 (F or N)

Which would serve you more,
better plans or better ideas?
 (N or U)

Which would you prefer, a day to do
whatever you want or a day at a spa?
 (F or C)

Process

write the three answers
which have the the same
priority on top here

from the remaining answers,
write the two with same
priority on top here

write the remaining
answer here

social priorities

Notes

Positively Biased

Social Priority Question Set 2

©2005 Steven Paglierani The Emergence Alliance Inc

Social Priority Questions		**Choices**	

Which would be better,
to produce a lot or be soothed a lot?
 (N or C)

Which would you rather be, an
outspoken critic or an expert witness?
 (F or U)

Which would you rather do, study in a
great library or relax in a candle-lit bath?
 (U or C)

Which would you rather be,
a bank manager or a freelance artist?
 (N or F)

Which is more important, to get an
education or to have an occupation?
 (U or N)

Which feels better, to curl up on a couch
or to sit on a log by a camp fire?
 (C or F)

Process

write the three answers
which have the the same
priority on top here

from the remaining answers,
write the two with same
priority on top here

write the remaining
answer here

social priorities

Notes

Positively Biased

Social Priority Question Set 3

©2005, Steven Paglieranj The Emergence Alliance Inc

Social Priority Questions	**Choices**
Which would you rather be, well fed or well read?	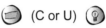 (C or U)
Which feels better to you, having no rules or having clear rules?	 (F or N)
Which feels better to you, to do a lot or to learn a lot?	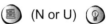 (N or U)
You're eating out. Would you rather eat, exotic food you pick, or tasty food someone else picks?	 (F or C)
Which feels better, to get a good night's sleep or to do a good day's work?	(C or N) 
Which would you rather get, challenging homework or no homework?	(U or F)

Process

social priorities

write the three answers
which have the the same
priority on top here

from the remaining answers,
write the two with same
priority on top here

write the remaining
answer here

Notes

Positively Biased

Social Priority Question Set 4

©2005, Steven Paglieranj The Emergence Alliance Inc

Social Priority Questions	**Choices**
You're getting a gift. Which would you rather get, a great book or a great meal?	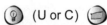 (U or C)
You have a to-do list. Which would feel better, to complete it or to just tear it up?	(N or F)
You're hiring an employee. Should this person be insightful or committed?	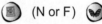 (U or N)
You are redecorating your home. Do you focus on beauty or on spaciousness?	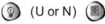 (C or F)
You are applying for a job. Which would you prefer, a secure job or an easy job?	(N or C)
Same situation. You're applying for a job. Which would you prefer, flexible hours or a stimulating mission?	(F or U)

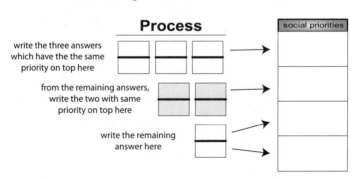

Notes

Positively Biased

Social Priority Question Set 5

Social Priority Questions	**Choices**

You're applying for a job. Is it better to be well groomed or well schooled? 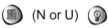 (N or U)

You're going on a date. Which would you rather be, unique or calm? 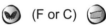 (F or C)

You're buying shoes. Which is more important, good fit or good wear? 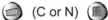 (C or N)

Which would you rather be, an inventor or a rebel? (U or F)

It's your day off. Would you rather relax or learn? 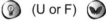 (C or U)

You're in school. Which would you rather have, no assignments or neat assignments? 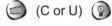 (F or N)

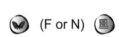

Process

write the three answers which have the the same priority on top here →

from the remaining answers, write the two with same priority on top here →

write the remaining answer here →

social priorities

Notes

Positively Biased

Social Priority Question Set 6

©2005, Steven Paglierani The Emergence Alliance Inc

Social Priority Questions	**Choices**
Which would you rather do, study or straighten up?	(U or N)
Which do you prefer, wearing casual clothes, or wearing your kind of clothes?	(C or F)
Which would you rather do, clean the kitchen or take a bath?	(N or C)
Which would you rather be, spontaneous or perceptive?	(F or U)
Which would you rather be, insightful or calm?	(U or C)
Which would you rather be, focused or frank?	(N or F)

Process

write the three answers which have the the same priority on top here

from the remaining answers, write the two with same priority on top here

write the remaining answer here

social priorities

Notes

Positively Biased
Social Priority Question Set 7
©2005, Steven Paglierani The Emergence Alliance Inc

Social Priority Questions	**Choices**
You're looking for a new apartment. Should it be cozy or have a lot of closet space?	(C or N)
You're first child is about to be born. Would you rather the baby be intelligent, or independent?	(U or F)
Which appeals to you more, to be snug and warm or to be savvy and perceptive?	(C or U)
Which would you rather be, outrageous or efficient?	(F or N)
Which would you rather be, tidy or wise?	(N or U)
Which feels better, to be bold or to be serene?	(F or C)

Process

write the three answers which have the the same priority on top here ⟶

from the remaining answers, write the two with same priority on top here ⟶

write the remaining answer here ⟶

social priorities

Notes

Positively Biased
Social Priority Question Set 8
©2005 Steven Paglierani The Emergence Alliance Inc

Social Priority Questions	**Choices**
Which sounds better, massages or seminars?	(C or U)
Which sounds better, to do it your way or to do it well?	(F or N)
Which would you rather get, an expensive vacuum or a good professor?	(N or U)
Which would you rather be, outspoken or well cared for?	(F or C)
Which would you rather be, rested or organized?	(C or N)
Which would you rather be, bright or blunt?	(U or F)

Process

write the three answers which have the the same priority on top here

from the remaining answers, write the two with same priority on top here

write the remaining answer here

social priorities

Notes

Negatively Biased
Social Priority Question Set 1
©2005 Steven Paglieranj The Emergence Alliance Inc

Social Priority Questions	**Choices**
Which feels worse, being uncomfortable or being unorganized?	 (C or N)
Which feels worse, being wrong or being forced?	(U or F)
Which do you dislike more, having a cold or being bored?	(C or U)
Which is harder for you, to have to follow rules or to have to leave a mess?	(F or N)
Which feels worse, having something break or making a mistake?	(N or U)
Which feels worse, working long hours or working in the rain?	(F or C)

Process

social priorities

write the three answers
which have the the same
priority on top here

from the remaining answers,
write the two with same
priority on top here

write the remaining
answer here

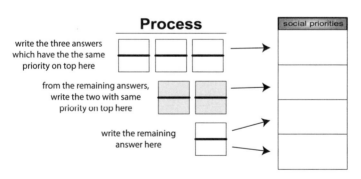

Notes

Negatively Biased
Social Priority Question Set 2
©2005, Steven Paglieranj The Emergence Alliance Inc

Social Priority Questions	Choices
Which feels worse, being messy or being tired?	(N or C)
Which feels worse, being pressured on a job or having a mindless job?	(F or U)
Which would you dislike more, not knowing or being damp?	(U or C)
Which is harder for you, being unable to clean up or being forced to clean up?	(N or F)
Which is worse to have, a boring recipe or a dirty oven?	(U or N)
Which is harder for you, to miss lunch or to miss your break?	(C or F)

Process

social priorities

write the three answers which have the the same priority on top here

from the remaining answers, write the two with same priority on top here

write the remaining answer here

Notes

Negatively Biased

Social Priority Question Set 3

Social Priority Questions   ## Choices

Which is harder for you,
not eating or not knowing?   (C or U)

Which is worse, working on your day
off or losing a day's pay?   (F or N)

Which is harder for you,
clutter or confusion?   (N or U)

Which is harder for you, being told not to
turn up the heat up or being cold?   (F or C)

Which would feel worse, having no time
to sleep or having no time to clean?   (C or N)

Which would feel worse, having nothing
to learn or having no free time?   (U or F)

Process

social priorities

write the three answers
which have the the same
priority on top here

from the remaining answers,
write the two with same
priority on top here

write the remaining
answer here

Notes

Negatively Biased

Social Priority Question Set 4

©2005 Steven Paglieranj The Emergence Alliance Inc

Social Priority Questions	**Choices**
Which would be worse, getting a bad teacher or getting a bad massage?	(U or C) 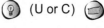
Which would feel worse, living in a dusty home or working for a controlling boss?	(N or F)
Which would be worse, being unable to learn or being unable to plan?	(U or N)
Which would be worse, being sick or being forced to take medicine?	(C or F)
Which would feel worse, having dirty hands or having chapped hands?	(N or C)
Which do you dislike more, feeling trapped or feeling confused?	(F or U)

Process

social priorities

write the three answers which have the the same priority on top here

from the remaining answers, write the two with same priority on top here

write the remaining answer here

Notes

Negatively Biased

Social Priority Question Set 5

Social Priority Questions   ## Choices

In school, which is worse, forgetting
your pens or forgetting an answer?   (N or U)

In life, which is worse, friends that try
to control you or houses that smell?   (F or C)

With clothes, which is worse,
scratchy material or mismatched colors?   (C or N)

With teachers which is worse, a
boring teacher or a bossy teacher?   (U or F)

At work, which is worse,
no time to relax or no time to learn?   (C or U)

With jobs, which is worse,
too many rules or too much to do?   (F or N)

Process   social priorities

write the three answers
which have the the same
priority on top here

from the remaining answers,
write the two with same
priority on top here

write the remaining
answer here

Notes

Negatively Biased

Social Priority Question Set 6

©2005, Steven Paglierani, The Emergence Alliance Inc

Social Priority Questions   ## Choices

Which would feel worse, having no time to study or no time to straighten up? (U or N)

Which would feel worse, having sticky hands or being told to wash your hands? (C or F)

Which would be more upsetting, a dirty bathroom or a bath with no hot water? (N or C)

Which would feel worse, being unable to be spontaneous or unable to be perceptive? (F or U)

Which would be more upsetting, to lack insight or to lack sleep? (U or C)

Which would be worse, to be unfocused or unable to be frank? (N or F)

Process   social priorities

write the three answers which have the the same priority on top here

from the remaining answers, write the two with same priority on top here

write the remaining answer here

Notes

Negatively Biased

Social Priority Question Set 7

©2005, Steven Paglieranj The Emergence Alliance Inc

Social Priority Questions   ## Choices

Which feels worse, being
uncomfortable or being unorganized?   🖐 (C or N) 📖

Which feels worse,
being outsmarted or being forbidden?   💡 (U or F) 🦋

Which is worse,
a lumpy bed or a bad movie?   🛏 (C or U) 💡

Which affects you more,
restrictions on your time or wasted time?   🦋 (F or N) 📖

Which feels worse, losing your keys
or losing your interest?   📖 (N or U) 💡

Which would be worse,
being trapped or being sick?   🦋 (F or C) 🛏

Process

write the three answers
which have the the same
priority on top here

from the remaining answers,
write the two with same
priority on top here

write the remaining
answer here

social priorities

Notes

Negatively Biased
Social Priority Question Set 8
©2005, Steven Paglieranj The Emergence Alliance Inc

Social Priority Questions	**Choices**
Which is harder, being hungry or being ignorant?	(C or U)
Which is harder, losing a day off or losing a day's pay?	(F or N)
Which is worse, a cluttered closet or a dull book?	(N or U)
Which would you struggle with more, being restricted or being overtired?	(F or C)
Which is worse, tasteless food or tattered clothes?	(C or N)
Which is harder, being outfoxed or taking orders?	(U or F)

Process

social priorities

write the three answers which have the the same priority on top here

from the remaining answers, write the two with same priority on top here

write the remaining answer here

Notes

Section Four—the Decision Tree Tests

These tests are simple and easy to administer. Just picture the positions of the Decision Tree map quadrants while asking the following questions.

Question One

As you begin decisions, do you feel in charge of making these decisions (internal locus of control). Or do you feel like someone else is in control of these decisions (external locus of control)?

Question-One Answers

If, as people begin their decisions, they feel like they're in charge, then their decision tree is in the right half of the map—either the Bluntness tree or the Precision tree. Whereas if they feel like this decision will come from someone else, then their decision tree is in the left half of the map—either the Correction tree or the Digression tree.

Alternative Question-One

No clear answer? Then ask if they feels like their decisions begin at the beginning or at the ending—whether they feel like they've already been made or are just beginning to be made.

Alternative Question-One Answers

Already made? Then people's decision tree is in the left half of the map—either the Correction or Digression tree. Just beginning to be made? Then people's decision tree is in the right half—either the Bluntness or Precision tree.

Question Two

When you begin decisions, where do they start, with something physical or with something mental?

Question-Two Answers

If, as people begin their decision, physical things influence them more, then their decision tree is in the bottom half of the map—either the Bluntness tree or the Correction tree. Both of these processes focus more on physical factors than on mental factors. Whereas if they feel like they base their decisions more on what their mind says than on what their body says, then their decision tree is in the top half of the map—either the Precision tree or the Digression tree. Both of these trees focus more on mental influences than on physical influences.

Personalizing the Test Question Settings

Admittedly, some folks will find these questions hard to answer. If this happens, ask them to imagine a decision. Even mundane decisions such as what movie people want to see or what they want for lunch can work here. Simply have them picture the event. Then have them answer the two test questions while imagining this event.

Testing for the
Four Primary Decision Trees

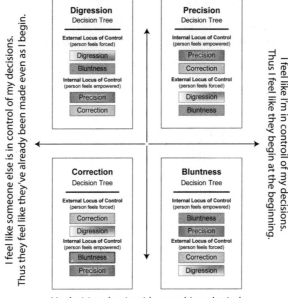

Still no clear answer? Then ask them to decide something simple such as which is better, a pencil or a pen, while watching them make this decision. Here you will need to use what you observe to arrive at answers for the two test questions.

Picturing the Quadrants of the Decision Tree Map

Finally, if you remember to picture the map while you're administering these tests, you'll feel more confident about your results. Here Bluntness is located in the lower right quadrant and is physical, internal, just beginning, and fixed. Correction is located in the lower left quadrant and is physical, external, already made, and changing. Precision is located in the upper right quadrant and is mental, internal, just beginning, and fixed. And Digression is located in the upper left quadrant and mental, external, already made, and changing.

Section Five—the Gender Identity Tests

The first thing to know about administering the gender identity tests is that you'll need to let the test form guide the process. In all, you're going to be measuring thirty-two tipping-points. Thus the testing process is far too complex to contain in your head. On the other hand, you'll be using the same two questions throughout the tests. So once you get the hang of asking these two questions, administering the tests will be easy.

The two questions?

Question One

In this setting, do your need-meeting urges/efforts tend to be assertive (outwardly moving) or receptive (inwardly moving)? This is the direction question.

Question Two

In this setting, do your need-meeting urges/efforts tend to be meek or bold? This is the degree of need-meeting force question.

With regard to the direction question, either people tend to go after what they want (assertive). Or they tend to try to draw the solution to them (receptive). And with regard to the degree of need-meeting force question, either their urges/efforts tend to be careful and cautious (meek). Or they tend to be intrepid and daring (bold).

Of course, the key to getting accurate test results is to make sure these questions stay tipping-point based. And with the direction question, doing this is easy. Either people's urges/efforts focus inward or outward. But with the degree of need-meeting force question, doing this can be hard, especially if they intellectually ruminate on the difference between meek efforts and bold ones.

The thing to keep in mind then will be the word "tendency." Either people tend to execute need-meeting decisions fearlessly or carefully. Remember too that these measures can focus in two places—on people's need-meeting urges and on their efforts. So either you're measuring only their urges to make these efforts, or only the efforts themselves.

What's the difference?

Efforts exist physically. Efforts are things you actually do. How you dress. How you talk. How much space you take up around your friends. Whereas urges do not exist physically. Rather they are what your inner voice tells you. Things like what your head tells you to wear, what you morally think you should say, what you feel pressured by society to do, and so on.

Why measure both? Because much of our suffering stems from mind body mismatches—from behaving a certain way while having urges to behave in an entirely different way. Here people may have urges they never act on or efforts they halfheartedly execute. Either way, when this happens, there will be significant differences between their behavior and urges. Indeed, they may hide these urges so well that not even their closest friends know. In which case, they'll likely suffer from self doubt, fear of discovery, and so on.

These kinds of conflicts—or the lack thereof—are one of the main things these tests reveal. Indeed, testing for them is one of the more significant differences between the wise men's personality theory and other theories. No previous personality tests offer a way to accurately measure real world differences between urges and behaviors, let alone a theoretical framework within which to understand these differences. And to see what I mean, let's examine the test form.

An Overview of the Test Form

To begin with, take a look at the blank form located on the following page. Notice how it's divided into two sections. In the upper section—the Core Gender Orientation section—you measure people's urges; what they experience inside. And in the lower section—the Gender Presentation section—you measure how they behave; what shows on the outside.

Now notice how both sections contain four double-headed arrows. These four arrows represent the four settings in which people look to meet needs—in physical, sexual, psychological, and social settings. Now notice how each of these arrows has two segmented bars associated with it—one above it and one below. You record the answers to the test questions on these segmented bars.

Realize too that each bar will end up with only one mark. At the same time, this one mark will represent the combined response of the two test questions. Here the direction question determines which side of the midline this mark goes on—to the left of the midline (receptive) or to the right (assertive). And the degree of need-meeting force question determines the length of this mark—whether it's short (meek) or long (bold).

What's the difference between the upper and lower bars?

Marks on the upper bars represent people's need-meeting experiences in friend-type relationships—the urges they feel and efforts they make in relationships with people whose character type starts in the same place as theirs does. Either two Me-first people or two You-first people. Whereas marks on the lower bars represent people's need-meeting experiences in family-type relationships—the urges they feel and efforts they make in relationships where their character type starts in the opposite place from the other person. A Me-first person with a You-first person and vice versa.

Gender Identity Chart   name: date:

Core Gender Orientation - your *inside gender* / your *urges*
(This section is required)

more yin → Receptive   Assertive ← more yang

Social Gender
friend-type relationships   friend-type relationships
family-type relationships   family-type relationships

Psychological Gender
friend-type relationships   friend-type relationships
family-type relationships   family-type relationships

Sexual Gender
friend-type relationships   friend-type relationships
family-type relationships   family-type relationships

Physical Gender
friend-type relationships   friend-type relationships
family-type relationships   family-type relationships

meek   bold

Gender Presentation - your *outside gender* / your *efforts*
(This section is optional)

more yin → Receptive   Assertive ← more yang

Social Gender
friend-type relationships   friend-type relationships
family-type relationships   family-type relationships

Psychological Gender
friend-type relationships   friend-type relationships
family-type relationships   family-type relationships

Sexual Gender
friend-type relationships   friend-type relationships
family-type relationships   family-type relationships

Physical Gender
friend-type relationships   friend-type relationships
family-type relationships   family-type relationships

meek   bold

Must You Complete Both Sections?

Some may be wondering if they need to complete both sections. After all, if determining someone's core personality is all you're looking to do here, then only the first section—the Core Gender Orientation section—is required. And in truth, if this is what you decide to do it will be fine. To be honest though, the best way to administer these tests is to alternate your questions between the two sections, one relationship/setting at a time. Typically, you'd begin by asking the two questions for the Physical, friend-type setting in the Gender Presentation section. Then you'd ask the same two questions for the Physical, friend-type setting in the Core Gender Orientation section.

Why would you want to do this? Because when you alternate between the Presentation and Orientation sections, people find it easier to discern between their urges and behaviors. More times than not, this will improve the accuracy of their answers. In addition, this honors the part of human nature which needs to warm up before revealing secrets. Urges, which are internal things, are often more secret than behaviors. Lastly, utilizing the interplay between urges and behaviors (the outside self versus the inside self) makes these tests even more tipping-point based, in that these two sections are also complementary opposites.

Now let's look at how to administer the test.

Doing the Mental Pre-Test Warm Up

If you're going to administer both sections, start with the bottom-most setting of the Presentation section; physical gender. Now take a moment to get a sense of this person's physical presentation (efforts)—clothing, body, voice, etc. Now remind yourself of what you're looking for in question one. In this setting, do this person's need-meeting efforts tend to be assertive (move outward) or receptive (move inward)?

What does it mean to ask this question about someone's appearance?

People whose efforts move inward tend to place much importance on how they appear. They do this to draw attention to themselves in hopes this will get others to want to meet their needs. People whose efforts move outward however are more concerned with making things happen. So rather than draw things to them, they tend to go after what they want.

For example, physically receptive women tend to wear sexy dresses, flowing clothing, more makeup, and heels—in hopes they'll draw attention to themselves and in doing so, get what they want. Whereas physically assertive women care less about this attention and more about not having to wait. So they tend to wear more functional clothing like jeans, pants, tailored clothing, little if any makeup, and pumps, flats, or sneakers.

Conversely, physically receptive men tend to dress to fit in. They do this in hopes they won't make waves which prevent their needs from being met. Whereas physically assertive men dress to stand out from the crowd. They do this in hopes they'll be seen as powerful and thus, be able to take what they need.

When it comes to gender and physical appearance then, men's and women's appearances get interpreted differently. What is considered receptive for women is considered assertive for men, and vice versa. Now add to this that depending on the situation, the same clothing on the same person can tip either way, and you begin to see why we've been struggling to understand gender.

For example, a woman wearing a man-tailored, conservative suit to a business conference would likely tip towards the assertively female end of the spectrum. But if this same woman wore this suit to a wedding, she'd likely stand out, tipping her towards being receptively female.

Speaking of male and female, some may have noticed this form makes no mention of these words. Admittedly this may seem odd in a test for gender. However since limiting the difference in genders to people's genitals would be woefully inadequate, with few exceptions, the questions on this form have nothing to do with genital gender. Physical appearance is one of those exceptions.

This then is the one thing you need concern yourself with here—is this person trying to draw attention to him or herself—or not? With regard to women, if yes, then she tips towards the physically receptive end of the spectrum. If no, then she tips towards the physically assertive side of the scale. And with regard to men, these two answers get reversed.

Admittedly, this is not the way most people use the word *assertive*. Or the word *receptive*. But if you keep in mind how I've defined these two words—as the direction of a person's need-meeting efforts—you'll do fine. In general, receptive people look to *draw* attention to themselves and in doing so, get their needs met. Assertive people don't care about this attention. They look to *assert* their way into getting their needs met. And yes, there is one exception—with regard to physical appearance, men and women are opposites. Other than that though, this rule holds true.

As for question two, it's simple. After determining the direction of these efforts, you then assess their degree-of-force. Are these efforts meek or bold? Remember, you're looking only to tip this answer one way or the other.

What would doing this look like?

Say we're talking about a woman. Does she go to the supermarket looking like a fashion model? These are bold receptive efforts. Nice skirt and blouse at the PTA meeting? Meek receptive efforts. Pants and sweater at the office? Meek assertive efforts. Conservative business suit at the sales meeting? Bold assertive efforts.

And a man?

Does he dress like a suit model at the business meeting? Gangsta rapper at the hip-hop club? These are bold assertive efforts. Dress slacks and shirt at the office? Perfectly creased uniform at the job? Meek assertive efforts. Nice jeans and a short-sleeved shirt at the family function? Meek receptive efforts. Raggedy shorts and tee at the picnic? Bold receptive efforts.

Asking Question One for Physical/Friend Presentation

Okay. You've completed your mental pre-test warm up. Now you're ready to begin the tests. Know it's often a good idea to explain to the person what you're looking for. For instance, you might start with a brief explanation as to what friend-type relationships are.

Is this necessary? Not really. Most times, saying "friends" will suffice. At the same time, people should be clear as to the tipping points involved. With friend-type relationships, people's character types start in the same place. With family-type relationships, they start in the opposite place.

How might you say this to the person?

You could say something like, "I'm going to be asking you some questions about how you physically present yourself in and around friends, everything from what you wear and how you carry yourself to how much physical space you take up in public places."

Realize it may make it easier if you don't use the words *assertive* or *receptive*. Instead, try saying things like, "do you tend to try to wait for things to come to you, or do you tend to go after things?"

For example, you might say something like, "When you decide what to wear, do you tend to want people to notice you? Remember, women who dress to impress draw attention inward (receptive). Men who do this push attention outward (assertive). Whereas women who tend to dress to fit in look to avoid drawing attention to themselves (assertive female). And men who do this tend to want people to look past them as well (receptive male).

Another question you might ask is, "When seeing friends, do you tend to make a statement, or do you tend to dress like everyone else? In other words, do you tend to be flamboyant and want to be noticed, or do you prefer to dress similarly to your friends?

Here again, when it comes to physical appearance, remember, men and women are opposites, direction wise. Flamboyant men are assertive. Flamboyant women are receptive. Conservative women are assertive. Conservative men are receptive.

Oddly, when it comes to managing personal space, this difference doesn't exist. Men's and women's answers indicate the same thing. So for instance, say you ask, "When going with friends to a restaurant or a movie, do you tend to ask where you should sit (receptive)? Or do you tend to just take your seat (assertive)?" The answers apply to both men and women.

Remember, you're looking to do only one thing here—tip the direction of this person's need-meeting efforts in physical settings one way or the other. People who look to—or wait for input from—others look to draw attention to themselves (receptive). People who tend to just take their seat prefer to do things for themselves (assertive).

Now here's a brief list of possible questions.

- When you travel with friends, do you usually drive (assertive direction) or does someone drive you (receptive direction)?
- Regarding sports and friends, do you usually play (assertive direction) or watch (receptive direction)?
- Regarding your appearance in and around friends, do you tend to make a statement (assertive male/receptive female) or fit in (assertive female/receptive male)?
- When you talk with friends, do you generally speak softly (receptive female/assertive male) or loudly (assertive female/receptive male)?
- Regarding meals with friends (and if you can cook), would you rather prepare the meal (assertive direction) or be served the meal (receptive direction)?
- When you're at a restaurant with friends, do you tend to shrink inward and take up little space (receptive direction), or spread out and take up a lot of space (assertive)?
- Regarding friends visiting your home, do you prefer your home feel spacious (assertive direction) or cozy (receptive direction)?
- When you're out walking, hiking, jogging, or skiing with friends, do you prefer relaxed trails (receptive direction) or vigorous trails (assertive direction)?

Obviously, there are many other questions you could ask. Also, given time to ruminate, some folks will turn this into a mental clusterfuck. In reality though, if you keep it simple, even one or two questions should suffice. Indeed, the simpler you keep the process, the more accurate the results will be.

At this point, you're almost ready to mark the form. But before you do, silently ask yourself if this person's answers match what you see. Moreover, if your sense of this person doesn't match her answers, then gently probe a bit. Indeed, if need be—and if it feels appropriate and safe to her—you can even let her know what you see. Before doing this though, be sure to tell her that her answer is what matters most.

Asking Question Two for Physical/Friend Presentation

Once you've arrived at an answer, locate the friend-type, physical setting in the Presentation section and mark an "x" on the appropriate side. Receptive folks get charted to the left. Assertive folks get charted to the right.

Why just an "x?" Because you've yet to ask the degree-of-force question. Here getting an answer will be easy as long as you remember that you're only looking to tip the answer one way or the other.

The question? How forceful are these efforts? In other words, how much do effort does this person make? Not much equals the meek degree-of-force. A lot equals the bold degree-of-force.

Now extend the "x" marks you previously made to reflect this strength. Meek marks are about three clicks long. Bold marks are about five.

Asking the Questions for Physical/Friend Orientation

Next you'll need to see whether this person's physical friend *behavior* matches her physical friend *urges*—in other words, whether her physical Presentation (her outer self) in friend-type relationships differs from her physical Orientation (her inner self). Here again, it may be helpful to set the stage with a few examples.

For instance, you might say something like, "You told me, when you're out with friends, you dress conservatively. Do you feel this is truly you—or do you secretly wish you could dress with more flair? In other words, is there a difference between the way you feel inside and the way you feel outside? Or does your outer self match your inner self, physical appearance wise?"

You'll also need to ask a physical space question, something like, "when sitting with friends in a restaurant or at a movie, do you tend to want them to decide where to sit, or do you decide?"

Here again, this person may want to just take her seat (assertive direction) but wait anyway (receptive direction). Or she may just take her seat. Either way, after you get a clear answer, record an "x" on the appropriate side of the physical friend Orientation part of the form.

Now ask Question Two. "How forceful are these urges? In other words, are your urges meek or strong?"

Not much equals the meek degree-of-force. A lot equals the bold degree-of-force.

Now extend the "x" to reflect this degree-of-force.

Asking the Physical/Family Setting Questions

Now go through the same two-question sequence for the two physical/family settings. But this time, start with the Orientation section (urges). Here you'll ask the same two questions, but with romantic relationships in mind. For instance, you could ask, "when traveling with your husband or boyfriend, do you usually drive (assertive direction), or does he drive you (receptive direction)?"

Again, tip question one then mark an "x." Then tip question two, then extend the length of this "x."

Finally when you've completed this setting, do the same for the physical/family Presentation section. And when you're done, you'll be ready to explore the four sexual situations.

Asking the Sexual/Friend Presentation Questions

Hopefully, by the time you get to these questions, you'll have established a connection with this person, as some folks feel uncomfortable answering sexual questions. Fortunately, all you need get in the way of responses are head nods and single word answers. Receptive or assertive. Meek or bold.

What are you looking for with regard to sex and friends? Essentially, how open the person is with them regarding sex. Does she openly discuss sex with friends or does she hang back and listen? You're also looking to see how open she is to making sexual innuendoes and joking about sex. Here you'll need to ask things like:

- Around friends, do you tend to initiate casual talk about sex—jokes, stories, innuendo? Assertive folks do. Receptive folks would rather listen, then respond. Or not talk about it at all.
- Do you share the sexual aspects of your relationships openly with friends (assertive direction), or do they know little to nothing about that aspect of your life (receptive direction)?

- When you're out with friends, are you sexually adventurous, meaning, do you tend to flirt, kid about sex, and ask others sexual questions (assertive direction)? Or are you the quiet one—more laid back and generally more conservative when it comes to talking about sex (receptive direction)?
- When you're around friends, are you more likely to be a flirt (assertive direction) or watch someone else flirt (receptive direction)?
- When you're watching a movie with friends and a sexy scene comes on, do you feel excited and show it (assertive direction), or do you get embarrassed and try to hide your reaction (receptive direction).
- How would you feel about going to a sex-toy store with your friends, excited (assertive direction) or embarrassed (receptive direction).

Again, when you're done, mark an "x" on the appropriate side of the midline. Then ask the degree-of-force question and extend this "x" to reflect either meek or bold.

Asking the Sexual Orientation Section Questions

Now ask these same questions for the sexual/friend setting of the Orientation section. Then ask the sexual/family questions listed below. As with the physical setting questions, you're looking for discrepancies between urges and efforts, and between friends and romantic partners.

Again begin by asking question one—the direction question. Does the direction of your need-meeting urges/efforts tend to move inward (receptive) or outward (assertive)? Mark the answer with an "x" on the appropriate side of the midline. Then ask the degree-of-force question, extending the "x" to the appropriate length—three clicks for meek or five for bold.

Asking the Sexual/Family Presentation Questions

Now ask the person these questions for her sexual need-meeting efforts in family-type relationships. Here you'll ask things like:

- When it comes to romantic interests and sex, would you more likely chase (assertive direction) or be caught (receptive direction)?
- Who is the dominant partner during sex? Assertive folks tip in the dominant direction. Receptive folks tip in the submissive direction.

- Around your husband or boyfriend, do you tend to initiate casual talk about sex—jokes, stories, innuendo (assertive direction)? Or would rather listen, then respond. Or not talk about it at all (receptive direction).
- Do you share the sexual aspects of your relationships openly with your partner (assertive direction), or does he know little to nothing about that aspect of your life (receptive direction)?
- When you're out with your partner, are you sexually adventurous, meaning, do you tend to flirt, kid about sex, and ask provocative questions (assertive direction)? Or are you the quiet one, more laid back, and generally more conservative regarding talking about sex (receptive direction)?

Know that this pattern is what you'll be using to advance through all four sections. For each setting, you begin by asking the friend-type relationship questions in the Presentation section. Then you ask the friend-type relationship questions in the Orientation section. Then you ask the family-type relationship questions in the Orientation section. Finally you ask the friend-type relationship questions in the Presentation section.

One final note.

Some folks might wonder why people's physical appearance isn't considered part of people's sexual gender? The answer? This would depend on the point for that low-cut blouse versus that buttoned-to-the-neck sweater. Is it meant to be visual foreplay? Or is it non-sexual attention-getting? To be honest, it could be either. Moreover, to make it easier, I'd suggest you leave the appearance stuff for the physical gender section, the social stuff for the social section, the psychological stuff for the psychological section, and the explicitly sexual stuff for the sexual section. And yes, there are explicitly sexual things people do appearance wise. So if it really sounds explicitly sexual, then make an exception and go ahead and use it. Otherwise, let this go.

Asking the Psychological Setting Questions

You'll proceed through the psychological part of the test the same way you did in the prior two sections—with the friend-type part of the Presentation section, followed by the friend-type part of the of the Orientation section. Then you'll do the family-type part of the Orientation section. Then finish up with the family-type part of the Presentation section.

What kinds of questions should you ask this time?

- When you're hanging out with friends, how much space do you take up in conversations? Taking up space is assertive. Making space is receptive.
- When you're with friends, would you more likely offer an opinion/express a belief (assertive direction) or seek an opinion/consider a belief (receptive direction).
- When one of your friends voices an opposing view, do you hold your own or push back? Assertive folks do. Receptive folks yield.
- When one of your friends asks you for your thoughts on something you know little about, do you venture a guess (assertive direction) or fold the question back on the questioner (receptive direction)?
- When the topic turns to things like politics or social issues, do you risk upsetting your friends? Yes (assertive direction) or not (receptive direction)?
- Which would you more likely do, offer advise to a struggling friend (assertive direction) or be a good listener (receptive direction)?
- Would you be more likely to give an oral report based on your opinions (assertive direction) or read someone's else's paper to yourself (receptive direction).
- If you were a therapist, would you more likely talk and counsel (assertive direction) or sit and listen (receptive direction)?
- Are you more likely to share your journal with a friend (assertive direction) or listen to a friend's journal (receptive direction)?
- Are you more likely to give a friend a recipe you came up with (assertive direction) or share someone's else recipe (receptive direction)?
- In learning situations, are you more likely to be the teacher (assertive direction) or the student (receptive direction)?
- If you did martial arts and were practicing with a friend, would you be more likely to suggest she try new things (assertive direction) or follow your friend's lead (receptive direction)?
- At a job, are you more likely to be your friend's boss (assertive direction) or your boss's friend (receptive direction)?

Over all, the thing to see this time is how receptive people more look to draw people out by listening, while assertive people more look to voice their opinions and be heard.

Asking the Social Setting Questions

Again, start in the Presentation section with friend-type relationships. Then contrast and compare this with the friend-type Orientation setting. Then do the family-type Orientation setting. Then do the family-type Presentation setting.

Here you'll need to ask questions like:

- When you're going to dinner with friends, who decides where you'll go, you (assertive direction) or your friends (receptive direction)?

- Regarding holiday get-togethers with friends, are you more likely to invite someone (assertive direction) or be invited (receptive direction)?

- When you're meeting a friend at the mall, who decides where you'll meet, what time, and how long you'll stay, you (assertive direction) or them (receptive direction)?

- When you're out with friends at a club with live music, who decides how close to the band you'll sit, you (assertive direction) or them (receptive direction)?

- When you go to a movie with friends, who decides how far back from the screen you'll sit, you (assertive direction) or them (receptive direction)?

- When you're at a friend's wedding, which are you more likely to do, make a toast (assertive direction) or be part of a toast (receptive direction)?

- When you're out with friends and it involves dancing, are you more likely to dance (assertive direction) or watch (receptive direction)?

- Regarding going on vacation with friends, are you more likely to plan the vacation (assertive direction) or be told the plan (receptive direction)?

- When it comes to friends and music, are you more likely to sing/play music (assertive direction) or sit back and listen (receptive direction)?

- When it comes to friends and playing party games like Charades and Pictionary, which is more like you. Outgoing and bold (assertive direction) or laid back and uncertain (receptive direction)?

Where Are the Rest of the Questions?

So where are the rest of the questions? Aren't personality tests usually long and detailed? Know I've purposely given as few suggestions as possible. And yes, I'm well aware people's answers will vary based on the questions they're asked. But as long as the questions are tipping-point based, you should have no problems.

My point? Focus your efforts on seeing the person in front of you. Your questions should more reflect what you see in this person than some intellectual sense of gender. An eighty-year-old grannie will probably not feel the same about questions about sex as an eighteen year old college freshman. Then again, the eighty year old could easily be more assertive when it comes to sex. You never know. And a forty year old Orthodox Jew will likely have little in common with an over-sexed eighty year old atheist. Then again, when it comes to urges, while their morals would likely be different, their fantasies might be quite similar—gender wise.

Also do remember to be respectful and make this person's dignity and comfort more important than filling out the test form. After all, you're asking people to reveal themselves to you. Finally, please be sensitive to how these questions can sound like judgments to some folks.

The Formal Order of the Sixteen Gender Situations

Finally, for those for who got lost during this somewhat lengthy explanation, here is the preferred order for the test questions.

1. Physical/friend Presentation (behavior).
2. Physical/friend Orientation (urges).
3. Physical/family Orientation (urges)
4. Physical/family Presentation (behaviors).
5. Sexual/friend Presentation (behavior).
6. Sexual/friend Orientation (urges).
7. Sexual/family Orientation (urges).
8. Sexual/family Presentation (behaviors).
9. Psychological/friend Presentation (behavior).
10. Psychological/friend Orientation (urges).
11. Psychological/family Orientation (urges)
12. Psychological/family Presentation (behaviors).
13. Social/friend Presentation (behavior).
14. Social/friend Orientation (urges).
15. Social/family Orientation (urges)
16. Social/family Presentation (behaviors).

One More Look at the Idea of "Receptive vs Assertive"

Few ideas in personality come with as much baggage as the words assertive and receptive. So before closing, I'd like to talk a bit more about these two words. Let's start with the idea that many people see being "receptive" as a sign of weakness. Conversely many folks interpret the word "assertive" as a sign of strength.

The problem is, non-violent people can be mistaken for folks who are afraid and so, are making excuses for not acting. And this sometimes is the case. But Gandhi was overwhelmingly receptive. So was Martin Luther King. But neither man was weak.

At the same time, men and women who violate others—either physically or mentally—are often mistaken for people who are strong. In reality though, it's fear and weakness that make them act larger than life. So while the word *assertive* is often used to describe the forceful part of what people do, in truth, this word more refers to the outwardly moving direction of these forces and not to how strong they are.

Along the same lines, some folks may misinterpret marks placed closer to the ends of the double-headed arrows as being stronger than those placed more towards the midline. Ironically, if these were conventional forms, this could be true. The thing to remember here is that each mark on these forms records two answers—not just one.

So for instance, say you're talking about physical gender. Say you're also talking about people's efforts not urges. What does it mean to say that gender wise, people are meekly receptive versus boldly receptive when it comes to their physical gender?

At the risk of confusing you more, I'm going to resort to two more words we tend to misuse—the words *masculine* and *feminine*.

So for instance, what does it mean to say a woman is physically receptive? Does this mean she is feminine?

If a woman tips toward the receptive side, her appearance could be seen this way—as being generally feminine as opposed to being generally masculine. Realize though that this says nothing about how she feels or acts sexually, socially, or psychologically. All it says is that she generally prefers wearing things like skirts, dresses, heals, and makeup. As opposed to wearing pants, boots, and little to no makeup. And that she's generally calm, quiet, and soft spoken as opposed to being more straight forward, matter-of-fact, and firmly spoken.

Of course, were you to voice this difference as a caricature of the word *feminine*, you might say this woman was "girly" looking. However, this word carries even more baggage—most of it bad. In truth then, to many folks, even saying someone looks feminine can imply that you're saying this person is weak. Or gay. Yet despite the stereotype, being gay has nothing to do with appearance or overall gender, only with sexual preference. Moreover if you think girly women are weak, watch how they get people to do things for them. Or spend money on them. Or simply get people's attention.

My point?

If you stick to the meanings I've assigned these two words, you'll do fine. Receptive people's need-meeting urges/efforts tend to move inward, towards themselves. Assertive people's need-meeting urges/efforts tend to move outward, towards other people.

Trusting the Accuracy of Tipping-Points

Usually when you see segmented lines on test forms, they indicate things like amounts. These lines extend from the small amount at one end of the line to the big amount at the other end. In addition, these segments generally represent equal increments. And this makes sense. These lines look to record a single linear measure.

The lines of the wise men's gender form are designed differently. Here the position of a mark on a line does not indicate an amount but rather whether this measure is receptive or assertive. Whereas the strength of this measure is charted by the length of this mark. Thus unlike traditional forms—where each mark represents one linear measure— on the wise men's gender form, each mark represents two tipping-point based measures. Here you make a mark on one side of the midpoint on a two-directional line, and this mark indicates direction. Then you extend this mark to a long or short length to indicate a degree-of-force.

Why make such a big deal out of this?

Because at first glance, there appear to be only eight measures on this test form, when in reality there are thirty-two. There are sixteen lines, each of which records two measures—direction and strength. Moreover, rather than being linear measurements, these measurement are fractal and tipping-point based. In other words the lines on conventional forms are one dimensional and linear, and they flow in one direction in even increments. Whereas the lines on the wise men's gender form are two dimensional and fractal. Thus they flow in two directions with two degrees-of-force.

Some might ask why I've chosen not to place marks at the midpoint of these lines. The answer is, to be tipping-point based, an answer must land on one side of the midline or the other. A flipped coin that doesn't land doesn't have an outcome. This is not to say you must place these marks at the quarter and three quarter points either. You can. But you can also choose to add a dimension to your results by allowing your sense of the person's answer to guide the placement of the each mark within the left or right side.

Finally, some will ask why I've chosen to put increments on the recording lines if these lines aren't linear. The answer? I've done it merely to accommodate those who favor the materialist wise man. In reality, nothing in the real world occurs in even increments. At the same time, I'm sure you are more than capable of sensing change within these increments. So if you do choose honor these changes, don't be shy about expanding or contracting the degree-of-force sizes either. It's tendencies you're looking for, not increments, remember?

Devising Your Own Tests

Obviously, the tests I've presented here are only a basic guideline. As such, they're not intended to be a comprehensive set of test questions. Moreover as I've said, I've done this on purpose. Human beings are like snow flakes. Fragile. Special. And inherently individual. So no personality test should treat people like rats being measured in a maze.

The goal here is simple—to get to know people. How they work. How they love. How they take up space in life. How they wait or push ahead. And while the questions I've offered here will do fine in most cases, personally creating your own questions would be even better. As long as these questions are based on the test guidelines, of course.

Speaking of this, nothing would please me more than for someone well versed in the wise men's personality theory to devise a set of tests aimed at children. Should you be so inclined, please keep in mind that children younger than seven do not experience cause and effect. For them things only connect by association, as here and now time is all they know. This means questions which ask them to imagine how things may unfold in the future will likely fail, as young children have no sense of how things change over time.

Does this sound too hard? All I can say is, try anyway. You never know how you might make the world a better place for your having lived.

I for one think you just might add a lot.

Warmly,

Steven